B Black
Black, Michelle.
Sacrifice : a gold star widow's fight
for the truth.
$28.00
on1184236119

O9-BTM-331
HARRIS COUNTY PUBLIC LIBRARY

WITHDRAWN

Sacrifice

Sacrifice

A GOLD STAR WIDOW'S
FIGHT FOR THE TRUTH

Michelle Black

G. P. Putnam's Sons
New York

PUTNAM
— EST. 1838 —

G. P. Putnam's Sons
Publishers Since 1838
An imprint of Penguin Random House LLC
Penguinrandomhouse.com

Copyright © 2021 by Michelle Black
Penguin supports copyright. Copyright fuels creativity, encourages diverse voices, promotes free speech, and creates a vibrant culture. Thank you for buying an authorized edition of this book and for complying with copyright laws by not reproducing, scanning, or distributing any part of it in any form without permission. You are supporting writers and allowing Penguin to continue to publish books for every reader.

Hardcover ISBN 9780593190937

Printed in the United States of America
1st Printing

For
Bryan Black, Dustin Wright, LaDavid Johnson, Jeremiah Johnson,
and their families, who deserved the truth.
Also for the men who survived the ambush;
may this book bring you the peace and justice you deserve.

Author's Note

Sacrifice is a work of nonfiction based upon events that occurred over the course of several years. My depictions of these events are based either on my own experiences or on interviews I conducted with surviving members of Green Beret Team 3212 and some of the mid-level and senior officers who were involved. I was unable to interview one of the survivors who was on assignment in the Middle East and did not interview two survivors who preferred not to be involved. The actions on the ground were pieced together from interviews with survivors, video taken by the headcam of J. W. Johnson, conversations with a member of the investigative team after the ambush, and narratives given by the military to survivors and to the families of the fallen. A copy of the redacted report provided to my family can be found at michelleblacksacrifice.com.

Direct quotes found in this book, including my own, are not verbatim but are intended to capture, to the best of my ability, the essence of what the speaker was saying based on the recollections of the people I interviewed.

Some names have been changed to protect the privacy of service members, e.g., those who remained on active duty after the incidents described herein. I have not changed the names of individuals whose names have appeared in the media in connection with the incidents.

Sacrifice

Prologue

The day my husband was buried, his casket pulled by six black horses, the sun shone brightly. With my boys on either side of me, I wept for their loss, and for mine. I had always assumed that Bryan and I would grow old together. Surely a folded flag was never meant to be mine. But here I was.

Twenty-six days earlier, ten Green Berets fought a lethal battle on the ground in Niger, Africa, against ISIS militants. The ambush, which resulted in the death of my husband and three of his fellow soldiers, was the largest loss of American life in that region since the Battle of Mogadishu—also known as Black Hawk Down—in 1993. After being ambushed by an ISIS-affiliated group outside of the village of Tongo Tongo, six members of Green Beret Team 3212 would emerge alive but forever changed.

What most Americans remember about the Niger ambush, however, is the argument that erupted over a phone call between the president of the United States and one of the three widows. The poor handling of the phone call, coupled with a media firestorm and a handful of callous tweets, and the resulting feud took the focus from the soldiers and placed it firmly on American politicians. Because of this, the four

American and five Nigerien soldiers who died in the attack were forgotten within a couple of weeks.

But not by us. Not by my family and the other families of the fallen.

We were shocked by the attack and wanted to know how and why it had happened. Niger was not meant to be a dangerous assignment. Teams like my husband's conducted missions on the continent using a "by, with, and through" strategy to train their partner forces by having their partners take a lead role.

Knowing this, we had questions about the ambush: Why was the team out near the Mali border by themselves with no backup and so poorly equipped? Who had made the decisions leading up to these terrible events? General Thomas D. Waldhauser, the commander of AFRICOM (United States Africa Command), quickly started an investigation to learn the facts surrounding the mission that led to the ambush. I knew there was a process to military investigations, and I was certain that the Army would probe every decision that led to this heartbreaking loss of life.

I expected the story of the ambush would be simple, and the investigation truthful. However, over the months of waiting I was surprised and confused by how the team was being treated. The Army referred to the Green Beret soldiers as a team that went rogue and acted like cowboys in order to go after a risky target, putting their lives and teammates in danger. They were disparaged in the media and their captain was blamed and vilified for his decisions during the operation. I counted on the investigation's results to clear up my confusion. But after the family briefing in April 2018, I found that I had more questions than I'd had going in.

I had thought the day my husband was buried, when my sons saw him put in the ground, would be the worst thing I could survive. But somehow, life had become less bearable. I needed to know the truth, to hear every detail of the ambush, to find out what AFRICOM had failed to tell us. What exactly happened to the men before, during, and after the ambush? The men of Team 3212 knew what had happened on the ground, but due to gag orders put in place by the military, they were not able to speak about it.

I was faced with an overwhelming task, one that I had no idea how to begin. In late spring of 2018, I began talking with the remaining members of Green Beret Operational Detachment Alpha (ODA) Team 3212. When the gag orders were lifted, many of the survivors came to my home one at a time and allowed me to record them as they told me every moment of those fateful three days. They answered every question; I wrote their story. Simply by listening to the men of ODA 3212 and not blaming them, I had earned their trust. That trust meant the world to me—and I knew I couldn't let them down. I had become the key to telling the true account of what happened in Niger.

I often say I'd prefer to hear an ugly truth than a beautiful lie. In the year following my husband's death, I was told plenty of both. *Sacrifice* details many of the ugly truths I faced following the ambush and the lies I was told in the aftermath. It tells the story of what happened to ODA 3212 in October 2017 in Niger, and shows how that account differs from the official narrative. I have aimed to share that truth—and to honor the men who lived it.

PART ONE
Life and Death

1

Bryan

Since the day Bryan left for Niger, I'd had a horrible feeling deep inside. We'd been through several deployments and long separations, but none had made me as nervous as this one.

In many ways I enjoyed my routine when Bryan was gone. I woke up early, got the kids to school, went jogging, worked on a house project. At night, when I wasn't reading or painting walls, I caught up on all the "girl shows" Bryan hated, like *The Bachelorette*. I hadn't felt uneasy when he left on his two previous deployments, and neither of us had ever seen the need for long goodbyes. A quick hug and a kiss; "I love you" and then "See you in six months." But this time was different. I suppose some people would call it a premonition, others would call it God's voice whispering to warn me, and others would say it was just my imagination. All I know is that as I stood at the curb of the small Fayetteville Regional Airport in North Carolina that sunny Saturday morning in August 2017, I desperately wanted to tell him to stay. For the first time in six years of watching him leave for training or deployments, I couldn't let him go. He seemed to feel the same way, pulling me in a second time for a stronger embrace. I began to tear up, which had never happened before, and he promised he'd be home soon, but he faltered as he picked up his bags and walked away, turning back for a second glance. He called out, "I love you. I'll call you as soon as I can."

It was the last time I saw his handsome face, heard his deep voice, held him in my arms. I didn't feel right about letting him go that day, but there was nothing I could do to stop it. I was more in love with him than ever, and I willingly let him walk out of my life when every fiber of my being was screaming at me to stop him. But what could I have done? Who can stop the tide from going out, even if you know a tsunami is what it brings back in? So I let the Army pull Bryan out of my arms that day.

I met Bryan fifteen years earlier in Mammoth Lakes, California, a ski town in the winter and a hiker's paradise in the summer.

After graduating college, I'd wanted some time off from reality to have fun. I learned I had epilepsy after having a seizure my first day of college classes, and it had taken me longer than expected to graduate as I adjusted to taking daily medication and managing my condition. When I treated it correctly, I could completely prevent my seizures. But I could not party, go without sleep, or take on heavy loads of schoolwork like most college students. Upon graduation, I was proud to have proved to myself what I could do—but I was ready for a break. I went skiing.

Every morning I'd walk a mile to the village, where I would take a gondola up to the ski lodge and teach children my favorite sport. I loved walking in that crystal cold air as the sky lightened. After a day on the mountain, I'd head down to my next job at a fur-and-leather shop in the village, where I'd make espresso for customers and run the register. At night, sitting by the woodstove while my roommates socialized and watched movies, I crocheted colorful hats for local boutiques that sold them to tourists.

Mammoth was a daily adventure. My jobs were enjoyable, and in my free time I explored the surrounding mountains and lakes with my friends. Some nights we would hike up local peaks to snowboard down in the full moonlight; other times we would sneak into condominium hot tubs or seek out hidden local hot springs. I wasn't looking for anything or anyone when Bryan came along.

Like me, Bryan moved to town that fall after finishing college. He planned to ski, and he played online poker at night. He'd found a room for rent online and had accidentally moved in with the town drunk. In an effort to get out of the house one night, he wandered into the church I attended.

I spotted Bryan standing at the back by the coffeepot. He was hard to miss at 6'2" and 230 pounds, with a neck as big around as my thigh. He stood with his arms crossed in front of his massive chest and gave no hint of a smile. He seemed like a tough guy with a bad attitude, but his outfit intrigued me. The ski-bum crowd usually wore saggy pants and fur-lined jackets, but Bryan was wearing fitted jeans and a blue crewneck sweater. I decided to say hi and find out what his deal was.

When I introduced myself, I was met by a deep monotone and a goofy smile. "I'm Bryan."

"Well, it's nice to meet you, Bryan," I said, smiling back.

"It's nice to meet you, too." Already I could see there was nothing tough about this tough guy.

"Have you been in town long?" I asked.

"No, just a couple weeks," he said, continuing to smile at me in silence. I couldn't decide if he was dumb or simply to the point.

As I was leaving church, it was snowing and the roads were covered in solid ice and lined with four-foot snowbanks. There on the steep main street that ran directly in front of the church, Bryan was gliding and sliding fearlessly down the icy road on a bike that looked two sizes too small. I would find out later that he had recently backed his truck into a park barbecue—and even though he had gotten out and bent it back into shape, he had been charged with a hit-and-run by an officer who had witnessed him "fleeing the scene." The resulting rise in his insurance had led to him parking his truck for a year.

A few months after we met, I arrived home from work one night to find Bryan in my living room watching a movie with my roommates. Having been raised in a large family, I generally liked such gatherings, but that night I needed quiet, so I opted to stay in the front room crocheting. As I gathered my wool, Bryan came over and said he wanted to learn.

I tried to teach him the basics. As he sat cross-legged on the floor in front of me, he awkwardly held a crochet hook and pink yarn in his large hands. I thought it was the silliest thing in the world: a muscle-bound wrestler taking a night off from playing poker to take a crochet lesson from me. We giggled and joked back and forth, insulting each other as he worked on the knotted mess that he handed me proudly at the end. I liked that Bryan took the lesson seriously and learned a few skills despite the challenge that holding a small needle and yarn posed to his strong fingers. We decided the hat he made was actually more like a doily, but still called it a success.

The more Bryan talked, the more interesting and fun I found him to be. I appreciated that he was able to laugh at himself as he sat making a mess of my pink yarn, and in the years that followed I don't remember a time when he cared about his image or what anyone thought of him. He was certain of who he was and more secure than anyone I have ever met, and yet he rarely talked about himself. I would find out later that he was a child chess prodigy and tied for second in the nation at just eleven years old. He continued to compete in national chess championships throughout his teen years.

At the end of ski season, we all looked forward to the Poodle Prom, a dance party with an open bar that was put on by Mammoth Mountain for all the instructors. I had broken my foot, landing me on crutches. As my friends partied and danced, I hung out at one of the tables, bored, trying to avoid advances from some of the drunker guys.

Bryan playing in the National High School Chess Championships.
(Henry Black)

Bryan had been dating one of my coworkers for a while, so it came as a surprise when about halfway through the night I saw her up on the back corner of the bar swinging her long blond hair around and dancing suggestively for a couple of guys I didn't recognize. I watched in bewilderment, wondering what had happened to Bryan. Then I saw him sitting alone at a table looking bored, with two full bottles of beer for company. Dressed in a light blue button-down shirt that complemented his eyes, he looked handsome.

He glanced up at me on my crutches, then smiled and asked if I wanted a beer, pointing to one of the bottles. I paused and looked back at the bar, where his girlfriend was dancing.

"Don't worry, she's already drunk and is too busy trying to make me jealous to notice either of us," Bryan said matter-of-factly, then chuckled a little.

I put my crutches against one of the free chairs and laughed, too. "Well, okay, then." Then I asked him why he wasn't joining his girlfriend on the bar.

His answer was simple and direct: "I don't dance. I'm bad at it."

"Well," I said, "I'm sorry to hear that, but I'm glad I've got someone to talk to."

As we drank and joked, the hours flew by. Before I knew it, I was regretting having to leave.

In the summers, most people left town and the ratio of men to women changed to around ten to one. One night I was the only girl at a condominium rec room playing pool with a group of male friends of mine. It was loud and raucous. I loved playing pool and knew I was good at it. I had just won a game as Bryan walked in. I asked, "Well, does anyone else want to play?"

"I don't think any of us can beat you," one friend replied.

Bryan walked right past everyone and said, "I can beat you," in his booming voice.

I laughed at him and said, "Really? I doubt that."

Bryan smiled his big, warm smile and said, "Okay, then if I win you have to make me dinner."

The room got really quiet. Then one of the guys yelled, "Hey, you can't do that, that's a date!"

To which Bryan responded, "Next time, you ask her first, then."

Trying to lighten the situation, I turned to the guy who'd objected and said, "Well, technically it's not a date if you're buying the food."

As Bryan and I racked the balls, I told him that when he lost he'd be making the dinner, and it had better be good. I took the first shot and sank two balls. I knew I had gotten lucky, but I tried to play it off as pure skill. As I leaned in for my second shot, I gave Bryan a triumphant smile and asked him if he knew how to cook a roast, because I really could go for some prime rib.

I carefully aimed and took a deep breath before hitting the cue ball, sending it straight past the green 6 ball I had been aiming for and ricocheting off a bumper.

Bryan smiled at me and said, "Prime rib does sound good."

Annoyed, I handed the stick to him. He leaned over and set up his shot, pulled the stick back, then paused, glancing up at me before easily sinking his first ball. "I like horseradish, too." He set up his second shot, angled the cue ball to send it straight past all his balls and directly into a bumper, where it bounced. I was smiling, thinking he had missed his shot, when I realized it was heading for a ball near the corner pocket. It hit the ball dead on, sending another of Bryan's balls into a pocket. We were tied. Bryan continued to sink one after the other while I sat there watching helplessly. I got one more turn, but I missed my shot and Bryan won easily. I made sure to let him know that he'd just gotten lucky and that next time I would be handing his butt to him. Bryan told me that the only way I would ever win against him was if he let me.

The very next night I made everyone fettuccine at my house, since we couldn't actually afford prime rib. Just when we finished dinner, my college boyfriend called to catch up. As I looked across the room to where Bryan sat talking to everyone, I told my boyfriend I was not going to be moving back.

Living in Mammoth during the summer meant being surrounded by stunning scenery and backcountry hiking. Pick just about any path and you would soon find yourself ten thousand feet up and completely secluded in the rugged beauty of the Sierra mountain range. The countless paths, high mountain lakes, and peaks of the John Muir Wilderness and Pacific Crest Trail were a playground to those of us who lived there.

Bryan and I began planning backpacking trips with others from our church. We often left after dark with headlamps after working all day and were poorly equipped with our Eddie Bauer sleeping bags bungee-corded to our JanSport school backpacks. Sometimes I wonder if it was age or the lack of oxygen at that altitude that helped us consistently make such ludicrous decisions, always going out underprepared. It wasn't long before the number of people interested in going dwindled.

Midway through summer it was common for just me, Bryan, and one or two other friends to go on each trip.

By late in the season, Bryan had become one of my best friends and my constant companion, so it should not have surprised me one night when he called me his girlfriend. It was now August and we were walking across the parking lot from church toward my car. The air had a sharp chill to it that night and the scent of pine needles mixed with the fine mountain dirt. I was commenting on the beautiful purple and red hues in the sky when Bryan said, "I'm just glad I get to enjoy it with my girlfriend."

It was clear he was testing me, hoping to see my reaction. I slowed my pace as I looked him over, my eyes narrowing. There was a moment of silence between the two of us, during which the word seemed to hang in the air.

"What do you mean I'm your girlfriend?" I said to him. "I'm no one's girlfriend." I had always hated not only the word but the idea of it; I felt it gave another person permission to think they owned me.

Bryan stopped and looked back at me, goofy smile in place, and simply said, "Yes, you are." He paused for a moment before continuing. "Besides, I've already been telling everyone that we have been dating."

"Really?" I asked, dumbfounded. We had both stopped walking and just stood in the center of the parking lot. "And how long have you been telling everyone this?" Bryan looked entirely unaffected by my disbelief, which served only to annoy me more.

The streetlights began to turn on one by one while I tried to hold my glare at Bryan. I unlocked my car and we climbed in. Looking over, I saw Bryan could barely contain the smirk on his face.

"You can't just go around telling people we are in a relationship. That's ridiculous," I told him.

"It's not ridiculous if it's true," he argued. "We are in a relationship."

Clearly, I was not getting through to him. "Why in the world do you think we are in a relationship? We've never even talked about it."

"Well, we are talking about it right now . . . and we *are* in a relationship."

"How? Define *relationship*, Bryan, because I'm completely confused, and I think you are wrong."

I tried everything I could that night to prove to Bryan we were just friends, and instead of getting his feelings hurt he thought it was funny and just kept on arguing with me in his annoyingly analytical way. "I'm not wrong, *you* are wrong. We hang out every day when we aren't working. We are always together alone at your place or mine. We ditch everyone else and eat most meals together. We don't have to eat at a restaurant or watch a movie at a theater for it to be a date. If we are together and we are eating with no one else but us, then it is by definition a date. Besides, neither of us has the money to go out all the time, and people only do those things to spend time together and decide if they like each other. We already know we like each other, so technically we are in a relationship."

"Well," I said, exasperated, "*technically* we aren't in a relationship if one of us didn't *know*." But finally I said, "Fine. We are dating. But you cannot date someone if they do not know about it. So up until this moment, I had not agreed to date you or be your girlfriend, so, *technically*, we were not dating until now. As of this moment, we are officially dating—but no sooner."

Bryan smiled his huge grin and said, "Fine."

I laughed and said, "Okay, boyfriend, let's go."

Bryan corrected me: "*Man*friend."

I rolled my eyes as I started up the engine and drove the five miles back to Bryan's house.

The following weekend, Bryan and I set out on a backpacking trip we had been planning for some time. Our goal was to hike thirty miles to reach a set of natural hot springs in the backcountry somewhere between the Pacific Crest Trail and the John Muir Wilderness Trail. We decided to leave on a Friday night after work and camp at one of the lower lakes before doing a big push on Saturday to get near the hot springs so we could enjoy them longer. We were more prepared for this trip, with larger, better-insulated sleeping bags and a tent we'd borrowed from a friend, as well as a water filter so we could safely drink from the lower lakes. I had even gone to the extra effort to buy real hiking boots rather than use my old running shoes, which had been my go-to the past few years.

We were excited as we switched on our headlamps and set out that night through the woods. Walking in the dark, we talked about why no one else wanted to come and how much they were going to miss out on. That's when Bryan said the pastor of our church had pulled him aside and suggested the two of us alone shouldn't go. Being twenty-six years old, I was shocked that the pastor felt it was any of his business.

Bryan said matter-of-factly, "I told him we aren't rabbits."

I started laughing. "You seriously said that to the pastor?"

"Yep."

I suddenly could picture all the rabbits in the woods that surrounded us, millions of them listening in on our conversation and multiplying. In the pitch-dark forest, with only a tiny headlamp for light, my laughter grew louder and echoed in the darkness. Bryan was grinning from ear to ear but saying nothing. I started laughing so hard that I had to stop walking for a minute and try to breathe.

At the midway point to Duck Pass, we set up camp for the night. When I awoke the next morning Bryan was already up and arranging things to make us breakfast. That morning, enjoying the incredible view, we talked at length about the future. Bryan unabashedly began telling me his dream the night before: In it, he had proposed and I had asked him what took him so long.

"Maybe you should just propose already, then," I said.

We laughed and began to talk about marriage, and that set the tone for the conversations that continued as we hiked that day. I remember being terribly excited at the prospect of spending the rest of my life with Bryan; I knew that no matter where we went, life would be a great adventure together. Bryan was just my type, a strong and silent leader who loved God and was both kind and formidable. When I was with him, I always felt safe, adored, and respected. I never tired of being around him, with his quick wit and his deep interest in the world, and I finally admitted to myself that I had been falling in love with him for weeks. But that trip was the first time I allowed myself to say it out loud.

Bryan and I stopped at an elevation of about eleven thousand feet and sat next to Purple Lake to eat our peanut-butter-and-jelly sandwiches before making the long descent to the floor of the valley below. It was a pristine summer day. At high altitude, the light feels brighter and stronger, and though the landscape is stark, the colors seem more vibrant. Even the sky seems bluer.

We had come such a long way in such a short time, and there was a certainty and security with him that I'd never felt with anyone else. I wouldn't just call it falling in love, I'd call it finding my equal. Someone I could enjoy every day, who I would not grow weary of. He already seemed like he *belonged* in my life.

After resting, we set out again in hopes of making it to the springs by sunset. Our biggest obstacle of the day lay ahead of us in the thousand-foot switchback descent. As we made our way down the mountain in the bright August sun, we shared tales from our pasts and discussed the future—but soon, pain in the middle of my right Achilles tendon started nagging me. My new boots were not as fabulous as the store clerk had said; they were breaking down along the spine after only one day of hiking. By the time we reached the valley floor near Fish Creek, I was limping badly and could go no farther. That night, we set up camp in a beautiful spot hidden in a patch of aspen trees made even more peaceful by the sound of the creek as it snaked its way past our tent. Bryan wouldn't let me do a thing but sit with my foot submerged in the cool creek water as he set up the tent, made a fire, and cooked us a meal.

That night as we lay in our tent, I remember staring at Bryan and thinking how much I loved his funny face. His big blue eyes, his long chin, even his teeth. He jokingly but proudly told me he'd had people compare his looks to Shrek's. That made me laugh and I said, "A *hot* Shrek. But do you have layers like an onion?" I reached up and put my hands on his cheeks and stroked them gently, then smiled. "I like you," I whispered to him.

"I like you, too," he whispered back before reaching over and kissing me.

The next morning, I woke up with my heel no better than it was the day before. We realized there was no way I could continue on to the hot springs. We'd have to turn back and head home, and my only pair of shoes was useless. But as the saying goes, necessity is the mother of invention. For some odd reason—with Bryan, there was often an odd reason—Bryan had packed an unreasonable number of socks, which ended up working to our benefit. We pulled the laces and insoles from my useless new hiking boots. Then, poking holes in the insoles and attaching the laces, we created flip-flops of sorts. On top of the flip-flops, we layered several knee-high socks to provide cushioning. And then we set out, with me looking completely absurd but feeling far more comfortable than I had the day before.

We slowly made our way back up the thousand-foot ascent to Purple Lake. It was late afternoon by the time we arrived, and we decided to camp there for the night. We were surprised to find that we were the only people in the area that day. As the day settled into night and the colors of the sky changed from pink to purple to black, Bryan and I sat at the water's edge and held hands.

"Look over there," Bryan said. "Do you see that?"

An eagle floated majestically through the sky, then dipped down, landing on the far end of the lake near a collection of large boulders and pine trees.

"That's amazing!" I said.

"Not as amazing as you," Bryan said, and I turned to see that he was giving me fake puppy-dog eyes.

"You are such a dork," I said and laughed.

Soon darkness engulfed us and the sky became a sea of stars that stretched from one mountain horizon to another. It felt like we were sitting in a snow globe filled with stars. Just me and Bryan, the lake and the universe.

Four months later, I opened a huge present from Bryan on Christmas day. It was a box of the most beautiful yarns I'd ever seen. I pulled them out one by one, thrilled by the soft texture and the bright colors of each skein, imagining the hats I would make. At the bottom, I found a small velvet box, inside of which was a beautiful diamond ring. Bryan got down on one knee. I told him I couldn't take him seriously on his knees, so he should get up and kiss me and I'd say yes.

On July 23, 2005, Bryan and I were married under an old oak tree in my parents' front yard in Tehachapi, California. As the band began to play the wedding march, I reached for my dad's arm while taking a deep breath. He squeezed my arm and smiled at me as we started to walk the aisle. My dad handed me off to Bryan as the wind gusted and large rain droplets landed on my cheeks and eyelashes. The massive chandelier hung high up in the tree began to sway wildly back and forth, casting across the wedding party and the guests light and shadow, light and shadow. Then there came a loud clap of thunder and the preacher bowed his head and prayed against the wind and the impending rain. As he prayed, a sudden calm set in: The wind stopped, the rain subsided. And as he finished, the sun peeked out, revealing a magnificent rainbow.

It was beautiful, almost eerie. The storm had come right up to the very edge of the property and stopped. As Bryan and I turned to look at the golden fields behind us, we saw a white horse with its head bent, grazing in the field. We took pictures—rainbow, horse, and all—then headed to the backyard for a good party.

Just married and standing under a rainbow with Bryan and our families. *(Copyright © Rich LaSalle 2020)*

2

Family

After honeymooning on Kauai, Bryan and I returned to Mammoth in August and began our lives as husband and wife in a tiny apartment. By October, we were excited and nervous to find out that we were expecting a baby. I was considered a high-risk pregnancy because of my epilepsy and needed to be constantly monitored. While the epilepsy was controlled by medication, blood volume changes in the body during pregnancy made it more difficult than usual to control. To make things more complicated, my regular medication was not safe to use while pregnant, since it could cause severe birth defects. So I was put on a different medication that was safe for the baby—but it turned out it was not as effective at controlling my seizures. Bryan, worried about my health, worked from home playing online poker for a living so he could keep an eye on me.

Late one night I woke up to Bryan carrying my seven-months-pregnant self through the snow. We had been working on a project for a friend's wedding when I collapsed and had a seizure. In typical Bryan fashion, he calmly picked me up and carried me down the road to the local hospital and told me we were going to have to move closer to better medical care. We stayed with my family during the last few months of the pregnancy before our son Ezekiel was born at a hospital in Bakersfield, California.

Bryan and I were instantly in love with our little baby human. He had this wild look in his big blue eyes, and I knew from the beginning that he was going to be my biggest life challenge yet. Much like his dad, Ezekiel feared nothing and no one. Because my seizures were caused by a lack of sleep and the presence of stress, Bryan would often stay up at night with Zeke, then get up early to work.

That summer, when Bryan and I took our new baby back up to Mammoth, we started to notice that things were not quite right with our son. Ezekiel had significant issues with feeding, was overly sensitive to sound, and seemed to have a heightened startle reflex. He would scream—not cry, like normal babies do, but scream—until I thought he'd run out of air. He kept us up day and night; he hardly slept. He also appeared to have little interest in people and loved to just stare at the lights and toys on his bouncy chair rather than play with them. Neither of us had been around infants before, so we thought all the struggles we were having with Ezekiel would subside with time. Two months before Ezekiel's first birthday, Bryan and I faced the fact that with a growing family and astronomical insurance prices, we could no longer afford to live in our favorite ski area. We moved to Redding, California, a good midway point between his parents near Seattle and my family near Bakersfield.

Not long after arriving in Redding, we discovered we had another baby on the way. Once again I needed to be constantly monitored, which meant Bryan had to work from home. When he wasn't working, he was monitoring Zeke and me, constantly on alert in the event I had a seizure. At the same time, I started to have real concerns about Ezekiel's progress. At first he spoke a few phrases, but then he slowly quit using the words he knew and began to simply make repetitive noises.

Ezekiel was very loving with me and Bryan and he enjoyed socializing with other family members, but he made little to no eye contact.

He enjoyed just sitting in his crib alone, staring at the wall. When he was two, I took Ezekiel to his pediatrician and asked about the potential for autism and was told I had nothing to worry about. He'd grow out of it, the doctor said. In April 2008, our second son, Isaac, was born. At that time the United States' economy was in a downward spiral, and the regulations on Internet gambling tightened. Suddenly, Bryan was having trouble making as much money as we needed. So we left California and headed north.

For a year we lived with Bryan's parents in Puyallup, Washington, while Bryan tried several different job options, but in the end nothing worked. Meanwhile, the signs of autism that Ezekiel displayed were increasing. Several times a day, he would have meltdowns that would last between two and three hours at a time. We tried everything we could to help him. We read books on raising strong-willed and difficult children. Nothing worked.

Having a three-year-old who couldn't speak and a one-year-old who was beginning to walk was a challenge. When Isaac wasn't crying, Ezekiel was. I rarely knew why Ezekiel was upset or how to fix it. My only time to myself was during Isaac's long afternoon naps, when I would plop Zeke in front of the TV.

After a year in Washington I visited a pediatrician. I was desperate for a diagnosis or some explanation that would help me with Ezekiel. Once again, I was told that he just needed more time. According to the pediatrician, Ezekiel showed too much affection toward me and too much interest in socializing with others to be diagnosed as autistic. I didn't know how much longer I could take the daylong meltdowns and lack of communication with Ezekiel. I could see that Isaac was progressing quickly enough that it was plausible he would speak before his older brother did. I felt heartbroken and overwhelmed.

By April 2009 I was back on the old medication for my epilepsy, so Bryan no longer needed to be home with me all the time, which opened up new job options. From the time he was a teenager, Bryan had thought about becoming a SEAL or a Green Beret. We knew that if he joined the military, our family would be covered under full military insurance, and we agreed that joining the Army was the best option to stabilize our finances. When Bryan signed up for four years of military service in 2009, I remember feeling a huge amount of relief. I could see how happy joining the Army had made Bryan and how much stress it had lifted from him. While I had been raised about as far from the military world as one could be, Bryan's father had been an officer in the Marines, so he understood exactly what he was committing to—and if that made him happy, then I was happy. The rest I would adjust to.

In August 2010, when Bryan finished Army infantry training, we

Bryan and me in Texas after his graduation from basic training. *(Karen Black)*

moved to Colorado Springs, where he was stationed at Fort Carson as a medic with a combat support hospital.

I was extremely nervous as I arrived at the base. I had never known anyone who was in the military before meeting Bryan's dad. I didn't understand even the most basic of military functions, like how to get on base or what a PX, a commissary, or a Class 6 was. Going on base felt like arriving in a foreign country; it even had its own language, as everyone used acronyms for everything.

The first time I went to get gas and liquor at a Class 6 on base, I remember looking around and seeing fried chicken, soda, and coffee to the left and a whole lot of alcohol to the right and I realized, *Okay—it's a 7-Eleven with a lot of alcohol!* Then next door at the PX, I saw that they had clothes, electronics, beauty products, and household items, and thought, *Aha, we've got Walmart here.* Beside the PX sat the Commissary, which was a military grocery store with really low prices. For months after that, I would drive the strip featuring the Class 6, the Commissary, and the PX and think to myself, *So basically, here we've got 7-Eleven, Safeway, and Walmart, but cheaper. That's awesome.*

Bryan had gotten a small two-bedroom apartment for us located off the base, and the kids started preschool at the local public school. Ezekiel was now four years old, and after more than two and a half years of seeing multiple doctors and unsuccessfully trying to get a diagnosis for him, I vowed to get professional help once and for all.

In June 2011, I took Ezekiel to see a nearby psychologist. As I sat on a long, light brown leather couch in his office watching Zeke play with blocks, I cried silently. The psychologist observed Zeke, then brought me into his office alone. He explained to me in a soft and sympathetic voice that after spending only thirty minutes with Ezekiel, he was sure my son had autism. Ezekiel displayed all the classic signs except the lack of affection and the desire to socialize.

"Autism is a spectrum," he told me, "meaning there is a wide range in which children who are diagnosed can function. Those on the lower end often must live at home their entire lives, may never speak or be able to dress themselves. Those on the high end often function fine on their own, moving out, going to college, even getting married and having families of their own. The higher-functioning may only have slight social issues, making them seem odd because of the way they process the world around them, but they become fully functioning adults. After assessing Ezekiel, my guess is that he is on the lower end. Not so low that he won't be able to dress himself, but probably never living away from home and certainly never fully functioning or being integrated into regular education classrooms."

Upon hearing his assessment, I was crushed. "With therapy and hard work, that can be changed, correct?" I asked, almost pleading.

The doctor hesitated. "Well, yes, that can help, but it is rare to see any real marked changes, especially at an older age. Usually, children who are diagnosed at two or three and undergo intensive therapy have a higher likelihood of being helped by therapy. Intelligence also plays a huge role, but the level of intelligence is hard to determine when a child is significantly lacking in speech, as Ezekiel is."

As I sat in the psychologist's office, I felt a huge shift happen inside of me. I'd had professionals telling me for years that Ezekiel was fine when I knew he wasn't, but I believed them because they were experts. Now I had another specialist telling me I had been right all along, but it was too late. Suddenly I didn't care that he was a professional. A fierceness came over me and I told him he was wrong. "I believe with therapy and hard work he will be just fine. I know it."

I knew my son better than any doctor; he was more than capable of overcoming whatever challenges he faced. When Bryan came home from work that night, I told him that Ezekiel had been diagnosed with autism. Bryan's straightforward response was the best reassurance ever: "Well, we already knew that. At least now we have the diagnosis so we can get him some support, so this is a good thing." I loved him even more for that.

Receiving the official diagnosis of autism gave us the piece of paper necessary to get Ezekiel the speech and behavioral therapy he so desperately needed. Ezekiel was placed in a special-education kindergarten classroom and assigned a paraeducator who would take him to a regular education classroom at intervals throughout the day. He began doing around ten hours a week of speech and behavioral therapy that I would augment at home. Most days at around 10:00 a.m., I would get a phone call that Ezekiel was having a meltdown and needed to be picked up. I was the only person who knew how to calm him down. Those first few months, it was rare for him to make it past midmorning, but as the year progressed he had more successful days at school.

For two years, my days in Colorado consisted of taking care of Isaac and running Zeke back and forth to school and therapy appointments. I had next to no social life and was an emotional mess. Fortunately, Bryan had a lot of days when he was able to come home early from base or take some time off in the morning and spend it with me. That year, our bond as a couple grew stronger. Some days we would go on slow jogs, not talking until the end, when we would walk back to the car holding hands and joking with each other.

"Did I ever tell you that I like you?" I would ask.

And he would say, "I like you, too."

Other days we would find a hole-in-the-wall coffee shop or a diner and spend a couple hours just talking about our future hopes and dreams, not just as a couple but as individuals. Our marriage was about us, and our kids were a product of our love, but we knew they could not become our complete focus. Those mornings spent together allowed Bryan and me to forget our difficulties for a moment and enjoy life.

Nearly a year after Ezekiel's initial diagnosis, I found myself back in the same psychologist's office for a follow-up. I'll never forget the triumphant feeling when that doctor smiled at Ezekiel in amazement. After nearly a year of intensive behavioral and speech therapy, which I backed up at home with a lot of extra practice, Ezekiel had been able to slowly integrate into a full-day classroom setting. He was speaking beautifully and reading on grade level. The psychologist said that he now had no doubt that one day Ezekiel would be fully integrated into regular-education classrooms and perhaps go on to college and live on his own. I cried as relief flooded my soul. I finally had confirmation that my little boy was going to be just fine.

Things in the Army weren't going quite as well for Bryan. After a year of working at a combat support hospital (or CSH, pronounced "cash") at Fort Carson, he was growing restless. He decided to try out for Special Forces selection. I was excited for him to finally be going after the very thing he had long wanted: to be part of an elite military unit.

To become a Green Beret takes more than desire; it requires full mental and physical commitment. The selection process necessitates countless hours of physical preparation. Then, if the soldier is chosen, he and his family have to move to Fort Bragg, in North Carolina, where Green Beret qualification courses are held. Bryan spent several months in Colorado preparing for the long-distance ruck (weighted backpack) marches and nighttime land-navigation courses he would be expected to successfully complete. He joined an orienteering group to navigate courses in the woods and find various points using only a compass and a map. On weekends, we'd meet up with large groups of orienteering enthusiasts in the woods of Colorado.

Bryan was running uncountable miles each week, doing strength-training exercises and body-weight exercises, climbing ropes and doing push-ups and pull-ups and marching long distances while wearing a hundred-pound ruck. He seemed never to stop moving, and every night he came home starving.

After months of exhaustive preparation, Bryan left for North Caro-lina and my waiting began. Twenty-four days later he called from Camp

Mackall, ecstatic at being selected. He was exhausted and ready to come home, but he was getting his chance. I was so happy for him that he would get to see this longtime dream realized, and proud of him for all the hard work and commitment he had put in.

When he arrived home, I was shocked at how exhausted and thin he was. I knew the selection process was grueling, but I had not expected Bryan to look like he'd been starved. He lay around the house for days trying to recover but was only getting worse. He would lie on the ground, alternating heat and cold packs on his stomach, running in and out of the bathroom and heaving up anything he'd eaten that day.

Twice I took him to the ER on base and twice they gave him fluids and released him. It scared me that he couldn't keep down any food and could keep down very little water as he continued to lose weight. He was so weak that he would go to work each day, find a couch, and sleep until it was time to come home. While he was preparing for training, he had craved fruit and he had frequently eaten melons. I knew that melons from the store where he bought them had been linked to a listeria outbreak, but the Army hospital wouldn't run the test and told him he had the flu. He just needed to wait it out, they said. Over the next two weeks, he continued to lose weight and get weaker.

Fortunately, his unit was preparing to deploy to Afghanistan and was issued antibiotics to take with them as a precaution. As soon as they were issued, Bryan began to take the pills—and within a week was back to himself.

Knowing that all Bryan had needed was antibiotics, I became frustrated with the hospital on post that had not taken my husband seriously. I had learned to question authority in other realms, but this was the first time I found myself questioning the Army's judgment. I found myself wishing we had gone to a civilian ER from the start, even if that meant paying out of pocket. Being broke is better than being dead.

After recovering, Bryan jumped back into work as his unit began to prepare for deployment. We were excited to start a new adventure and see what life had in store for us. In July, we packed up our little apartment in Colorado and moved to Fayetteville, North Carolina.

We had just moved into our home in Fayetteville near Fort Bragg where Bryan was beginning the SF Q Course. *(Karen Black)*

I was excited to finally be moving into our first house and to be able to stay in one place for several years. It was a beautiful two-story split-level brick home, nearly three times the size of our apartment back in Colorado. We had half an acre of grass surrounded by dogwood and oak trees in a pretty southern neighborhood. Bryan spent the next three years going through what's known as the Q Course—the Special Forces

Qualification Course—while I learned about schools and the community surrounding Fort Bragg.

When Bryan would leave to complete a portion of the course, I would invent a house project to occupy my mind and time while he was gone. I still needed to be available for Zeke at a moment's notice in case he had a meltdown at school. I was not yet comfortable going back to work knowing that I would often have to leave to cope with school situations. I invested my time learning about the world of special education: terms such as IEP (Individualized Education Plan) and BIP (Behavior Intervention Plan), and laws that pertain to children with special needs at both the state and federal level. I worked closely with Ezekiel's teachers and school over the course of the next several years to make sure he was getting everything he needed to succeed.

Bryan meanwhile was out in the most punishing and grueling of conditions, trying to prove his mettle and earn his green beret. For as long as I had known him, Bryan possessed a do-or-die mentality. When Bryan made a choice, he never wavered on it, even if it might kill him. Throughout our marriage this was displayed time and again; it was one of the qualities I most respected in him.

When Bryan came home after a twenty-four-hour final training exercise in the Q Course, he pretty much fell through the door. He had lost a significant amount of weight in just one night. He was pale and looked as though he might pass out at any moment. I helped him up the stairs into our kitchen, where he laid himself down on the floor. He asked me to help him set up an IV bag by attaching it to the pot rack on the ceiling. Bryan had taught me how to do IVs in the past, and he walked me through the steps again as he lay there on the floor. I cleaned the injection site and set up an IV port for him, then made him two sandwiches. As he lay there trying to recover, he began to tell me about the previous night.

He'd had a cadre (the term for a Q Course instructor) with whom there existed a significant and mutual dislike. The cadre was a Navy corpsman and there had been problems with that cadre several times, but with this being the final night of the course, the instructor decided to target Bryan in an attempt to get him to quit. He caught Bryan early in the night making a tactical mistake. As punishment, Bryan was given a dummy weighing sixty pounds and was told to run up and down the stairs of a building carrying it. This would have been a challenge, but not impossible, and even possibly an appropriate punishment for Bryan's mistake—if there had been an end time set or water breaks allowed. Instead, this instructor watched the entire night to make sure Bryan did not stop except to pee behind a tree. Hour after hour, Bryan climbed the stairs, sweating throughout the night and into the morning with his muscles spasming as he became severely dehydrated. At one point the cadre whispered to him that he could quit or die. Bryan made his choice and nearly died.

I was enraged that one man was allowed to wield so much power over my husband that he could nearly kill him, and no one would step in. The fact that the cadres who were responsible for the men they were training would look the other way while one of the soldiers under their care was nearly killed was incomprehensible to me. I can appreciate that there is an unspoken rule among the cadres not to get involved in one another's business, but surely there had to be a line when it came to a soldier's life or a clear abuse of power. When I brought all of this up with Bryan he told me that it didn't matter and he swore me to secrecy. All that mattered to him was that he had bested that cadre and would still get his green beret. That was extremely hard for me to accept, but I had to respect Bryan's wishes.

In the spring of 2015 Bryan graduated the Qualification Course, trading his maroon beret for a green one.

His first deployment, in August, was to Afghanistan. Just before he left, we celebrated our tenth wedding anniversary by taking a trip to Asheville. Bryan's dad came to watch the kids for us. For three days, Bryan and I enjoyed some of the best food, beer, and street art in the

Bryan and me after his Special Forces graduation ceremony. *(Karen Black)*

mountains of North Carolina. It was the first time we had been kid-free in years. We felt like a couple of teenagers with no curfew and a credit card. We bought what we wanted, drank what we wanted, and stayed out as late as we wanted. It was silly how much that little bit of freedom meant to us.

Two weeks after our wonderful trip to Asheville, Bryan left on his first deployment on a Green Beret B-Team. The kids were now nine and seven, and Ezekiel no longer needed me to be so involved with him at school. I finally felt I could want more for myself and contribute to our household income. I found the perfect job for me: working online for a Chinese company as an English tutor. I could make my own hours and work as much as I wanted, but still be available for the kids when Bryan was deployed.

Upon returning from his first deployment, Bryan immediately attended three months of Ranger school. After earning his Ranger tab, he was recruited by ODA Team 3212, a Special Forces A-Team, which was slated to leave for Africa in a month and a half. His two subsequent deployments would be with this team. The A-Teams do missions, while B-Teams run support and communications. Each day he would go to work and spend hours organizing the medic area of his team room. Before deployment, the team spent several weeks training to prepare, and often Bryan would be gone all night for training. By the end of May 2016, Bryan was gone again on his first deployment to Niger, Africa.

Bryan working with the Nigerien partner force. *(Ondo)*

Unlike when Bryan was in Afghanistan and we spoke several times a week for hours, when he was in Niger we hardly spoke. During the entire six-month deployment, Bryan and I spoke on average twice a month, and most of the time it was after the kids were in bed. He missed them so much. By the time he returned at the end of October, he was talking about getting out of the military after his contract ended in April.

At that time, Bryan began developing a stock-analyzing program based on research he had been doing since he was sixteen. One of Bryan's favorite pastimes was to read stock-trading books and follow the markets, and he spent hours online in trader chat rooms. He dreamed of creating a program that could pick stocks with a reasonable degree of predictability for success. He wanted to create a website geared toward the general public who had minimal understanding of the markets and offer stock picks for a small monthly fee. He would often test his program on me, despite the fact that I have never been interested in finance. He would ask me to look through the information, then pick what I felt was a good stock to buy. In response, he would slowly adjust his program, making it easy for me to understand and to navigate. He believed that with a little success and a solid following he could get out of the military and build a long-term business. As the program began to come together, Bryan and I talked about the pros and cons of remaining for one more stint in the military and using the signing bonus to help get his business off the ground. In the end, we chose to take the bonus and he signed up for another four years.

After so many years of struggle, it felt like we had finally reached a point of near-perfect balance in our lives as Bryan prepared for a second deployment to Niger in 2017. We had spent Bryan's recent leave on vacation in Washington, D.C., with the kids and his parents. We loved watching Ezekiel and Isaac explore the landmarks they had chosen for the day and seeing them have such fun with his parents as they made their way through museum displays, the boys taking turns reading about their favorite ones. For the first time, there were no meltdowns and the boys were somewhat independent, or at least not in need of our constant supervision. Bryan and I often hung back behind his parents and the kids as we walked the National Mall, holding hands, enjoying the sights in blissful silence.

When we returned home to North Carolina, we started remodeling our house. Our plan was to turn the ground floor into our bedroom and living suite. Bryan had laid tile throughout and remodeled the bathroom, while I painted each room a light gray. The living room became our new bedroom, and the guest bedroom a massive walk-in closet. When Bryan was finished with the shelving and the closet, the room looked like a perfect little boutique, complete with custom lighting he had installed. I loved it. He told me that the space was mine, that he had made it just for me, so I should fill it with all my things first. If his things didn't fit, he'd store them in his office upstairs. I was completely taken aback by his thoughtfulness.

"Did I ever tell you that I like you?" I asked as I hugged him tightly. "I might even love you."

"I might even love you, too," he said.

Life seemed almost too good, and it scared me a little. I remember thanking God in that moment for allowing me to experience that level of love in my life and marriage, especially after twelve years.

Bryan and I went furniture shopping, and for the first time I picked out a bedroom set that wasn't handed down from someone else or bought secondhand. The bed frame was back-ordered, so the set would not arrive until the first week of September, a week after Bryan had deployed. The mattress we had picked out came three weeks later. One week after our bedroom renovation was complete, Bryan was dead.

3

Notification

For weeks after Bryan left for Niger, I worried. The calls I received were few and far between, and often we were cut off after only a few minutes. In one call he conveyed that a film crew for the National Geographic channel was there. Bryan said he had been enjoying getting to know some of the crew while they were staying on the base near the village of Ouallam. Being a Green Beret, Bryan felt it was not acceptable to be filmed in his work environment, so he'd been avoiding the camera. I had lectured him that he needed to get in there and to be excited for the opportunity. I told him no one would ever be that interested in *my* life and he should be grateful that people found him interesting enough to want to put him on such a cool show.

Not many days after that conversation came the last call I received from Bryan. Monday, October 2, 2017. He told me he had only five minutes to talk. They were getting ready to do another mission to a town near the border of Mali, so it would be a few days before I heard from him again. He also said he was busy working in the office and was using the office phone. Which let me know the other guys were nearby and he didn't want them listening in, so he wouldn't talk, but I could talk to him. For five minutes I spoke, telling him what was going on with the kids and me. Then he interrupted me and said he needed to go. "I love you and I'll call you soon." He hung up the phone.

As the next days passed, my anxiety increased by the hour. By Tuesday I found myself checking out my windows, looking for an unfamiliar car in my driveway or for men in uniform coming to knock on my door. I didn't understand why I was feeling this way and kept trying to calm myself down and convince myself it was all my imagination.

Midday on Wednesday, October 4, I was crossing my bedroom when suddenly I stopped in my tracks. What I can describe only as the spirit of God suddenly surrounded me. In that moment, I felt overwhelming calm and peace. A small voice whispered to me, "Trust me. Everything is going to be all right. You will be okay." I stood there for a moment, contemplating what it meant. The last time something like that had happened to me was the day before my dad died. Remembering that, I was scared out of my mind, so I breathed deep and willed that feeling of peace to wash over me again.

At 8:00 that night, I was in the kitchen finishing the dishes after the kids were asleep when my phone rang. It was Bryan's mom, Karen. I had been avoiding speaking to her all week. Due to the nagging worry for Bryan's safety, I'd decided not to call her until I heard from him again. I hadn't spoken with him in four days, which wasn't unusual, but this time it felt significant, and I didn't want to frighten her with my concerns.

As I answered the phone, I was cautious about how I came across. I did not want her to hear the tremor in my voice. After saying hello, she told me that she had seen a newswire on her phone saying there had been an attack on U.S. soldiers along the border of Niger and Mali.

"That was Bryan," I said, my voice shaking. "Bryan was there. That's his group." Karen tried to convince me that we did not know this for sure, and to ease her mind, I agreed. But I knew right then that my husband was dead.

I sat on the steps in my darkened front room trying to breathe as I waited on hold for someone with Bryan's command at Fort Bragg to answer the phone. My whole body trembled. I had closed the double doors separating my living room from the rest of the house so I wouldn't wake the kids. My mind drifted from Bryan to each of the other team members I had met or heard Bryan speak about. I prayed for all the men to make it home to their families. "Please, Lord," I said, "if Bryan didn't make it, I pray his new captain did and the communications sergeant with the young family. The team sergeant needs to come home to be with his wife and son. They don't deserve this. Please let him come home." Bryan's best friend on the team was Sergeant First Class Brent Bartels, and throughout that night I felt pressed to pray for him. I felt Brent needed to make it home—otherwise, another part of Bryan would not be coming home, and I couldn't handle that, as well.

Finally, I heard a click on the other end and a female voice told me that until next of kin were notified, they were not authorized to tell anyone—even a spouse—whether a deployed soldier had been killed. I was read a statement filled with words saying nothing. It only served to heighten my fears.

Next, I called the team sergeant's wife to ask if she had heard anything about the attack. "Well, I heard from Smith a little while ago and he said they were out on a mission and things went bad. Real bad. But he wouldn't say what and he said he'd call me again tomorrow because they needed the phone lines open. I'll try calling him, though, and see if he can tell me anything about your husband. Okay?"

"Okay. Thanks."

I hung up the phone. The last time we spoke, Bryan had called on the office phone in Ouallam, but I didn't have that number. There was nothing I could do but wait.

It was 9:30 at night when I heard the car drive up. It seemed to take an eternity for the knock to come. I paused for a minute before opening the door, realizing the moment I opened it nothing in my life would ever be the same. When I finally turned the door handle, I saw two chaplains standing there. They solemnly asked if I would please allow them to come in. We stood in my entryway, sorrow written plainly on their faces.

Protocol requires them to read the statement on a spouse's death. As the statement was read, the words seemed to come at me in slow motion, each one hitting me like a brick, heavy and deafening. "I'm sorry, Mrs. Black. I'm afraid we have some bad news. I'm sure you have some idea why we are here. Your husband and his unit were attacked. I'm so sorry, Mrs. Black, but your husband did not make it. Bryan was killed earlier today in Niger, Africa."

I backed away from the two men until I hit the corner of the wall. I took several deep breaths as I began to shake. My mouth went dry and my stomach lurched. This was real; this was happening to me, to my family. I looked up the stairs, terrified that the boys might have heard noises and woken up. I was so scared that they would come downstairs before I could be brave for them.

The chaplains asked if I had anyone who could come over and stay with me. I panicked and said I did not. That's one thing about being a military wife: You are far from family. Too far, when things go wrong. It took a few minutes for me to come to my senses and realize I could call a friend from up the street. When my friend answered her phone I could say nothing but "Something happened to Bryan. Can you come over?" She immediately said yes and hung up the phone.

I had promised Karen earlier in the night that if I found anything out about Bryan, I would call her, no matter what it was. I dialed Karen's number and steeled myself to tell one of my favorite people in this world that her baby boy was dead. The depth of pain I felt as I unleashed that monstrous truth on her is something I wouldn't wish on any person.

The phone's ring sounded hollow as I waited for Karen to answer. "Hi. What's going on, did you find anything out?" she asked.

Shock had wiped away my emotions and I responded robotically. "I did."

There was a sharp silence that came over the phone, like an icy wind. She knew. After a few long seconds I realized I needed to finish.

"Chaplains are here," I said. "Bryan is not coming home."

There was no use trying to speak further. There was nothing to say as the thing of every mother's nightmares settled on us both.

Finally, Karen broke the silence. "I need to go. I need to let Henry know."

I sat on my couch for the next several hours as my friend arrived, the chaplains left, and more people began to come over. I couldn't talk and I couldn't sleep. All I could do was sit in shock, staring at the wall. The realization of what my life now was ran like a loop through my mind. "I am a widow, I am a single mom, I am now the sole provider, my job doesn't pay enough . . ." Fear of my unknown future without Bryan was palpable. *Where do I begin a new life,* I wondered, *one without Bryan? How is that possible?* I couldn't wrap my mind around any of it. *Was there any chance some mistake had been made? He'd come walking through that door again, wouldn't he?* I sat up all night, holding vigil, thinking these terrifying thoughts and staring into an abyss of uncertainty.

The next day came in a haze. I had sent the kids to school without telling them about Bryan. I decided early on that first night after being notified that I needed a plan. The children had slept well and would come down the stairs in the morning happy and ready for another school day, so they would have one last good day. If this was all I could give them this year, I would do it. I would pretend everything was normal even if it killed me. And my plan would be to take the kids to school and wait for as much family as possible to arrive before picking them up. I knew the boys would need to see the support they had.

My cousin Gwen, who they know as their aunt, had arrived around 2:30 in the morning. Henry, who was in DC for work that week, would be arriving in Fayetteville after the kids were in school. I called the school to inform them of the situation so they could prepare the kids' homework packets with extra work so they could be absent. I also needed to make certain that if anyone was aware of the attack because of media reports, no word of it got around the school or to my children before I spoke with them.

Then I simply had to wait for Henry's arrival. When Henry got out of his car that afternoon it was clear he had not slept. Dark circles were etched under his eyes and his normally light and friendly manner was silent and solemn. It seemed like he had aged overnight. He didn't say hello, just hugged me tightly, then walked into the house.

It wasn't much later that the school day was over, which meant it was time. I was sick with the truth that I was going to have to unleash on my own children. After picking the kids up from school, Henry and I took them out to a deserted playground in a wooded area. I wanted to tell them somewhere away from home. Someplace where they could wrap up this nightmare and leave it. Home should hold happy and comforting memories, not memories of devastation. I wanted them to leave the ruin of that moment and come back home to family and positive memories of their dad. I didn't want them to think of the news every time they walked through the door from school or sat on their beds.

So here we were on a winding road driving deep in the woods on a cool October day heading for a deserted playground. They were so excited to find out why Grandpa had come to visit and what we were doing at the park with him. After parking the car, Henry and I hung back as the boys ran for the swings. A cool October wind blew, kicking up leaves all around us as we stared at the ground, slowly making our way toward the playground.

"Do you want me to tell them?" Henry asked.

I did want that, but it was my job. No grandfather should ever have to tell his grandchildren that their dad—his own son—is dead. I looked up at the tall pine trees around us and felt the far-off sun rays peeking through their branches as I tried to fight back the terror I felt. It took a moment, but the wave of fear finally passed. I stepped forward.

"Hey, boys!" I yelled. They came running and met us near a park bench on the edge of the playset. "Grandpa and I brought you guys here to speak to you. We have some bad news." The boys looked at me with confusion as I searched for the right words. "It's okay to be angry or sad. It's okay to cry or yell. Okay?"

Both kids nodded in understanding.

"You know how we've been praying for Dad's safety?" I asked. "You know how we prayed he would be safely brought home?" Suddenly I saw fear in their eyes and I could not stop tears from coming to mine. I took a jagged breath and pushed ahead. "Well, his unit was attacked." My voice began to tremble as I continued. "Dad and his friends were there." Now I saw panic in their faces. "Some of them died and some were injured." I could barely breathe as I whispered, "I am so sorry, boys."

I could no longer contain the torrent of emotion, and I heard myself make an awful noise as I began to cry and the tears flooded my vision. "Dad is not coming home."

Isaac let out a panicked shriek as his face took on the most devastating shape I'd ever seen. "He's *dead*?" Isaac asked, incredulous.

"Yes, he is dead."

By now we were all weeping and the kids began whimpering like injured animals. So did I. Henry turned away and shook. Isaac looked at me, desperate, and asked me a question I wish I could have given him a different answer to.

"No, not halfway dead," I answered him.

"All the way dead? Maybe he can still be fixed and come back?" he begged.

I responded shakily, "You know the answer to that. No. There is no coming back."

Isaac turned, wailing, and ran away from me.

43

"Please don't run away and hide. I'm sad, too, and I need you here." But it was no use; Isaac was gone.

Henry, Ezekiel, and I stood there in silence for a long while, crying. Then we all hugged, trying to ease the pain. Finally, everyone separated and went off on their own.

I found my younger son hiding under the slide.

"Isaac?"

Silence.

"Honey, I'm so sorry. Why don't you come out and let me give you a hug."

He couldn't even look at me or respond.

I glanced behind me at my older son, who was kicking at the dirt, sobbing. Henry followed one boy and I followed the other. Then we just sat and gave them time.

They say that time heals all wounds, but some scars are everlasting. Even in the moment, I knew that this would be one of those ugly scars seared forever on our souls. *Breathe,* I told myself. *Just take a deep breath and trust He who makes all things new. Remember, He can work all things for the good of those who love Him and are called according to His good purpose.* I repeated this in my head as I stood by the slide. Those promises were all I had left that day. The only hope I could cling to that offered some glimmer of light in such a dark place.

After a while, Isaac emerged and I gathered my children to me. Then my older son made the most honest comment, which brought the ugliness of the situation into glaring focus. "I can't believe my dad was murdered."

My breath caught in my throat and my heart ached on a whole new level. I did not know how to respond, mostly because he was right. An eleven-year-old autistic boy had more clarity on the situation in that moment than most people I know, including myself when I heard about the ambush.

After a few more minutes our tears began to subside. Henry and I coaxed them onto the swings and the boys finally began to calm down. The quiet solitude of the forest helped bring some peace to the situation and I finally felt a small amount of calm come over me. That is when Ezekiel looked at us and said, "Who is going to teach me how to do everything now? Dad was supposed to teach me to fish and wrestle and everything." He began crying again.

Desperate in that moment, I glanced at Henry, hoping he'd be willing to back up my next words. "Grandpa will. That's why you have Grandpa."

Henry and I locked eyes and I saw fresh tears well up as he said, "Yes."

We continued to push the kids on the swings in silence. After a few minutes, Isaac got off his swing and walked over to the jungle gym where he spent some time climbing. We gave the boys another half-hour to just be alone and cry before deciding it was probably time to get back to the house. I asked Isaac what he wanted.

"Can my friends come over?" he asked.

Bryan with our boys after the Special Forces Qualification Course graduation. *(Karen Black)*

"Yes. Absolutely."

I texted my friends who knew what had happened and asked if they could bring their kids by to play for a little bit. My sons needed their friends to feel like they would be okay. By the time we arrived home, the sun was setting and there were friends at my house waiting to support and be with us on the hardest day of our lives.

By the next day, family and friends started flying in from all over the country. The first to arrive was Karen, who was flying in from her and Henry's home state of Washington. Having been on the East Coast for business that week, Henry had driven in the day before. I couldn't contain my grief as I threw my arms around her and we both wept bitterly. Henry had picked her up from the airport, and as we sat in my house grieving, there was little to say, so I offered them something to drink. Henry wanted coffee, so I disappeared into the kitchen for a moment. From the other room, I heard knocking at the door.

Henry answered it and an unfamiliar male voice quietly said hello to him. I peeked down the stairs to see a tall, slender man in black slacks, a white button-down, and a black blazer. He looked disheveled, both kind and sad all at once. He looked up at me with grave eyes and climbed the stairs to introduce himself.

"Hi, I'm Major Alan Van Saun. I am so sorry to hear about Bryan. I knew him, and he was an outstanding man and soldier." He fought back tears. "I am the commander over Bryan's unit but was on temporary paternity leave due to the birth of my daughter, so I was unfortunately here in Fayetteville when the ambush took place. I just wanted to offer you my sincere condolences and tell you how very sorry I am. I wish I could do something. If there is anything you need at all, please let me know."

I didn't know what to say except "Thank you." There was a long stretch of silence until Henry asked him to come in and sit for a while. I left the two of them and Karen alone as I finished making the coffee. A simple task felt like the only thing I could do. Anything else, my mind couldn't process—certainly not figuring out what to say to the major. I listened as he and Henry talked in the other room, both men shaken and tearful.

As he left, Major Van Saun took my hand as he again offered any help we might need. When Henry walked him out to his car, I watched an intense exchange between them. Henry questioned the major: "I don't mean any disrespect, but why the *fuck* was Bryan's team sent out with no support?" Henry's career was in the military, so he understood that world and its procedures well. Major Van Saun looked at Henry sadly as he replied that Special Forces teams are often isolated without support. The major's head seemed to hang with the weight of the visit.

Tears streamed down my face as I stood at the kitchen window watching him drive away. I was devastated by what lay ahead for my family and pained as I watched Henry grapple with the loss of his younger son. I thought about my two boys and the unimaginable nightmare that losing one would be.

About an hour later, the wives of the Green Beret team members came over. We stood there in my kitchen that Friday morning, weeping for all that was lost. I had lost my husband; their husbands had lost their friends; we had all lost our peace of mind that this could never happen to us. So far, I had heard that only three men were dead: Bryan and Dustin Wright, Green Berets, and Jeremiah Johnson, a non-commissioned officer (NCO) from the support unit attached to the team. But a friend from the team mentioned how horrible it was that the mechanic was missing as well. She said that LaDavid Johnson, the mechanic from the support team, was now presumed dead. I was shocked. Bryan had thought of LaDavid like a little brother. A deep and guttural sob came from my throat as I leaned on my friend's shoulder and wept. I knew I was crying harder over the loss of LaDavid than I had over my own husband, but LaDavid was the youngest and the whole team was helping him train to go to Special Forces selection. Originally, he was not supposed to deploy with them, but the team had requested LaDavid join them on deployment again for a second year.

I knew the men on the team would have felt responsible for LaDavid. They all would have wanted to protect him, especially as he was there because of them. If Bryan had known LaDavid was dead, it would have destroyed him. It made me physically sick to think of him being gone.

By that night, the attack in Niger had begun to spread across every major news network. Back in Bryan's hometown in Washington State, reporters had surrounded his parents' home and began interviewing their neighbors. A segment aired in which a reporter standing in front of Karen and Henry's house stated who lived there and that they were out of state indefinitely because of the tragedy. Because the report showed the street and house they lived in, Karen and Henry had to contact local authorities to monitor the empty house.

By then we had all started receiving phone calls and text messages from members of the media requesting to speak with us. None of us knew what to make of it. I still could not even say out loud the words "Bryan is dead." So I just put my phone on silent.

The following week my house was overrun by an incredible number of visitors every day. Men who had been on previous deployments and a few from the team stopped by as they began to arrive back in-country, but they were all very quiet, almost standoffish. They didn't want to talk about the ambush and focused mainly on condolences and stories of my husband. I was too exhausted to care about the details those first weeks, anyway. More than anything, I needed to laugh, so I enjoyed hearing their stories about all of my husband's antics at work and overseas. The laughter helped to ease some of the pain and numbness I felt.

It's amazing how robotic and dead you can feel inside and still survive. My life had become an out-of-body experience as one nightmare after another played out. The news of Bryan's death. Telling his mom. Seeing his dad's face. Breaking my children's hearts. Making choices about a casket, where to hold a memorial. Discussing an autopsy. Wondering if he had a will. Making decisions in the event further remains were found and what that might mean. Wondering where he wanted to be buried, what songs to play at the church, which Bible verses to put on the leaflets we'd hand out at the service. To view or not to view the body.

The blur of meetings to schedule, documents to sign, and people to meet in the wake of Bryan's death was dizzying. I wanted to lie down and disappear but felt that everything I did reflected on the man Bryan was. So I woke early each day, put on my best dress, made my bed, did my hair and makeup, all before anyone could arrive and surprise me. Something in the routine soothed me. The details of dying in the military are complicated. A casualty assistance officer (CAO) is assigned to each family, and that same man stays with the family until all investigations and paperwork are complete. Without a CAO, I don't know how I would have managed to get everything done or how I would have understood half of the information being given to me. Each day my CAO would lay out the day's agenda before me and take meticulous notes as we addressed each item.

In the midst of the planning and paperwork, I was getting bits and pieces of what had happened to Bryan's unit. The first few news articles, quoting Army officials, reported that it was unclear who the enemy was that fired on Bryan's team. A spokesman for U.S. Africa Command (AFRICOM) confirmed that the ambush had occurred near the Niger/Mali border.

By the end of October, we heard that the eleven-member team had accompanied thirty-two Nigerien soldiers on a mission to gather information. *The Washington Post* reported that together they left from the capital of Niamey to travel to a deserted area near the village of Tongo Tongo, outside of which they were attacked. According to reports, the team had not expected resistance during their one-day mission. Fifty militants surprised the team when they set upon them with small arms and rocket-propelled grenades. An official looking into the ambush stated that the team did not request support for an hour, but once they did a drone arrived on scene within minutes—and an hour later, French Mirage jets arrived to assist the stranded team. Reports stated that four

U.S. soldiers had been killed, one of them having been separated from his eleven-member team. Indeed, Sergeant LaDavid Johnson was not recovered with the others and initially was unaccounted for. Survivors of the ambush said they felt the villagers of Tongo Tongo had stalled the team's departure and may have been complicit in the ambush.

I was grateful that following the attack there was only a little media attention to the ambush. Mostly there were articles reporting what officials looking into the incident had to say. I received a few phone calls, texts, and messages on Facebook from reporters requesting to speak with me. While I didn't like the attention and didn't respond, I was sure it would be short-lived. I never thought my husband's face would be on television. But soon that changed. Though I didn't have cable at home, and I didn't see what the nightly news shows covered, judging by the volume of articles appearing on the Internet it became clear that the story of the ambush was picking up steam. I tried to hide all of this from my sons as much as possible.

The increasing media attention stemmed from several things. This was the largest loss of life in that region since the Battle of Mogadishu, also known as Black Hawk Down, which took place in 1993—coincidentally, between October 3 and 4. Most Americans knew nothing of the U.S. presence in Niger, so it came as a shock to many to find out that Green Berets were operating in the region. Even Congress contended they were not aware of any military presence in the region, though the U.S. has had a presence there since 2013. Another issue was that LaDavid Johnson had gone missing after the ambush and it took forty-eight hours for his remains to be discovered under a tree not far from the ambush site. While he was missing, there was a lot of controversy surrounding the details of his whereabouts and remains.

AFRICOM, which is the combatant command responsible for all Department of Defense operations, exercises, and security cooperation on the continent, announced it would be conducting an extensive investigation into the circumstances around the ambush. My biggest concern was to find out what mistakes—if any—were made, and to be certain that the military would fix any shortcomings for future teams. I was relieved to know that the military was going to work hard to make sure every detail of the ambush was discovered and that they would share those details with the families of the fallen.

A week after Bryan's death, I was desperate to get out of the house and do something normal, so Karen and I took Isaac to his guitar lesson in downtown Fayetteville. As we parked my phone rang, so Karen took Isaac to his lesson while I answered the call.

There was a strange click and static and then a male voice that sounded far away. "Hello . . . uh, is this Michelle?"

"Yes. Who is this?" I asked, as I turned and headed toward the door.

"Hello, ma'am, this is Captain Mike Perozeni."

The name sounded vaguely familiar, but I couldn't place it.

"You . . . uh . . . you don't know me, but . . ." There was suddenly a nervous and intense edge to the voice. I had initially thought it was a reporter calling or someone from the military to give me more bad news. But there was something in his tone that made me think otherwise, some sort of vulnerability. "Ma'am, I am Captain Mike Perozeni . . . from your husband's team . . . I just needed to talk to you and to tell you how sorry I am."

Standing outside the music studio, I closed my eyes as I tried to process his words. They seemed to bounce from one side of my head to the other, not quite clicking. Finally, my mind cleared. This man was part of the unit. He was there that day outside of Tongo Tongo, in the firefight with Bryan and the other soldiers. Bryan had told me about a new captain being assigned to their team.

I could feel the fall sun heating up the air around me as a bead of sweat formed on the back of my neck, then rolled between my shoulder blades. I took a deep breath, fighting back tears before speaking again. "Are you back in the U.S.?"

"No, ma'am. I am in Germany in a hospital. I'm new to the team, so you probably haven't heard of me before, but I needed to let you know how sorry I am about Bryan." His voice broke for a second; he took a breath and continued. "I'm sorry that I didn't bring him home safely."

My head was spinning. He was wounded yet calling me from a hospital in Germany? As I stood there holding the phone, I was both confused and in awe of this man's character to call me from his hospital bed to offer condolences from the other side of the world. And my mind now zeroed in on the fact that Bryan had mentioned Captain Mike Perozeni to me a few times, and those conversations were now rushing back to me.

"Ma'am?" I heard Captain Perozeni ask as his voice broke through the heavy silence.

"Mike, I know exactly who you are. You don't need to apologize to me. I am just glad you are alive and safe—that is what Bryan would have wanted. Bryan told me about you. He said that he was glad you had joined the team and you were going to be an asset to them. He also told me that you were extremely intelligent and capable. Bryan didn't say that about many people."

There was another moment of heavy silence before Captain Perozeni finally said, "Thank you, ma'am. I appreciate you saying that."

I stood there fighting back tears. Grief threatened to overwhelm me; then, suddenly, I felt angry. Bryan would not want these men to feel guilty for surviving. They shouldn't be apologizing to me. I could feel Bryan and his strength, the essence of who he was like armor around me. I knew that he would have rather sacrificed himself for those men than allow any one of them to die in his place.

"You don't need to apologize to me, Mike. I am just grateful for each of you who survived and will make it home. That is what Bryan would have wanted, for as many of you as possible to make it home. Just get better and get home and I will be happy."

There was something—some sort of tension—that I could feel dissipate over the line. A sense of peace washed over me, flowing through my entire body like a river as I stood there staring out across the street to where a large elm tree grew. I watched as the tree's long branches began swaying in the gentle afternoon breeze.

"Yes, ma'am," Captain Perozeni finally said in a hushed tone.

"And, Mike, be sure to come see me when you get home."

As we hung up, I felt rooted to the spot for a minute, completely drained from fighting back the urge to cry. I hadn't wanted Captain Perozeni to hear my pain. Running the conversation over again in my mind, I began to weep uncontrollably. I had to put my hand on the side of the building for support as my knees threatened to buckle and my whole body shook with the weight of the conversation. Bryan would have been proud of me because I had stayed strong and offered comfort to someone I believed needed it more than me. Life is hard, and even more so when you feel the need to patch everyone else's wounds. In that moment, I realized I wanted to do just that: patch up all the wounds caused by the ambush. The most difficult part of that task was that, at times, it meant I had to hide my own pain.

4

Airport

Something about wearing the right dress and the right shoes helped convince me that I could be strong when my husband's body arrived at Raleigh-Durham International Airport from Dover.

The week before, I had sat in tears in a department store dressing room as my mom, sister, and cousin pulled every suitable dress they could find and brought them to me to try on. I needed three outfits that day. The first was for going to the airport to collect Bryan's body, the second for the visitation at the funeral home, and the third for the memorial service at our church. Bryan's memorial service. My husband's. This thought ran through my mind on a loop, but I couldn't grab it. I felt numb inside that dressing room, staring at the cream-and-white dress that my mom felt was the most appropriate thing to wear to the airport. *Who knows?* I thought. *Maybe it will help me feel brave.*

Bryan's body was being returned to us from Dover Air Force Base. The Charles C. Carson Center for Mortuary Affairs located at Dover is where the remains of U.S. service members are prepared. We were scheduled to go to Raleigh-Durham to meet the flight. The Army had told me he was in a cargo hold, which made me feel sick. He was now a thing, a cold body. Until now, I had never considered the steps that went into the arrival of bodies back in the United States when soldiers are killed overseas. Like most people, I had seen countless pictures of men in uniform carrying caskets from the cargo holds of airplanes, but my imagination had wandered no further.

I knew nothing of what families went through, the sorrow that day held. I had never thought of how they were forced to face the confused and curious travelers stopping and staring at them on what would be the worst day they'd ever live through.

As I stood in the dressing room, my mind raced through what I would be facing in the next few days. Overwhelmed by those thoughts, I stared at myself in the mirror. The widow. It was no longer just me, Michelle Black, staring back. This was a widow with empty eyes. I no longer recognized myself.

Like a life-sized doll, I was zipped and unzipped, spun and analyzed by everyone around me. I bent to every whim of those who were there and was grateful for their help. That day I hated every dress my family showed me, as each one signified the end of my future. I was doing only what I needed to do to survive each day.

At 11:00 a.m. on Monday, October 16, I stood ready in my cream-and-white dress, pearl necklace, and cream heels. The CAO picked us up for the hourlong drive to Raleigh-Durham International Airport. As we pulled up to the curb at the airport, three representatives from the USO escorted us through a private security line and across the airport to a small room inside the USO lounge.

There was a beautiful spread of food laid before us, so we ate as we waited for the plane carrying Bryan to arrive. I took my boys' hands in mine as we rode down the glass-walled elevator and whispered to them that everything would be okay. I kept my eyes straight ahead and tried hard to walk purposefully, to keep from panicking or crying as we stepped into the crowd of travelers moving through the terminal. My children would follow my lead, so I needed to set an example of strength.

When we reached the gate, we glanced behind us to see twenty-two soldiers in dress uniform marching down the main thoroughfare of the airport walkway, making their way toward us. Curious travelers stared at the procession of soldiers in their dress blues, the ceremony's purpose dawning on them slowly. Some people snapped to attention to show us respect; some even saluted. Others ducked their heads, as though they'd been caught staring at a car wreck, then hurried off or turned their backs.

I wished I could turn my back, too. It shakes you to your core when it's you they are marching for. I couldn't breathe. Looking around, I saw Bryan's parents with tears rolling down their faces. There was so much hurt there, I had to look away.

The soldiers continued marching until they reached our gate, where they came to a stop and marched in place, doing an about-face to turn toward us. Then the leader made a call and they stopped marching and saluted us before lowering their arms.

We were ushered to the door of the gate, where we lined up. I looked each of my children in the eyes, steadying them, steadying myself. The soldiers to my right began to march in place again as an announcement over the intercom at the gate explained who we were and why we were there. I was focusing on holding my head high and staring straight ahead when I felt the tears flowing freely down my cheeks. This wasn't supposed to be me; this wasn't supposed to be Bryan. We were supposed to be one of those families standing in the walkway on our way to a vacation, in awe of the somber ceremony we had happened upon. We weren't supposed to be finding out how a soldier is brought home firsthand.

I could feel myself shaking as I moved toward the door. Ezekiel squeezed my hand. When I looked down at him, my eleven-year-old autistic son was giving me a reassuring stare. He nodded seriously, then stepped forward, leading me. I squeezed both kids' hands and we stepped through the door. Walking the long, narrow hallway that led us to the tarmac was a surreal experience; everything felt slowed, each step took effort.

My husband was coming home five months early, in a casket. And while I wanted to shield my children from the nightmare we were about to confront, the truth was that we all needed to see the box draped in a flag carried by his friends and teammates. We needed that finality so we could fully grasp that this was real; this was permanent. There truly was no coming back from this.

With a storm forecasted to move in that day, it was breezy and the air was crisp as we stepped through the door into the bright light of day. I pulled my sweater tight around me as one by one we filed carefully down the metal steps to an area where we were to await the plane. We were offered earplugs for the noise. I helped the boys put theirs in, but I declined any for myself. I wanted to feel and hear the full impact of everything, just as Bryan had when he died. No comforts, nothing to soften the blow. I needed to stare this beast down, even if it brought me to my knees.

I repeated in my head the thoughts that had kept me going since the beginning of October: *I am heartbroken, but I am not broken. I will face this with fury and let every ounce of it hit me full force and dare it to break me. I've heard it said that you marry your equal; if that's true, I'm a beast. A force to be reckoned with. I will do Bryan proud. This is my mantra. I will take deep breaths, hold my children close, and handle things. I will not be another victim of the men who took my husband's life and those of his fellow soldiers. Those men were left in a desert without a choice, but I have a choice. My children and I will not be further victims of this tragedy; we will be victors.*

I was brought back to the present by feeling cold water on my skin. Two fire trucks were using their water cannons to create what is known as a water-cannon salute, which made a rainbow in the middle. An airplane suddenly emerged from under the arc and I realized our life together was ending as it had begun: under a rainbow.

Just twelve years before, Bryan and I had stood outside under a rainbow as we said our vows. Now I stood under another rainbow without him, thinking to myself, *I am cold and empty.* All of the pain and sadness I'd had to handle the last few weeks had built up to a coldness that had allowed me to keep a handle on things.

Then I saw Bryan's casket covered in a flag and I realized that I was about to lose that handle. The weight of what my children and I were gazing upon hit me like a sledgehammer to the stomach. A man I'd never met in a green vest with an orange marker was weeping as he stood facing us on the other side of the flag-draped casket.

A wave of violent emotion swept over me and I could no longer stem the tide as wave after wave shook my body and I cried out for the father of my children, for my husband, for my broken heart and his lost dreams, our lost dreams. My hands on his casket, his flag, I felt my face contort from the pain as the grief welled up from deep inside. My knees threatened to buckle as I tried to catch my breath and quiet my sobs. At that moment, I wanted no one but his mom, his dad, and my children. I found them and held on tight.

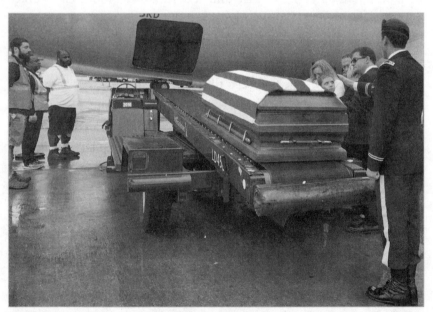

Receiving Bryan's body from Dover. (*Anonymous*)

Only those who loved him like I did could possibly understand the depth of the despair and pain I felt in that moment. Those who loved him—and apparently the ground traffic controller. Suddenly this thought made me laugh a little, and I remembered Bryan and all of our laughter. I looked up just in time to see the mortician standing next to the hearse, adjusting his hair as he checked himself out in the reflection of the back window, and I laughed a bit more to myself through my tears. Bryan would be loving this.

God, I was going to miss him.

As we stepped away from the casket, my tears began to subside. The soldiers stepped forward once again and moved the casket to the hearse. Then a chaplain called for a prayer and we all bowed our heads. The prayer was short and before I knew it we were being ushered toward the stairs to take us back inside.

Walking across the large lobby near the entrance to the airport, I saw a woman whose presence caused me to slow. She was a small woman with dark hair carrying an instrument case. As everybody else walked by, hurriedly going about their business, she stood alone, saluting us as a family. She did not move, did not make eye contact, just stood at attention, saluting us and honoring our sacrifice. I glanced over at Karen, and it was apparent she had seen this woman, too, because there were tears streaming down her face as well as a hint of a smile.

We made our way out to the curb of the airport and were greeted by the military-issued van parked along the street. As we piled into it, I felt completely exhausted, but the day had only just begun. I was soon confused as we pulled into a parking lot near the airport. I looked to the right of the van and realized there were several dozen men dressed in biker vests lining the sides of the parking lot we had just pulled into. They were standing at attention and some were holding flagpoles up, American flags waving in the wind.

Multiple Harleys and street bikes were parked, waiting for us to pass. It dawned on me that this was the Patriot Guard Riders, an organization whose members attend the funerals of members of the United States military and first responders at the invitation of the family. Someone had contacted us the week prior and asked if we would like them to escort us home from the Raleigh airport and we had said yes, but I'd had no idea what to expect and was shocked by how many riders had shown up to support our family.

I was unsteady on my feet as I held the boys' hands again while we followed Bryan's parents toward the front of the line of men. In the center of the cluster was one large, tough-looking man without a flag. He stepped forward and presented each one of us with a woven bracelet made to honor those who have fallen. He shook our hands and gave us each a hug.

The green braided bracelet was thick and heavy on Isaac's wrist as he proudly put it on. Isaac loved his new bracelet, and it would become a permanent fixture on him. We began to shake hands with some of those present, but there were so many and I was so exhausted that I could hardly stay on my feet. The emotional toll of the day was catching up to me. I looked back over at Henry, who was continuing down the line, shaking hands with people. When Henry returned from shaking hands and thanking those present, he climbed back into our vehicle looking completely drained, but calmer from talking to the men.

The Patriot Guard was not the only group who came and showed support. Both Bryan and Jeremiah Johnson returned home that day, flying into the Raleigh-Durham International Airport at different times. No media seemed to catch it, but the American people did. Everywhere I turned, it seemed someone was saluting or had set up a tribute to honor Bryan and Jeremiah and to show their support for our families.

As we pulled onto the freeway, the Patriot Guard drove alongside us and we were led by a police escort with flashing lights that went ahead of the hearse. While we followed the hearse carrying Bryan's body down the first section of the freeway, Karen's breath caught in her throat.

"Look at that!" She pointed ahead to the freeway overpass.

I could clearly see a fire engine with a large American flag displayed on its side. Lined up along each side of the fire engine were several firefighters who were standing at attention. How did these first responders know what time we'd be there to be certain we would see them? What had motivated them to do something so selfless for us? I was overcome by their gesture.

I was both smiling and crying when we approached the second freeway overpass. There was a display set up by a paramedic truck and several EMTs. They, too, had a flag displayed and were standing at attention as we drove by.

Approaching the third freeway overpass, I watched as several cars pulled to the side of the road. The drivers exited their vehicles, and they stood at attention. I was yet again taken aback. What was happening? For the entire hour and twenty minutes between Raleigh-Durham and Fayetteville, every single overpass had a display set up and people standing at attention. Cars continuously pulled to the side of the road as they saw us coming and saluted as the motorcade passed by. We were in awe of what our community had done; the gesture was beyond anything I could have imagined. I spent the entire drive home crying tears of gratitude.

When we finally pulled into our hometown of Fayetteville, a storm had moved in and it was cold out and drizzling. Despite the weather, the main road was lined with strangers, friends, and local media cheering and holding signs expressing love, condolences, and support. These wonderful people were showing me what it meant to honor the fallen. They showed up even though it was freezing and miserable outside. For hours they lined the roads and ignored their misery to recognize mine.

I wish I could give back to those who showed so much love and support, but the gesture was so big and made by so many that there is no way to repay it. As the days, weeks, then months rolled turbulently by, there was one thing that stayed consistent: the outpouring of support from the American public. Not one of these people cared what my religion or political leanings were; they were simply sending letters, calling, or showing up. It was during that time that I realized this is what makes our country so amazing. America is truly a country of the most generous individuals on this earth. We may not be a perfect nation, but which nation is? We are a nation of individuals who take pleasure in serving others, and that is why we are great. To give and to serve others is to sacrifice. To sacrifice for others is to love them.

Love is what I needed that day as the military van pulled up to the funeral home behind the hearse. Standing outside the mortuary, my body felt stiff with the horror of what was unfolding.

My family and Bryan's and those lining the streets of Fayetteville were enveloped by a chilly fog and drizzle. We stood at attention at the entrance to the mortuary, facing the flag-draped casket as a bugle began to play, low and melancholy, a song well known in a military town: "Taps."

When the song finished, Bryan was moved inside and we filed into the funeral home behind him. We were surprised to find ourselves in a small chapel the funeral home had built for just such an occasion. We were told to wait there as they prepared the body for viewing. Up until that moment, we weren't certain if we were going to see Bryan's body that day. It was a relief to hear that his body was viewable.

While we waited in the chapel, we sat in pews and my boys pretended to be preachers. They climbed up into the pulpit and managed to get the adults laughing through their tears with some ridiculous antics. It wasn't long before the funeral coordinator and my CAO came out and said they were ready.

Suddenly, Isaac turned to me and said with conviction that he wanted to see his dad. When I said no, Isaac launched a barrage of arguments, petitioning me to let him see his father's body. I had seen my own father after he'd suffered a heart attack, and for years I couldn't get the image out of my mind. I was thirty-two when that occurred, and until that moment in the chapel I had always wished I hadn't viewed my father's body, which had looked like an empty shell and not the father I adored. And heart attacks don't leave nearly the marks bullets do. I did not want the image of my husband's damaged body burned into the memory of my nine-year-old son.

As a parent I have always believed in leading by example. If I viewed Bryan, I would have to allow my sons the same choice. I desperately wanted to see Bryan, but I also knew the impact of what I might see. I decided that I wanted my last image of Bryan to be a happy one and I wanted the same for Ezekiel and Isaac. So I made the decision for me and my children not to view Bryan's body.

Bryan's brother, dad, and uncle talked among themselves and decided they would all go. They apprehensively followed the CAO through a door and into another part of the funeral home. When they returned, the men were clearly rattled and haunted by having seen Bryan in the casket. I was instantly relieved that I had made the decision for me and my kids not to view the body. Henry turned to Karen and simply stated with a tremor in his voice, "He still looks like Bryan." This knowledge brought me and Karen tremendous peace.

After the CAO closed the casket and put the flag back in place, the entire family could go in and spend time in the viewing room with Bryan and say our goodbyes. We gathered around the flag-draped casket, and the heaviness of the day coupled with the finality of Bryan's death seemed to overcome us all. There was complete silence; the sound of our combined suffering was deafening.

I placed my hands on Bryan's casket once more, closing my eyes as I let the tears flow down my face. I realized I wasn't yet ready to say goodbye. I needed more time. But Bryan's had run out. Backing away, I looked down at the cream-and-white dress I was wearing before glancing around the room at my family and Bryan's. It wasn't the dress that had helped me make it through that day and given me the strength I needed to face that nightmare, of course. It was everyone there in that room, outside on the streets, saluting at the airport, and those on the freeway overpasses. It was my pride in the remarkable country we live in and my need to prove myself worthy of the phenomenal man I had married as I prepared to lay him to rest.

5

The Call

The next day, I was sitting at my dining table with Bryan's parents, Ezekiel, Isaac, and Bryan's uncle Bob, waiting for my cell phone to ring. At 2:45, President Trump was calling to express his condolences for Bryan's death. We were all looking forward to the call, as it was a welcome distraction from the heartache of the previous day's events.

When the phone rang, I took a deep breath, trying to remember my manners the way my mother taught me. I let the phone ring twice so I would appear far more collected than I actually felt. When I answered, a White House operator said he was connecting me to the president of the United States. Standing there holding the phone, I felt humbled and amazed that this was truly happening.

"Hello, Michelle, it's Donald Trump and I just wanted to call and pay my respects. Your husband was an impressive man. I have a letter before me written by his team and those who knew him well. Your husband was a great man. He was loved and respected by everybody."

I was lost for a brief moment before I finally found the correct words. "Thank you, Mr. President," I said, my voice echoing oddly in my ears. "I appreciate that."

"So, tell me, Michelle, how are you doing?" President Trump asked.

"As best as can be expected. He was probably the best . . ." I began to respond, when President Trump asked, "This is a tragedy you never expect, right?"

I responded truthfully. "You know? Being a military wife, it is and it isn't. You're always prepared, so . . . It's definitely a heartbreak, but . . ." I was so emotionally exhausted that I couldn't think of the right words.

I was grateful that President Trump is a talker and just plowed ahead with what he wanted to say. "You're always prepared, but you never think it's going to happen, right?"

I knew that Bryan and I were keenly aware of the possibility he might lose his life when he signed up for the Army, but we both agreed he should join anyway, so I responded, "Exactly, it's a sacrifice he was aware of and he still accepted so . . ." I trailed off and the sentence hung in the air for a minute.

President Trump went on: "So, how are the kids doing?"

"They are okay. They are heartbroken."

He asked if the kids understood that Bryan was brave and died defending the country and that the whole country was grieving the loss along with them. I assured President Trump that my kids understood and knew how brave their dad was and that the people of this country grieved with them. I told him, "My husband was an amazing man, so they are strong, and they will be okay." Our conversation wrapped up when he said, "Well, I'm sure they will be. And if there's ever anything that I can do for you, please don't hesitate to ask."

In the wake of devastating loss, people always say, "If you ever need anything, please don't hesitate to ask." Despite people's sincerity when offering their assistance, the grieving person rarely asks for help or what they need. After losing Bryan, I learned to take advantage of these offers on the spot so they would not be forgotten. I found that things that would normally give me pause no longer did. I felt I had nothing left to lose, and it gave me a boldness I've never had before in my life. When he stated that if there was anything he could ever do for us that I should not hesitate to ask, I didn't. I stopped him and said that I had a request.

In the summer of 2017, before deploying to Niger, Bryan and I took the boys for our first family trip to Washington, D.C., with his parents. We saw the famous monuments and museums, touring the city by bus and on foot. It was an exciting and magical trip and one of the best family vacations we ever had. One day as we were walking through the city, we passed the Trump Hotel in downtown D.C. Ezekiel became overwhelmed with excitement, demanding we take pictures of him at each entrance holding on to the doors as though he were entering as a guest. At every sign saying Trump, Ezekiel stopped to pose with a huge grin.

During the 2016 election, Ezekiel had become obsessed with Trump and politics. He was in fifth grade at the time and his teacher was a Clinton supporter, as were most of his classmates. Ezekiel had come home one day and told Bryan and me that he was voting for Clinton and only stupid people voted for Trump because he was terrible. Bryan told Ezekiel that all politicians are terrible, and he should make up his own mind. We sat him down and listed all the pros and cons about both Clinton and Trump. We refused to give Ezekiel our opinions; we only gave him the facts about each candidate. Eventually, Ezekiel decided he liked Trump better because Trump was funny. He began to spend all his free time watching Trump memes and constantly quoted all things Trump.

So by the time we made our way to D.C. the following summer, Ezekiel was obsessed. Ezekiel's excitement over the hotel was both endearing and hilarious. He insisted we ride up the historic elevator of the hotel and look out over the Capitol from the rooftop. He begged us to stay a night at the hotel, but Bryan and I knew it was way outside of our budget. We promised him we would save up and come back to stay one night after Bryan returned from his next Niger deployment. Ezekiel's excitement at the possibility of staying at "Trump's hotel" was ridiculous, and

Bryan and I agreed we would absolutely have to follow through on our promise.

Now, only months later, it felt like a lifetime had passed since that carefree summer ride up the elevator. But in my ear resounded the question asked by the man who owned that hotel.

"Okay, I do have one request. One of my sons absolutely adores you and would love to stay in your hotel when we go to Arlington to bury his father, if that would be okay."

Without hesitation President Trump responded, "Yes, okay, absolutely. Let me get somebody on that."

He turned from the phone and started talking in the background with staff about a hotel stay for us. President Trump then came back on the phone and asked the ages of the kids and if two rooms for two nights would be enough. He told me he would be certain the rooms were connected so the boys could have their own room and I could have some rest. Then he asked if he could speak with Ezekiel and Isaac.

For a child on the spectrum who had been harassed to no end at school for supporting Trump unashamedly since 2016, this was a huge moment. Here was President Trump on the phone with Ezekiel calling him by name and telling him that he really had a great name. "I love that name. Listen, when you come to Washington, I would like you to come stay at my hotel as my guest. Okay?"

Ezekiel tried to contain his excitement as he responded, "That's really awesome. Thank you."

Trump continued, "Ezekiel, you have a great legacy. Your dad was a hero and a great man. You have got great genes, and now it is your job to protect and take care of your mom. Okay? You have an amazing legacy. Okay?"

"Okay. Thank you, Mr. President."

President Trump then asked to speak to Isaac. He told Isaac how brave and strong and smart his dad was and invited him to stay at his hotel in Washington as well. Finally, he told Isaac to take care of his mom and then Isaac handed the phone back to me as the president told me again how sorry he was and that he looked forward to having us as his guests in D.C. After hanging up, I looked around the room and for the first time since Bryan died, we all had smiles on our faces.

I remember when my own father died. While it shook my entire life, everyone else went about their days not noticing that an amazing man had just left this world. It bothered me that someone so incredible could vanish with no fanfare, no news article, no person outside his family and small town mourning his death. When Bryan passed away so suddenly, I understood how important it would be for my kids to know that many people across the country mourned his loss. Their dad had mattered enough that everyone was talking about him dying, everyone was sad, and even the president of the United States was calling because of it.

At 6:00 that night we went to the funeral home again, this time for the visitation. The line seemed to stretch without end as people came to express their sympathy. Teachers, military wives, families from my children's wrestling club, friends and teammates of Bryan's, and friends of mine stood patiently in line. For three hours I shook hands, hugged, and cried. The sheer number of people who came out on that first night blew my mind and melted my heart.

That night was the first time I met Hanson, another member of the team. A Green Beret weapons sergeant, Hanson came with his parents and his girlfriend. I was surprised by how young he appeared to be. He looked to be around twenty years old with his curly dark brown hair and large brown eyes. Though he forced a smile when he stepped forward to introduce himself, his eyes—filled with tears—told another story.

"Hi, Michelle. I was on the ground with Bry . . . with your husband . . . when . . . when everything happened. I'm so sorry."

He was clearly shaken and struggling to keep himself together. I, too, smiled through my tears, and I hugged him. I had so many questions I wanted to ask him, but he seemed nervous and it wasn't the right time, so I introduced him to Henry, who pulled him out into a hallway for a conversation.

After returning home from the visitation, Henry, Karen, and I sat in my living room discussing the day's events. Henry told us that he and Hanson had discussed the last few minutes of Bryan's life and he shared how Hanson had seen Bryan firing his weapon at the enemy with deadly precision. He also told us that Hanson seemed uncomfortable and very hesitant to talk about the ambush. We agreed it was probably difficult for him because it was still so fresh in his mind and painful.

As we sat there talking, Karen was searching on her phone for new articles about the ambush. "This is interesting," she said.

She called our attention to an article about a condolence call Trump had made at 4:45 that day to the widow Myeshia Johnson. According to a Miami news station, President Donald Trump told Myeshia Johnson over the phone that her husband, LaDavid, "knew what he signed up for . . . but when it happens, it hurts anyway."

Suddenly my words came back to me: *It's definitely a heartbreak, but . . . it's a sacrifice he was aware of and he still accepted so . . .*" While not verbatim, the president's words seemed to echo mine. I felt a knot take shape in my stomach. Karen looked up at me and said, "That sounds awfully similar to what you told him on the phone during your call. Don't you think?"

I've often wondered since if President Trump simply echoed my sentiments when he spoke to Myeshia Johnson, the widow of LaDavid, later that same day. If I had known similar words might be repeated to another widow, I would have been more cautious with what I said. But speaking to the president that day, I was simply talking from my heart. Bryan and I had discussed this possible outcome many times. All that night I was awake, thinking over what I had said, wondering if I had caused the president to say what he did to Myeshia.

By morning, I decided that maybe it was just a misunderstanding and would blow over. I secretly hoped that the president hadn't said those things and the paper had just gotten it wrong. I had so many other things demanding my attention that I decided not to worry about it and instead focus on the memorial I had ahead of me.

WEDNESDAY, OCTOBER 18

We took our time getting dressed and sipping coffee before heading to the church at noon. The church had made a beautiful lunch for our family so we could relax and eat before the day's events began. At the 1:00 pinning ceremony, we would officially receive our Gold Star pins and step into our new identity as a Gold Star family. It was not something I had ever wanted; it was not something anyone would wish for. Yet there we stood, as thousands upon thousands before us have stood, accepting an honor we would gladly give back if we could. We stood as we shook hands with commanders, majors, and generals, who pinned us and thanked us for our sacrifice.

The large sanctuary of our Southern Baptist church was jammed with people. Up on the stage were two large portraits of Bryan, one in his Green Beret uniform and one taken that previous summer at an ice-cream parlor in Washington, D.C. He looked so handsome and happy in a red shirt with his sunglasses pushed up on top of his head. We had just gotten off a ferry tour of the Potomac. As I thought about these happy moments, tears began to stream down my face. Now Bryan was a portrait on a wall, a memory I would replay in my mind, hoping to hear the exact tone and inflection of his voice. One by one, friends who had flown in from all over the country and men from the various teams came onstage to speak about Bryan. Their words were both heartwarming and soul-crushing. Then I heard Isaac, for the first time since finding out about his dad's death, weeping.

He had begun quietly crying the moment we sat down, and he cried throughout the entire service. The crying ebbed and flowed but never ceased. When I began to cry, Isaac became even more upset and he began kicking violently at the side of the pew by his seat. He was inconsolable. He turned away from me, pulling his feet up and pushing against the side of the pew. His weeping was loud and heartrending as it echoed around the walls of the large sanctuary. Though the church was filled with people, it felt empty to me as all sound faded against Isaac's violent cries. I have never in my life felt more helpless than I did at that moment. There was nothing I could do to ease his pain or take it from him. He is a child who never misbehaves or makes a scene, but on that day he could not be calmed or contained. A few times, Ezekiel reached around me and tried to pat Isaac's back to calm down his little brother. He handed him tissues and stroked his arm, trying to help.

When the service finally ended, we walked out the back of the building to where a hearse awaited the casket. The boys were crying as they both stepped in to help Henry load their dad's body. It was then that I saw all the cameras. They remained at a respectful distance, but that was the first time I realized my tragedy had become national news.

While I sat watching my child fall to pieces, talk of President Trump's phone call with the widow of LaDavid Johnson was consuming the nation. The words exchanged that day and in the coming weeks among the president, Myeshia, and Florida congresswoman Frederica Wilson ignited a political blaze. Before the week's end, all the privacy I once enjoyed had disappeared. My Facebook account and cell phone were overloaded with requests from reporters, each of them wanting me to weigh in on the controversy. My CAO had his phone ringing off the hook as the media tried to go through him to access me. Did I get a call from President Trump? Was I insulted by President Trump as well? What was my reaction to President Trump's call to Myeshia?

What the president said to Myeshia had upset her—and when she responded publicly to say that, President Trump took to Twitter. Myeshia's husband was dead, her young children were fatherless, she was pregnant and grieving, and whatever she felt at this horrible moment was justified. She should have been able to voice her hurt without coming under attack. Unfortunately, President Trump chose politics over mercy, and that was paid back to him tenfold by the media.

In the weeks that followed, hundreds of articles were written about the call between Myeshia and President Trump. The reactions of senators and congressmen were reported; even celebrities weighed in. Many pieces on the topic pitted Democrat against Republican—and in some instances, Black against White. Some were even callous enough to turn on Myeshia and call her names.

The only thing I wanted the media focusing on was discovering the truth of what had happened in Niger. Until the media circus over the phone call developed, coverage of the ambush seemed to have dropped off. Initially, the media called Bryan's parents and even sent reporters to my brother's work to get a quote. After they received little response, however, the media seemed to have lost interest.

Now I couldn't go to restaurants, my gym, or anywhere else without seeing my husband's face pop up on television screens. Both my cell and the landline rang around the clock. My social media accounts exploded with friend requests and private messages from strangers wanting to interview me. Text messages seemed to arrive every hour from different news organizations. One left a note on the door offering me muffins if I appeared on their morning show. Another reporter called from a local ABC affiliate and asked Isaac where he lived, making him fearful that someone was trying to kidnap him—maybe even the men who had killed his dad. I was so upset I unplugged the landline and forbade my kids from using the phone. It was all too much to deal with in the middle of my grief while simultaneously planning and attending visitations, memorials, and burials.

I had never in my life interacted with the media and I didn't know how to handle it, so most of the time I just ignored it. Until I couldn't. On October 23, Myeshia Johnson went on *Good Morning America* to talk about her phone call with President Trump. Myeshia recounted that

President Trump told her that LaDavid "knew what he signed up for." Then *PBS NewsHour* reported Myeshia Johnson saying that during Trump's call to her he "couldn't remember my husband's name." *Time* magazine reported that Myeshia's phone call with the president made her cry even more and feel worse.

That same day, President Trump took to Twitter to defend what he said on the call, and then every news site in the country was running the story of the phone call and the ensuing argument around the clock. *The Washington Post* tried to bring attention back to the actual ambush by mentioning the other three men killed, including my husband. I was shaken by how little the world knew about these men and how much they cared about a phone call.

The few articles focused on the ambush seemed to show a changing narrative and even contradictory stories. There was talk of the team having stayed a night out near the Mali border. CNN reported that they left the village of Tongo Tongo and stayed outside because they were uncomfortable with the feeling they got in the village. Other news reports were saying the team had stayed the night near Niger's border with Mali, then entered the village for the first time the following morning. There were also reports that the team was not wearing their body armor and were poorly equipped. Another report quoted an official speaking on the condition of anonymity who said that the truck carrying Bryan, Jeremiah (who went by "J.W."), and Dustin had gotten separated from the rest of the group. Now it seemed that not only had LaDavid been separated but so had my husband. I spoke with Bryan's parents and we began to discuss our concerns about these competing and constantly changing narratives. There were important questions that needed to be asked, and with the distraction of the Trump phone-call controversy, these questions seemed to fall by the wayside.

On October 24, I called the remaining men on the team to ask if they would be okay with me doing an interview and trying to focus the spotlight back on the men who had died in the ambush. They agreed and said they trusted me to speak on air. I called an anchor at Fox News who knew my uncle from high school. That night my interview aired, but unfortunately it went largely unnoticed. The primary focus of the press—and therefore of the public—remained the phone call.

It was infuriating to watch the media and those with politics in mind leave behind the four U.S. soldiers and the five Nigeriens who had died. It buried the real questions: What happened in Niger? Why was the team out there with no backup and so poorly equipped? How did the team get separated twice? I was looking forward to AFRICOM providing these answers and more when their investigation was complete. Waiting until January—when AFRICOM's report would be done— seemed impossible.

I decided it was best to focus on surviving the days ahead. We would be in Washington before we knew it, and I confirmed with my CAO that our plans to stay at the Trump Hotel were set in stone. I both looked forward to seeing Ezekiel's and Isaac's excitement when we arrived at the Trump Hotel and was scared to face the day that they had to say good-bye to their dad. I had no idea how we were going to get through that.

6

Arlington

The same week I did my interview with Fox News, preparations began for Bryan's burial at Arlington National Cemetery. We needed dress coats for cold weather and the boys needed suits, so shopping was a welcome distraction for us. We flew to D.C. on October 29 and spent the first night in a hotel near Arlington before Bryan's burial the next day. Realizing we had two days in Washington, my CAO asked if he could arrange a tour of the Capitol or something that would interest the boys. I laughed and said, "Well, we are staying at the Trump Hotel as guests of the president. I think we should go to the White House and hang out with him for the day while we're at it!" I was joking, of course, but my CAO responded, "Let me see what I can do." Two days later my CAO called to ask for my family's various Social Security numbers. He had gotten approval for us to have a tour of the White House.

October 30 was the first time I ever set eyes on Arlington National Cemetery. It was the one stop we hadn't made the summer before on our trip. Looking back, I am glad that I did not know the sobering environment I was about to step into.

That morning, Arlington spread out before me, its beautiful green rolling hills lined for miles with rows of white headstones. The sight of

Preparing to walk to the graveside ceremony. *(Copyright © Rich LaSalle 2020)*

it was stunning but also chilling. The smell of the 639 acres of fresh cut grass covered in dew seemed to muffle every word spoken, every cry, and every footstep. Bright fall light fell through the trees and across the sacred grounds, casting haunting shadows upon the countless stones.

I gazed at those stones, some as old as me, others as old as our country. I was overcome by the volume and magnitude of sacrifice. Had I not stood there myself, I could never have fathomed the weight of what Arlington represents. The expression "all gave some and some gave all" seems too small, too simple, after seeing the hundreds of thousands of grave markers.

I think of the Gold Star pin given to me as a tribute recognizing the loss of my young husband. That pin doesn't represent only the loss of my husband and the sacrifice he made, it represents a community of those who have lost loved ones who made the same sacrifice in the name of protecting our freedom. That crisp October day, I was overwhelmed by the staggering number of people who had stood where I was standing and had experienced what I was experiencing. The amount of grief and loss the place contained changed me.

For the first time in my life, I understood exactly how much freedom had cost each family who had lost a loved one in service to our country and I was humbled. I was not only heartbroken for those families and service members who had made the ultimate sacrifice, but I was grateful for each one who'd served and been willing to pay the price simply so I could live my life free and safe. No war has come to our shores in many generations, and these men and women who gave their lives overseas are the reason why. Most Americans will never know their names, but all know the freedom they afforded. They are not people of great fame or fortune; they are people of great sacrifice.

That Monday I stood silently watching the black caisson bearing my husband's casket and a black carriage pulled by six large black horses. Everything was black except for the wooden casket covered with an American flag, which contained my husband's body. With my children on either side of me and my family grouped tightly behind us, my whole body shook slightly. How was it that the sun was shining that day? Surely the day you bury your husband it should be raining or at least cloudy. But October 30, 2017, was a beautiful and bright fall day at Arlington National Cemetery.

Before me, soldiers saluted each other and marched in place as "Taps" was played. We've all heard "Taps" many times, but I came to learn that it is a twenty-four-note bugle call that was born as a revision to the U.S. military's original signal to extinguish lights at the end of the day. On military bases across the U.S., it signals lights out. At military funerals and memorials, "Taps" is played as the final salute to the fallen.

The sound of the bugle moved slowly and mournfully through the air like a fog settling across the grounds creeping into the skin, piercing the soul with its chill. It is such a lonesome and sorrowful tune that the sound of it seemed to suck all warmth from the world that morning.

When "Taps" drew to a close, the sleek black horses began to step forward as the soldiers in full dress blues started to march.

Slowly at first, then gathering surprising speed, I realized my shoes were going to be a problem. I could feel my toes wedged too tightly into the front of my high-heeled shoes—and my heels, having too much room in the back, were threatening to slip out.

I don't know how I hadn't realized the shoes were too big when I bought them, but there I was with no other choice than to cross my fingers and hope for the best. From where we stood to where the graveside services were held was a walk of about a mile. We were told to move briskly in order keep up with the caisson as it moved the casket to the grave. All eyes were on me as the widow in the lead. I needed to move swiftly, but my shoes simply were not cooperating. That is when I realized my shoes might actually have to come off so I could run to catch the caisson. Surely there is a rule against that. I could feel Bryan loving that image: me, running through Arlington shoeless, my pantyhose tearing as I run. Suddenly I felt myself smiling as I clutched my children's hands and hurried forward with a new determination. I would

Waiting while the casket is moved from the caisson to the grave site.
(Copyright © Rich LaSalle 2020)

take the blisters, the pain, even a rolled ankle, but I refused to let Bryan catch me burying him in bare feet and ripped pantyhose. I would win this battle. I managed to move swiftly for the entire mile, and somehow I made it. Not painlessly or gracefully, but I made it nonetheless.

Once we were sitting by the graveside, the relief of having made it ebbed and the realization of what we were doing hit me like a wave. My children were staring at their father's casket, waiting for it to be lowered into the ground. There was no way to avoid this now. I had to face it; this was real and it was happening to me. I stared down the line and saw Bryan's mom and dad, the grief etched into their faces. I couldn't fix this or make it go away. The tears streamed down my cheeks, unrelenting, as each person stood before us speaking. I don't remember a single word from that entire day. There are no words for watching your nine- and eleven-year-old boys place white roses on their dad's casket.

Bryan would forever be thirty-five. I had always assumed that Bryan and I would grow old together and that the Army would be a stage in our lives, not the nail in Bryan's coffin.

Before that moment in Arlington, there were so many things I saw differently than I do now. One glaring example is how I respond to the national anthem. I once saw it as a symbol of my patriotism. I would hear it play and I would stand, proud, with my hand over my heart and my head held high. For most of my life, hearing the anthem play was like hearing a call to duty. It was my chance to stand up and show that I loved my country. But not anymore. Now my knees shake, and I am barely able to stand as the tears well up when the national anthem plays before my children's sporting events. I cast my gaze down and try to hide my eyes as a flood of memories overwhelm me, as I'm reminded I am swearing loyalty to a country that cost my husband his life.

I fight to remain on my feet as I hear about a battle, lives lost, a flag that waves because of the brave men who died fighting, defending our nation. I think about the families left behind, the countless children left fatherless and motherless. I think about my own children, and about

Bryan, and then I fall to pieces. Only now do I fully understand exactly how much that flag costs.

As I sat there that day in Arlington, the surviving team members of ODA 3212 were lined up at the back of the crowd behind me at the grave site. Though I knew most of the team members, that day I didn't see them. Hidden by the large crowd of mourners were the men who had gone through more than I could ever comprehend. They stood silently, waiting for everyone to leave before they took turns paying respects to one of their own. One who had laid down his life for theirs.

The men of ODA 3212 and other 3rd Group soldiers pay their respects. *(Arlington National Cemetery)*

When the ceremony finally ended, I walked with the kids over to the road where a white government van waited. Shivering, I climbed inside the van and I sat in a stupor as we were driven from Arlington National Cemetery to Downtown Baptist Church in Alexandria, Virginia. There we were met by many who had been at the ceremony in Arlington. The members of the church had made a wonderful meal and served us before joining in as we talked about Bryan and celebrated his life. It had been a terribly hard day, and the warm meal and fellowship helped to ease some of the pain.

After several hours we thanked our hosts and said our goodbyes before heading to the Trump Hotel. As I walked up the wide stone staircase outside the hotel, with its gold handrail and large black sign hanging overhead, I felt conspicuous. My eyes were red and puffy from the long day filled with heartache and I was certain I looked like the human version of a used tissue, entirely disheveled and tear-soaked. Exhaustion was written all over my face as I coaxed Ezekiel and Isaac out of the car and up to the hotel entrance. I felt anxious as I looked through the sparkling glass doors. But all my unease melted away as the two doormen swung the doors open wide and greeted us warmly.

As soon as I told the front desk receptionist my name she exclaimed, "We've been waiting for you! We love you here." She called over several other hotel staff to introduce us. They hugged us and gave the boys gift bags filled with hats, teddy bears, and other souvenirs. I was instructed not to pay for anything while I was there. If I wanted to visit the spa or order room service or dine at the restaurant, it was to be charged to the room. As a person raised in a large family, I was hardwired never to charge anything to a room under any circumstances unless I wanted to face certain death. So the idea that I could charge a spa visit seemed completely insane. I thanked the receptionist and told her I would, knowing deep down that I would never use the spa. Perhaps a good stiff drink, though. That did seem vital for my survival at the moment.

Walking into our hotel rooms was like stepping into a dream. The sheets on the bed were a soft white linen, the pillows large and downy, and together they seemed to promise me my first full night of rest in a month. I smiled to myself when I noticed the personal note and the plate filled with berries and chocolate welcoming me to the hotel.

The boys in their room next door were already snacking on the berries and lounging on their twin beds, watching TV. They had found two matching kids' bathrobes in the closet and told me they were going to wear them after a bath that night.

I called my mom and invited her to come over to check out my room and to have a glass of wine. Breaking rule number one, I grabbed a bottle of red out of the minibar, then grabbed some glasses, which we took to a little table in the hallway outside my room. We sat there sipping wine and enjoying the quiet until Isaac came out of his room with a sheepish look on his face.

"Uh, Mom? I have some kind of bad news. We sort of locked the door between your room and our room so we can't get back into your room. Can you let us in? I left my bag in your room."

I swiped my key card through the lock and while the light switched from red to green the door wouldn't open. I tried again. Nothing. I tried again and again, but the door didn't open.

"Hey, Isaac," I said, "did you or Zeke lock the top lock on the door? The dead bolt?"

Isaac's eyes darted to the ground. "Well . . . I think maybe I did."

I started laughing. "Okay, well, you get to go down to the lobby and find help. Take your brother and go talk to the lady at the front desk. Tell her you locked yourself out of the room."

For the next two hours my mom and I sat outside that door as multiple people tried to figure out how to undo what my kids had done in under ten minutes of us arriving. Despite my exhaustion, the situation struck me as hilarious. Here I was sipping wine, desperately ready to relax at last, and within minutes everything had come undone. In situations like these, my dad had always said, "If you don't laugh, you'll just have to cry." After spending the day crying, I was done with it. So my mom and I sat outside and laughed at it all. Eventually the door was opened, I was able to get the boys and myself to bed, and one of the longest days of my life was over.

———

The following morning was our tour of the White House. We didn't know what to expect; we had simply been given a time to be outside waiting. Our CAO would take us from there.

At 8:00 in the morning, the boys piled into the van with two of their cousins; Karen and Henry; my sister, Catherine; and me. We drove past the crowd waiting outside the White House for tours and were taken to a back entrance. A handsome young man dressed in a suit came and introduced himself as Rick, military aide to the president. We were taken to a small room with dark wood-paneled walls. It contained several antique chairs and a couch with a curved back and plush red velvet fabric that appeared to be from the 1920s.

We were the only people in the room, and I was confused because we seemed to be on some sort of private tour. After a few minutes, an older gentleman introduced himself as the White House historian and instructed us to follow him. He showed a breathtaking wealth of knowledge by pointing out everything from the flooring to the paint on the wall to each vase and piece of art.

There seemed to be no place we couldn't go. If an area was roped off, the aide moved the rope for us. One of the first places we ventured into was the presidential theater normally used by presidents and their families. We propped our feet up on the footstools and sat back in the opulent red seats as we listened to Rick tell us about watching movies with the president. President Trump hated when Melania and Barron were out of town because he enjoyed watching movies in the White House theater but didn't like to watch them alone. Rick laughed as he told of sometimes receiving phone calls to join the president for a movie in the theater.

We were led downstairs to see the florist's refrigerators filled with beautiful fresh flower arrangements that would be put out later that week. Then the bowling alley, where we took a break and the boys and their cousins were given special Halloween cookies and bottled water. As we left, we saw the blackened stone on the underside of the White House from the fire that had been set by the British in 1814 during the War of 1812.

From there we went to the Diplomatic Reception Room in the Executive Residence of the White House. The large oval room on the ground floor is used as an entrance to the White House from the South Lawn, where the helicopter Marine One often lands. Rick led us out of a set of double doors and we found ourselves between the six large columns and two sweeping staircases that are the most recognizable features on the face of the White House. We walked out onto the lawn that overlooks the landing pad for Marine One and the south fountain, where we posed for pictures.

Once back inside, we continued on the tour by taking what is known as the forty-five-second commute to the West Wing across the colonnade with the Rose Garden to the left of us. I was surprised at how small the West Wing felt. We didn't visit any of the offices, but the hallways were narrow, and it reminded me more of the portable classrooms we had when I was in grade school than a building presidents and their administrations worked in full-time. As we squeezed past people, making our way down an especially narrow staircase toward the lobby near the back door, I noticed a black car outside and everyone making a fuss. Suddenly Vice President Mike Pence appeared in the doorway. He had been on his way to the Capitol building but needed to use the restroom, and there we were, blocking his way. Rick told him who we were and Vice President Pence seemed to be sincerely moved.

He shook hands and when he got to me he gave me a hug, then stepped back and said, "I'm so sorry." Tears brimmed in his eyes. He hesitated for a minute, then began to move back down the line.

Once he finished giving his condolences, we exited through the door where Vice President Pence's motorcade waited for him. Rick suggested we wait for the vice president to return so we could watch the motorcade as it left the West Wing for the Capitol building.

When Vice President Pence got back into his car the entire motorcade began heading toward Capitol Hill. It truly was an impressive sight, with at least six police motorcycles moving single file, followed by several black SUVs, two limousines, and four more police vehicles, all with lights flashing, sirens blaring, and flags waving.

When the motorcade was out of sight, we headed up the wide steps of the Eisenhower Building into its impressive marble and limestone halls. The Eisenhower Building houses the majority of offices for White House staff, including a second office for the vice president. We climbed up the beautiful circular staircase and made our way to the vice president's office, where we were encouraged to sit at his desk and open a drawer where every past vice president had signed his name. We took pictures of each of us sitting in his high-backed brown leather chair pretending to be the vice president.

While I circled the office, marveling at its beauty, the White House historian came over and said, "You know we hold a prayer meeting in this office every week. We asked the vice president when he was first sworn in and he gave us permission, so several of us hold a weekly meeting here. We pray for many things, but one of our biggest focuses is those lost in war and their families. We have prayed heavily for you and your family and the families of the other three soldiers who were lost in Niger."

I was completely caught off guard by his sincere concern for those who have made the ultimate sacrifice. I didn't know what to say but "Thank you."

He continued, "I hope this is not too bold, but I would like to know, did you feel the prayers? Do you think they helped?"

Of course there was only one answer I could give him. "Yes. Absolutely, without strength coming from unseen places, I would not have survived the last few weeks. I can't tell you how much I appreciate your prayers."

Despite the surreal day we'd had touring the White House, I was still emotionally drained from the previous day at Arlington. Filled with so many competing emotions, I was left feeling numb as we looked at some of the most incredible pieces of our nation's history. We looked through one study, filled wall to wall with books, and I became curious what presidents kept in their private study. I walked over to read the titles and after ten minutes of staring at them realized I hadn't retained a single title or author. Vague impressions and a few pictures are all I have left from that remarkable day.

As we finished up the day at the White House, the historian and Rick surprised all four kids with a large jar of candy for Halloween. They passed out small mementos to each adult present as we shook hands and said our goodbyes. Rick handed me a commemorative collectible coin shaped like a football; as it turned out, he was the one who carried the nuclear codes for the president, also referred to as the nuclear football.

Walking back to the car, we discussed how impressed we were with the tour and what our favorite things were along the way. The kids loved going underneath the White House and seeing the bowling alley and the adults loved the stunning architecture and woodwork in the Eisenhower Building. Of course, meeting the vice president was a highlight for everyone. But all I could think about was Bryan. He was the reason we were there and he would have appreciated all of this even more than I had.

I couldn't escape the glaring contradictions of my emotions. Heartache threatened to cripple me with each breath, and yet the surreal experiences that we'd had in the last two days left me smiling in amazement. In one breath I was saying hello to a vice president; in the next I was saying goodbye forever to the person I loved most in this world. One moment found me watching a motorcade in all its glory speed away from the West Wing; another found me leading mourners through Arlington National Cemetery. We spent two nights immersed in luxury at the Trump Hotel while Bryan spent his first nights buried six feet down in the cold fall ground. All the magnificent wonder and all the horrifying cruelty that can be found in life were neatly wrapped up in a three-day trip. It was hours of devastation capped off each night with a whiskey or a wine and a tear-soaked smile as I thought about Bryan: how much he would have loved it all, how hard life was to love without him.

After the graveside ceremony. Placing a white rose on top of Bryan's casket and saying goodbye for the last time. *(Copyright © Rich LaSalle 2020)*

PART TWO

Conflicting Reports

7

Loss

We arrived back in Fayetteville on the first of November feeling exhausted but with one more memorial to attend. The last was the unit memorial, which was to be held on base. Since the ambush, I still had not seen Brent or Captain Perozeni, because of their injuries. After the earlier phone conversation I'd had with Captain Perozeni, I needed to tell him in person that I didn't blame him. I needed to be certain that he believed me. Brent had nearly died and was still recuperating from multiple surgeries. I had heard rumors that they were both at the memorial service for Bryan in Fayetteville and at the burial in Arlington, but I'd not seen them. I wasn't sure if they had been avoiding me or simply trying to give me space. But I was certain I would see them at the unit memorial.

On November 7, all the families gathered in the small chapel at Fort Bragg as each of the four fallen men was remembered with moving tributes by those who knew them best in battle. I began to weep as one teammate spoke of my husband: "Staff Sergeant Bryan Black was the measure of a man in my life. He was a professional poker player, junior chess champion, stock trader, master of carpentry, medicine, martial arts, and a speaker of three foreign languages. I could literally spend all day telling you incredible stories about Bryan, but when thinking back on how incredible this man was, there is one thing that sticks out to me. He was the father and husband we should all strive to be. Green Berets place mission successes above all else, often including their wives and children. I am standing before you today to tell you Bryan's wife and sons were his pride and joy, his heart and soul, his ultimate love. While a man like Bryan had every other reason in the world to brag about his many talents, the only thing this humble professional could ever bring himself to boast about was his amazing sons and his remarkable bride, Michelle."

After the service, everyone went outside, where tables with food and drink were set up under the trees. I was elbow-deep in a conversation with Dustin Wright's uncle, aunt, and cousin when I felt a tap on my shoulder. At last, here were the two men I had been waiting to see.

Brent stood there with one arm in a black mechanical contraption that ran from his wrist all the way up to his shoulder and kept his arm bent at a sharp 90-degree angle even as he went to hug me. I remembered Brent as the guy in the room making everyone laugh, the life of any party, with his muscular frame, wide smile, and boisterous personality. Now he was gaunt, his cheeks hollow, and all color drained from his face. Sorrow seemed to have pulled the breath from his body.

Brent's eyes were red as he fought back tears. "I'm so . . ." he started to say.

"No," I said firmly as my own tears welled up. "No. *You* don't apologize to *me*. Just don't. It's okay. I'll be okay."

He wrapped me in a tight hug as I said, "Bryan would have wanted you to make it home. He would be happy to know that you made it, that's what matters. I am so grateful for every one of you that made it."

I was weeping out of relief for finally seeing them, but also weeping because the level of pain surrounding me felt unbearable. Brent released me from the hug and introduced me to Captain Perozeni standing beside him. Captain Perozeni gave me a sorrowful half-smile as he, too, fought back tears. I couldn't imagine being in a situation like the one they'd been in, unable to stop my friends from being murdered and having to come home to face the families of each friend who had died. No matter how angry I was over Bryan's death, I couldn't blame anyone but those who had pulled the trigger. If Bryan had lived, I knew he would be in these men's places, apologizing to people for something he could not have stopped. Feeling guilty for things he did not choose and could not change.

Later that night, we converged on a local Green Beret bar. I was a bundle of nerves when I arrived. I had brought a gift with me for Brent and was worried it would feel like an awkward gesture. When I found myself face-to-face with him again, I nervously held the gift out, trying not to make it into a big deal.

First, confusion flooded his face, then tears filled his eyes, and he managed to fight them back as he shook his head, saying with his slight stammer, "You got me a gift? Why? I should be giving you a g-g-gift." When he opened it, a smile slowly spread across his face.

"I felt Bryan would have wanted you to have these. He had me order cigars for him a few times and he always had me order this brand so he could share them with you."

Shaking his head again, Brent looked into the gift bag, then gave me another hug.

We moved to a quieter section of the room and Brent and Captain Perozeni began telling me stories about Bryan. At one point Brent started laughing and pulled out his phone. "Bryan spent the entire first month in Niger zeroing in this grenade launcher. That thing could hit a fly from a mile away by the time Bryan was done with it. I've got this video you should see, he's wearing this horrible pink shirt and just launching this badass weapon like a b-b-beast." Brent handed me his phone and there stood Bryan in a hot-pink shirt with his camouflage boonie hat on. He had a huge smile plastered on his face and a weapon sitting on his shoulder. He pulled the trigger and then watched as a grenade flew from one end. I started laughing as I saw the sheer childlike joy on my husband's face.

"He was so happy," I said to them.

Brent became silent suddenly, and his smile slipped. "Ugh!" he said, sounding frustrated. "There is so much I want to tell you, but I can't."

He looked around the room. "We aren't supposed to be talking to anyone about what happened out there. There's an investigation and they don't want us talking to you guys or anyone else about it until it's complete. We have to keep our m-m-mouths shut. But there is so much I wish I could tell you."

That fast, my mind was reeling. The team was under gag orders? How did the Army not inform the families of this? And no wonder the guys had seemed standoffish the last few weeks.

Just then we heard the announcement that a picture-hanging ceremony was about to begin. The whole place exploded in loud cheers as people headed toward one end of the bar. I was suddenly being herded by Brent and other team members toward the front of the room as speeches began for each of the four men killed in the Niger ambush. First, J.W.'s friends spoke and hung his picture, then friends of LaDavid did the same. After the first two pictures were hung, a team member and friend of Bryan's got up and spoke while I took his picture to the wall. My hands shook so much that Karen and Henry stepped up beside me to help. We all wept as we placed Bryan's picture on a wall filled with the faces of so many who had lost their lives in defense of our nation. As we stepped away from the wall, Dustin Wright's family stepped in and they took their turn placing Dustin's picture upon the Wall of Heroes beside Bryan, J.W., and LaDavid.

The following morning, Brent's words came back to me. *We aren't supposed to be talking to anyone about what happened out there. . . . We have to keep our m-m-mouths shut.* Four weeks had passed since the ambush, and I was eager to hear the results of the investigation, but I'd been told it would take several months to complete. Could there be another reason why it would take so long?

November was a blur as we waited for AFRICOM to bring us the truth. The kids and I spent Thanksgiving with Bryan's family in Washington State, then returned to North Carolina so the kids could go back to school.

It was the first week of December when the chaos of the memorials and the holidays subsided. Things felt like they were settling down and I was starting to believe I could get through this new life. But I should have known that it's the things you don't expect that hit the hardest. I faced my first blindside the first weekend in December when the boys returned to wrestling.

Wrestling was a sport they had been learning the past few years, and Bryan had always been home during the wrestling season. He had taken them to every practice and every tournament. At home, Bryan and the boys would move our coffee table aside and go over wrestling moves at the foot of the couch as they practiced "shooting" on one another in our spacious front room. Now Henry was taking the boys to wrestling and the boys were having a hard time being there without their dad.

They had their first tournament of the season an hour outside of town and Henry agreed to go with me. The morning of the tournament came early. We were up at 4:00 and I was exhausted and running behind schedule. I knew we were going to be late, but then halfway to the tournament I realized I'd completely forgotten to factor in warm-ups. We were now far later than I'd realized and it was all my fault. I had failed my kids and I felt sick with guilt. Bryan had always taken care of all these details, and I was kicking myself for not paying better attention before, not being a better parent now.

We had run through the doors to the gymnasium and halfway up the bleachers before I realized I was overwhelmed and fighting back tears. I had just failed the first test of picking up where Bryan had left off. A full flashback hit me as I realized that this gymnasium was the same one we'd been to together last year for the boys' first-ever tournament.

I climbed the stairs and sat at the back behind everyone with my hat pulled low. The funny thing is that those first ones were the easiest tears I would shed that day. If I'd known what was about to transpire I probably would have packed up and walked right back out.

With the boys being nine and eleven, one would wrestle in the morning with all grade-school kids and the other would wrestle in the afternoon with all middle-school kids. What that meant was a long day lay ahead for us. It felt good to be out of the house after several months at home watching TV or playing video games, but one thing that did not occur to me until the wrestling had started was that while everyone else was training and getting stronger the past two months, my boys had gotten out of wrestling shape.

As anyone who has ever wrestled can tell you, going to a tournament when you are out of shape and ill-prepared can be incredibly brutal. Isaac wrestled two times, and, all things considered, he wrestled very well. In the end, though, he was reduced to tears and was more emotionally defeated than I had ever seen him. He needed a steady hand to encourage him. I looked around and was hit with the reality that the job was now mine alone.

I did my best and told him about all the things he did right and then ended it with telling him how proud his dad would be. That is when I watched Isaac fall apart completely before my eyes. We sobbed quietly in the back of the crowd, unnoticed. Fortunately, I've gotten good at knowing how long it takes for the "just cried" face to disappear. As soon as it was safe, I pasted a smile on, pulled my hat up, and walked down the steps to check on Ezekiel's afternoon bracket.

While walking down the stairs I ran into one of the parents from the team. She asked me if we were doing better now that it had been a couple months. How could I be honest? Unless you've be through this you don't understand that the first month is the easiest one. You have shock to numb the pain, the reality that he's never coming home hasn't sunk in, and people are still there. Two months in, everyone is gone and silence sets in. The reality of life without him comes to feel unbearable.

So I lied. "Yes, it's rough, but we are good. Thank you for asking."

Ezekiel had moved up a weight class, so he was now wrestling kids who were a year older than him as well as those in his age group. Today his competitors looked to be older and more muscular than any he'd wrestled the previous year. I watched as Ezekiel stepped onto the mat and got into position. The ref blew his whistle and Ezekiel was body-slammed and pinned in under ten seconds. He came off the mat dazed and in tears but determined to win the next one.

The next match went much the same as the first, but fortunately his competitor was not as rough and Ezekiel held his own for a little while longer. He fought hard, but still he lost. This time he came off the mat looking destroyed. He and I talked about changing his plan. "No more focusing on pins, focus on what your coach is telling you. Roll over, use your hands to move your competitors, bring your knees in and stand up, stand up, stand up."

The third and final match was an incredible improvement. The kid Ezekiel was wresting was remarkably strong and noticeably larger than him. When they first got to the mat I suspected this was going to be bad, but I held out hope regardless. As they began to dance, the kid shot and Zeke went down to the mat hard. He looked like he was pinned, but then he did it. Red-faced and determined, he rolled over. Elbow by elbow, he lifted himself up, brought his knees in. He used his hands and slowly worked himself loose and stood.

He had officially earned his first points of the season and, in my eyes, taken his first steps toward becoming a man. On his feet again, Zeke, feeling emboldened, shot hard. The kid sprawled, landing right on top of Zeke. The heated match went on back and forth, with Zeke fighting tooth and nail against this beast of a kid. You could see the pain and determination plainly on Zeke's face throughout the match. Unfortunately, sometimes no matter how hard you fight, you still lose.

Ezekiel walked off the mat that day bleeding, sobbing, red-faced, and hyperventilating. I walked him out into a deserted hallway to calm him. He began to yell that he was done. Never again was he going to wrestle. So we walked and paced as he continued breathing erratically and sobbing for another few minutes.

Finally I told him it was time to stop. Sometimes it just sucks like everything else in life, and today was one of those days. "It's okay to be upset, but it's time to calm down." Then, just like with his brother, I told him everything he did right as I cleaned the blood off his face and hands. I brought Zeke close and held him as I whispered that he had wrestled better than I had ever seen him wrestle. He had fought in a way that would have made his dad so proud. We sat hiding in the corner of that deserted hallway, clinging to each other until the tears subsided and we could breathe again.

On the way out, another friend stopped by to say hi and comment that I must be very tired, as I had been so quiet. I paused for a moment, then made the decision to lie again. "Yes, I'm very tired." Then again, was it really a lie? I was so emotionally drained I could barely speak.

We headed out to the car in the rain, grateful to be heading home. We had survived. Henry told me that day that he would come with me the rest of the season, which meant a great deal.

I took the boys to see my mom for the holidays to help them forget their troubles—and to do my best to ignore the whole thing, as I could no longer stand the sound of Christmas music. And once the holidays were over, my days at home in North Carolina were spent going to appointments with my CAO: attending to my taxes, having military pay changed over into my name, signing my family out of the military by changing our label from "active duty" military to "retired." All the while, memories and lost dreams ran on a loop in my head. I wasn't sleeping much, so I began trading sleep for writing. Night after night, I sat in the dark with a laptop as my companion, pouring myself into stories about the man I had loved. The husband I was supposed to grow old with. Did he know that when he died, so did I? I filled pages in the hope that his children would know their story of where they came from. It was on those sleepless nights when my writing became my obsession that I searched my soul and found a new strength. A strength that would carry me through the even harder times ahead.

8

Investigation

In the first few days after the ambush, as we sat at home stunned and grieving, several higher-ranking military personnel came to my house to offer condolences.

After Major Van Saun appeared that first day, Colonel Bradley Moses— the commander of 3rd Special Forces Group at Fort Bragg—came with his wife, Stacy, to see us. He also planned to brief us on what was known so far about the deadly ambush. Bryan's parents and I sat quietly in the living room as Colonel Moses explained that they had very little information so far, but as more became available we would be updated. "What we do know is that Bryan's team, ODA 3212, had been on a routine patrol and had not been expected to encounter any enemy forces when the ambush occurred." He pointed out that it was typical for teams like ODA 3212 to travel with little to no support, as that is how Green Beret teams are expected to be able to operate. Before leaving, Colonel Moses said to us, "If any of you ever need anything, please do not hesitate to ask."

That was the last formal update we would receive from the military for many months. News reports—all of which seemed to contain few specifics about what had actually happened to Bryan and his team—were what we depended on. I didn't have cable at home, so I was unable to watch the news, but Henry read any article he could find that might shed new light.

The official investigation by AFRICOM was due to be finished in January, but the wait felt impossible to me. Plus, the story of the ambush seemed to change every day. By the end of October we knew that the team had gone on a mission to the border between Niger and Mali and been attacked by fifty militants outside a village where they had stopped for water. The team had gotten separated at some point and the villagers were suspected of stalling the team, setting them up for the militants nearby.

Many articles contained conflicting information. Henry sent me an article published by *The Guardian* in November that stated, "Witnesses described seeing 200 heavily armed attackers swarming toward the soldiers on motorcycles—a far greater number than previously reported. The soldiers fought alone for around six hours despite the village chief's panicked calls to four separate Nigerien authorities, according to villagers."

How did the number of militants jump from fifty attackers against the eleven-man team to approximately two hundred? How had the men been alone on the ground for six hours when initially all reports said they'd been alone for only two hours? I would have to wait for AFRICOM to clarify these discrepancies.

By early November, as we became impatient, my CAO began updating us on the pace of the AFRICOM investigation. Despite our eagerness, however, Karen and Henry and I believed that the longer the investigation took, the better, because it would mean that AFRICOM was being as thorough as possible.

After burying Bryan and attending the unit memorial, Karen had returned home to Washington State to resume her job as a middle-school teacher, planning to return in January when the brief was presented. Henry had stayed behind to help me with the boys. Most evenings he and I pored over the most recent articles for new information. Henry's long history with the military allowed him to interpret the information and inferences from various reporters to tell me what he felt had happened, who might be at fault, and why. I needed to know with certainty the details of Bryan's last hours. Was he aware of what was about to happen? Was he for or against the mission? Had he died quickly and painlessly? Did he die for no reason? And could this have been prevented?

One November night, Henry sat quietly at my dining room table as I read an article he had found on the website of the Atlantic Council, a think tank covering international affairs for businesses and intellectual leaders. The article quoted J. Peter Pham, vice president for research and regional initiatives and director of the Africa Center: "Pham pointed out that it was only in October of 2016, one year after Abu Walid al Sahrawi, former senior spokesman and self-proclaimed emir of a Sahara-based al-Qaeda-linked group, pledged loyalty to al-Baghdadi that ISIS designated al Sahrawi's group as its 'Greater Sahara' division. [The group has been blamed for the deadly ambush on US troops on October 4.] ISIS only accepted al Sahrawi's 'oath of fealty' after his group carried out attacks in the borderlands of Burkina Faso, Mali, and Niger—the very same area where the US forces were recently ambushed—Pham pointed out." (Brackets are from the original article.)

I read these lines over and over, trying to fully process what they were saying. My mind was constantly foggy from fatigue and grief. "Henry, is this saying that there have been attacks by ISIS-linked groups in that region before?"

Henry looked at me sadly and said, "That is how it appears. But we have no way of knowing for sure. We'll have to wait until the investigation is complete and we are briefed so we can learn those details."

My heart ached. Did Bryan and the other men on the team know about these prior attacks? Did they know they might be in danger? Why was no other media outlet reporting this? If there had been previous attacks, why did the team go to the border with no backup? That didn't make any sense to me.

It was 11:00 p.m., but I knew I wouldn't sleep, so I pulled out some scotch and poured a drink for us both as we talked over the ambush yet again.

"Do you think there may have been a major blunder, or do you think this was just bad luck, as in wrong place wrong time?" I asked Henry.

"Well, that is hard to say for certain, but usually in these kinds of circumstances if you look hard enough you can find mistakes, because no one is perfect all of the time and most missions don't go perfectly. Even missions that are successful are rarely perfect and mistakes can be found. But as far as major blunders go . . . it's possible. I'd be more inclined to think they just ended up in a bad position without the proper backup that could have helped. If anything, my guess is that lack of support or backup was due to an incomplete intelligence picture. So that is really the bigger question."

By the end of November, through various news articles we had learned that Bryan's team had been on a routine patrol that should have had them visiting a town named Tiloa, then returning to their base in Ouallam in one day. At some point, there had been a change in plan, but no one seemed certain of how the change had come about. The new plan led them in search of a terrorist campsite in an overnight raid. The raid meant they were out for twenty-four hours, which caused them to be surveilled and ultimately hit by militants. There were conflicting reports about whether the team's captain, Mike Perozeni, had mischaracterized the mission in order to avoid getting the proper approvals.

During these months of waiting for the report, the team had not yet come under scrutiny by the media. What none of us knew initially was that a gag order had been placed on them. They were not permitted to speak with the family members of their fallen teammates regarding the investigation or the ambush. So at all the wakes and memorials, the silence of those who survived had begun to arouse suspicion and distrust from the families of those who had lost a loved one. This tension frustrated many family members, and it pitted everyone against one another, especially as media reports quoted anonymous officials who cast doubt upon Captain Perozeni's actions. Meanwhile, the first team of

AFRICOM's investigators had not visited the site of the ambush until November 12, more than a month after the events.

Chairman of the Joint Chiefs of Staff General Joseph Dunford was quoted as saying it was a reconnaissance mission and the U.S. was in an "advise and assist role." This meant that American military personnel were to train their partner forces and to advise and assist on missions while their partner forces took the lead. According to an ABC News article on November 2, 2017, "It was not a reconnaissance mission, as initially described by officials, but instead a kill or capture mission conducted without additional support as requested by Nigerien forces according to Nigerien officials."

In December, CNN stated that fifty ISIS fighters had attacked the team. The militants had rocket-propelled grenades, mortars, and heavy machine guns. The article claimed the team was gathering intelligence on a terrorist leader before it was attacked. According to CNN, officials claimed that Bryan's unit was not under orders to conduct a kill-or-capture mission on the ISIS-GS (ISIS in the Greater Sahara) leader.

From this time forward, almost every article agreed that there were fifty heavily armed militants. Other details seemed to change daily. Eventually articles claimed the team had gone rogue and without orders had gone on a kill-or-capture mission seeking out a notorious militant leader by the name of Doundou Chefou.

The tide turned in December, according to a BuzzFeed article:

"Socafrica [Special Operations Command Africa] has, in recent years, become increasingly secretive, unaccountable, clientelistic, and—as recent episodes suggest—reckless. Odds are they didn't have the granularity of intel to offset the risk of such a mission," said Matthew Page, a former Africa specialist with the State Department's intelligence arm. "I think the bigger issue at stake here is the degree to which Special Forces Africa is increasingly seen by US diplomats and defense officials as a 'rogue element' that is pushing the envelope on its missions and activities in the Sahel, and elsewhere in Africa, without explicit buy-in from US policymakers, diplomats, or even senior military commanders."

Questionable decisions were made in the hours preceding the attack. By the afternoon of October 3, the soldiers had reached their destination—a militant bush camp in a village called Akabar, located in a nature reserve some four miles inside the Malian border, a second Nigerien official told BuzzFeed News. A US Defense spokesperson would not comment on the exact nature of the operation but said: "We don't conduct any operations without the consent of the respective host nations." The US's military partnership in the region allows them to accompany Nigerien troops up to 50 kilometers inside the Malian border.

After destroying the deserted camp, the patrol made a puzzling decision: They decided to keep pursuing their targets by combing nearby villages, according to [a] Nigerien general and [a Nigerien government] anti-terrorist unit official. That meant, without prior planning or any contingency plans, they would be extending the time spent in territory full of militants and their informants—a basic error, say US officials with dozens of such missions under their belts.

"That's not how it's done," Donald Bolduc, a retired general who led Socafrica until June, said of what's known officially about the mission so far. Senior militant leaders are normally well protected, Bolduc said, with rings of security guards and layers of militants who communicate with one another via radio, he said. "The resources and planning didn't seem to be there for that kind of operation," he said in an interview with Reuters in October.

Long after nightfall, when the mission was due to be debriefed back at the base, instead US soldiers sent a radio call to those awaiting their return in Ouallam. That decision to stay, which was relayed in that call, proved to be a disastrous mistake. "They sent a message just around midnight saying that because their position was still around the border with Mali, and that's a high-danger zone, they would stay the night there," a second Nigerien senior military official briefed on the matter said. It's unclear whether that decision came from the soldiers on the ground or their commanders back at base.

This article was the first time I heard the claim that the Special Forces unit behaved recklessly. It left me completely baffled. The team was said to have made the decision to stay the night near the Mali border in a highly dangerous area. This didn't fit with anything I had yet read—with anything my husband would have done. Bryan had voiced to me multiple times, including the last time we ever spoke, that he did not like going on missions up near the Mali border because it was dangerous. He had also told me they did not have legal permission to cross into Mali and that they were ordered to always stay on the Niger side of the border.

From then on, a trickle of negative information became a flow of articles painting lower-level officers in a bad light—particularly team captain Mike Perozeni. Reporters alluded to information that it was not SOCAFRICA that had behaved recklessly, but rather the team. There were questions and innuendos about the team's ill intent for the mission. It wasn't long before the men of ODA 3212 found themselves under scrutiny by AFRICOM, the military, the public, and the media. In the following weeks and months, those questions turned into character assassinations as two active-duty Green Beret team members had their names leaked to the press, an unbelievable betrayal by the military. Special Forces soldiers and their families are high-value targets to any enemy of the U.S., so it is known that they are to remain anonymous while operational. Captain Perozeni was one of those whose names were released, then dragged through the mud. Every move he made during the ambush was publicly criticized.

While there were multiple anonymous sources and officials quoted in the BuzzFeed article and in similar pieces, I knew the men on the team and I knew my husband. I knew how much blood and sweat, and how many tears and years, they had each put into earning that green beret. No single Green Beret, let alone an entire team, would go rogue to hunt down a terrorist without proper approval. Misleading higher authorities would damage their careers and put their lives at risk. That was one thing I felt certain of.

Next, articles soon came out claiming that the team was young and that inexperience had led to mistakes. A Politico article read: "Derek Gannon, another Green Beret combat veteran, acknowledged that 'a lot of mistakes happened' during the mission. 'This was a young team and they were not expecting contact, and once the bullets flew, that team fell apart.'"

While there were a few new members on the team, there were also many seasoned soldiers who had been on the team for many years. One of the newest recruits had come to the team after serving for four years with the 82nd Airborne Division and six years in Ranger Regiment. He was a highly decorated soldier who had been in combat multiple times over the course of his career. He was on his eighth deployment when the team was ambushed. Several other team members had similar backgrounds both in combat experience and in deployments. Knowing these facts, I could not believe that the team simply fell apart.

I also could not believe that Captain Perozeni—who had just earned his green beret and joined the team—could have convinced any one of the men to go rogue. And even if I was wrong about the others, the one person I knew beyond a shadow of a doubt would never go rogue was my husband. Bryan would have stayed behind at camp if he had thought for a minute that they were going on a kill-or-capture mission without backup and approval.

Bryan was not averse to risk, but he was a thinking man, a master of chess. Even when he played poker for a living, he believed in calculated risk, and he never would have gambled with his life. Before making any move, he would run the numbers, consider all possible outcomes, and make his decisions based on probability. I knew he hadn't gone rogue, but I didn't know what *had* happened.

By January, articles mentioned possible reprimands for officers who had failed to follow procedures. Most of the media seemed certain that the villagers had not set up the team, so quotes from the villagers were scattered throughout many articles. While the investigation was still incomplete, I doubted a village mere feet from the site of my husband's death was uninvolved. To report on the village leader's version of events when they had not been formally cleared by investigators seemed to me like interviewing potential murderers and taking their word as truth. Many of the quotes conflicted with one another and with the overall narrative put forth so far.

For four long months the families of the fallen and the men on the team waited as the investigation unfolded. The men on the team believed, as did I, that once the investigation was complete we would be able to get on with our lives with the full truth out in the world. The team believed that they would soon be acquitted before the public—and, most important, the families of the fallen.

One day in late January I was driving to pick up Ezekiel and Isaac from school while the radio blared music. As the light turned, my phone lit up with a message from my CAO: "Can you take a call?" I was relieved, thinking that this meant the AFRICOM investigation was finally done. But when I answered the CAO's call, his heavy tone indicated something else.

"I have bad news and I will be going straight from work to your house tonight so we can talk."

I laughed darkly, thinking, *What can be that bad? My husband already died in a very public fashion! Nothing can top that.* As it turns out, something could.

"I'm sorry to have to tell you," said my CAO, "that there are rumors there may be video footage by ISIS circulating of the attack and the deaths. There may also be pictures . . . They are believed . . . well, they think some are of your husband. They are circulating on an online terrorist site. It's only a matter of time before the media uses these. For now, the government is trying to block the media's access to these so they will not go public."

As he spoke, I fought back the urge to throw up.

Pictures and video of my husband's death? I gulped in air as I tried to calm myself alone in my car. How was I going to hold myself together in front of my kids until the CAO arrived at my house? Henry had flown back home for a few days, and I was going to have to deal with this on my own. I saw my sons making their way across the parking lot, so I took a deep breath as the car door swung open.

"Hi, guys! How was your day?" I asked with a big smile under large dark glasses meant to hide my swollen eyes.

"It was good, Mom," Ezekiel said.

"How was your day, Mom?" Isaac asked.

"My day was good, too," I replied, realizing I'd become a rather convincing liar.

That night my CAO said he hoped the military would be able to keep the media from releasing the video. For a month we stayed tuned—then we began to feel confident that the video would never go public. Unfortunately, the video's existence changed the timeline for the investigation being finished. We were now told that AFRICOM was reviewing the video for the investigation, which meant the brief wouldn't be ready for families for another month or two.

During February and March more articles appeared containing more conflicting and confusing information. One February *New York Times* article stated that "AFRICOM poorly planned the joint patrol and then changed the mission three times while it was underway."

On February 26, the National Geographic channel aired the *Chain of Command* episode in which ODA 3212 was shown only months earlier going about their daily routine in Niger. I had not been following the series and was surprised when a friend messaged me to say she was excited to see our boys on TV. I realized in that moment the level of disconnect that existed between those watching whose husbands had come home safe and those of us whose husbands had been killed. I was not excited; I was terrified.

I wanted so badly to watch hours of footage of Bryan working in Niger, but I feared the reaction I would have to seeing him—or not seeing him. He had told me he'd done his best to avoid the cameras, and now I was heartbroken. I wanted to see him one more time. To hear him speaking Hausa, which he had learned before his 2016 deployment to Niger. He always told me how much he loved going into the villages and talking to the local people in their own language. I prayed that somehow National Geographic had filmed him doing that, but deep down I knew better than to hope. And I was right. The day I watched the episode I strained to see Bryan, to hear him, but all I got was a profile of him eating. He had successfully achieved near anonymity in his TV debut just as he had hoped. God, I loved him. He'd always hated attention and I couldn't fault him for that, but not seeing more of the man I loved hurt.

I did see a lot of the officers who had visited my home: Major Alan Van Saun, Colonel Moses, and the colonel's wife, Stacy. The colonel's kids had played with mine outside the church following the unit memorial. I appreciated that both officers took the time to acknowledge my family and our loss.

After watching the *Chain of Command* episode, I was left with mixed emotions and memories of the past few months. It seemed incredible to me that National Geographic had filmed, created, and aired the episode in such a short period of time. It seemed surreal that the show was already wrapping up, yet here I was still waiting for answers from the Army.

Only weeks after that episode aired, *The New York Times* put out another article about the ambush that read "according to the third Defense Department official, a lieutenant colonel in Chad had already approved both the helicopter raid based from Arlit, which was scrapped, and Team 3212's original reconnaissance mission, which had taken it just 15 miles from the ambush site outside the village of Tongo Tongo.

"Additionally, that official said, Col. Bradley Moses, the head of 3rd Special Forces Group in Germany, was informed of the two missions. The official was not authorized to discuss the missions or the investigation publicly."

Colonel Bradley Moses, who had come to my home with his wife just days after Bryan's death, had been informed of those missions. The very man who had sat on my couch that first week and told me he knew very little about what had happened and what led up to the ambush. Yet he had been part of the process of approvals for and was aware of the mission the team was being sent on before they were sent. The mission that had killed Bryan, LaDavid, Dustin, and Jeremiah. Why had Colonel Moses said nothing of the part he had played? I thought being a leader meant taking responsibility for your part in things even when they go wrong. My head spun, and I started to feel I couldn't trust anyone.

March came and there was no end in sight. I was more confused and had more questions than ever. I found myself wondering: Who was the officer that ordered the mission? I had never heard his name; I only knew that he was a lieutenant colonel located in Chad. Who else was part of the decision-making process? What was the chain of command?

It was ironic, really, that a National Geographic documentary series called *Chain of Command* had filmed an episode of my husband and his team only weeks before the ambush. The series' goal was to explore the chain of command from the Pentagon to the front lines. Now here I was needing answers about that very same chain of command and how they had operated from the top down in the days leading up to the attack on the team. Somehow, all those higher up the chain of command who were featured in that documentary were now conspicuously missing from the very real-life drama that their authorizations and command decisions had created.

9

Video

Exactly one week after the *Chain of Command* episode aired, the anonymity my husband had worked so hard to maintain was obliterated. On March 4, the murders of Bryan, Dustin, and Jeremiah were broadcast by CBS News and YouTube before spreading across Facebook and Twitter. I had been in bed that Sunday night when my CAO texted: "Michelle. The video footage of the ambush was released. Please, whatever you do, do not watch it. I've seen it and can tell you it's not something you want in your mind."

I felt paralyzed. I now had the option of clicking a button and watching my husband's death as often as I wanted, and so did the rest of my countrymen. I knew I would never watch Bryan's murder, but even so it sickened me. Who would be so cruel as to release such a horrific thing as entertainment and call it news? My husband's murder was not news, it was terror.

Even so, the footage streamed into thousands of homes across our nation and became fodder for discussion. People commented on what Bryan, Dustin, and Jeremiah should have done. How untrained they were, how stupid for not driving faster out of harm's way. I was sickened by the fact that many in this nation couldn't comprehend just how deeply personal and sacred a husband's body, dead or alive, is to his wife. A child's body is to his parents. A father's body is to his children.

Bryan's murder was broadcast on a Sunday night. I did not sleep at all. The next morning when I delivered my children to school, I went into the school office. Through tears, I informed the administration about the video and asked them to lock down YouTube and to keep my kids away from computers that day. If there was any talk about the video, I wanted to be contacted so I could pick them up immediately. It was Zeke's first day back after a suspension the previous week. Ezekiel had been having behavioral issues at school since Bryan's death and the school was not handling it well, so he had spent many days at home with me. They had a no-tolerance policy for cussing, a habit Zeke had taken up when Bryan died, so he was frequently suspended. I knew that day I needed time to myself to deal with what was happening. Two hours after dropping the kids off, the school called me.

Though there were now many contenders for the title, that Monday will go down as one of the worst days of my life. The school reported that Zeke had etched the word *NIGER* into a computer screen at school. I can only guess what he saw on that computer in those two hours when I had asked the school to keep him away from them. When I came to pick him up, the vice principal informed me that due to Ezekiel's recent language issues he was of the opinion that Ezekiel had actually meant to write the N-word. He began to lecture me on the inappropriate nature of that word. When Ezekiel had become defensive, the vice principal said it became clear to him that Ezekiel had definitely meant the N-word. My exhaustion suddenly disappeared and was replaced by fury. I asked him why in the world he thought Ezekiel meant the N-word as opposed to Niger, which he had actually written, when his dad *had died there* and today a video was circulating of his death.

"He is autistic and has been in trouble every day for the last three weeks," I said. "Of course he freaked out and couldn't explain himself when you asked him that!" Two of Ezekiel's closest friends at school are

Black and he'd gotten into fights with other kids when he heard them using the N-word, so to me the accusation was offensive, of course, but also off-base.

The vice principal backtracked, saying he was just worried that Ezekiel's "behaviors" that past week showed that he was becoming violent and aggressive. I honestly don't know how in that moment I didn't turn to acts of violence and aggression myself. I could feel my blood pressure rising and my cheeks flushing as I held myself back from saying everything I wanted to say to him.

Instead I said, "What exactly would lead you to believe he would ever be violent at school?"

I could feel myself teetering on the edge of screaming at full volume and tried to contain it, knowing that there were elementary school children on the other side of the thin walls.

The vice principal stumbled over his words before finally saying, "Well, I spoke with him about using inappropriate language. I had a long talk with him and made sure he understood how offensive that word is to those in the Black community and made it very clear it is not to be used."

I looked behind me and saw my son sitting in a chair outside the office. He looked completely destroyed. Dark circles and rings of puffy red skin surrounded his bloodshot eyes. He had been shaking and crying since I'd arrived, and he looked both ashamed and exhausted. By now I was surrounded by the vice principal, the principal, and a counselor, and they were all telling me about Ezekiel's dangerous and racist behavior.

"Each of you," I said, "have known my son for over five years and have never heard him use the N-word or behave in a racist manner. I came in this morning and specifically asked that he be kept away from computers and explained why. That to me is the real problem. If I'd known the school couldn't handle that, I would have never left him here this morning. So him writing the word *Niger* on the computer comes as no shock to me. If anyone is out of line here it is each of you with your failures to protect my son and your vile accusations."

The principal became quiet and changed direction. "Ms. Black, why don't you take Ezekiel home for the afternoon, because he cannot stay after destroying school property. Destruction of school property is a very serious matter. That is something that will need to be replaced so you will be expected to pay for the computer screen he destroyed. I will be sending you a bill."

"I'm fine paying for the screen he wrote *Niger* on. Please do send me a bill." Then I looked at each of them hard, trying to keep my composure. "No one in this room can help my son with anything they have to say to him. He needs time, compassion, and maybe some professional help, but certainly not yours. You are no longer allowed to speak to him without me present. I am taking him with me now and you are welcome to suspend him for however long you see fit. His dad is dead, he needs compassion from the adults in his life. Let me know when you think you can handle that and I will bring him back to school."

I was furious and certain that neither Ezekiel nor I had a single friend in that office. I grabbed my son and hugged him as I whispered in his ear, "You are not in trouble. I am on your side. I love you, sweetheart." I took his hand and we left. We stopped by the Veterans Affairs counseling office, but they couldn't make room to see us that day, so I made an appointment for the following morning. I spent the rest of the afternoon sleeping on the couch with my arms protectively around my children as they watched old movies.

The worst part is that this horrible day was actually far better than my mother-in-law's was. The night the video was released, an unsuspecting Karen had come home from work and flipped open her laptop, ready to relax and stream the day's top news stories from CBS News. As she sat on her couch, footage flashed across the screen of a soldier shooting a weapon. He was taking fire, he was falling. The world seemed to slow down as the familiar figure she had watched grow from an infant into a man, the figure she had seen only months before, fell. Tears flooded her face as she watched her youngest son die on national TV. CBS was the only media conglomerate that felt it was acceptable to air an ISIS propaganda video.

Karen was not the only person who cared about the fallen soldiers and saw the video unaware of what it contained. Ondo, a member of Bryan's team, had been in the ambush and lost his best friend, Dustin Wright. At the time, he was traveling first-class on a plane for the first time in his life. He'd never before indulged in such luxuries. He smiled as he saw the large comfortable seat with plenty of room to stretch out. He thought maybe he'd order a meal and a drink to see if it tasted better up there. He was happy to see that he'd been seated next to a man who looked to be in his thirties and seemed sociable.

Ondo stowed his bag in the overhead compartment and sat down in the seat next to the man staring down at his phone. As Ondo adjusted the air and put his seat belt on for the flight, the man looked over to say hello. Ondo smiled and asked the man how it was going. The man turned his phone toward Ondo and told him to check out a cool video he was watching. As Ondo turned his attention to the phone he was instantly taken back to the worst day of his life. He could hear the machine-gun fire, smell the sweat mixed with dirt and gunpowder. On the screen he saw Bryan fall. He remembered everything, things he would never forget, the metallic smell of blood pouring into the African dirt as they fought for their lives.

Repulsed, Ondo turned away from the phone, stopped a flight attendant walking by, and ordered a strong drink to calm his nerves before ordering six more. How was watching his friends die *cool*? These men had families. How could someone release that video? Since returning from Niger and burying his best friend and three teammates, Ondo had worn a bracelet on his wrist at all times. It was made of a dark metal and was engraved with the name of SSG Dustin Wright. Ondo's mind now went to Dustin and to the others. How would Bryan's boys handle this? What about Jeremiah's and Dustin's families? Ondo drank until at last he fell asleep, flying first-class over a first-world country with no class.

After the video's release, it felt like our lives had been shredded. No privacy remained, as the volume of messages from the press once again increased. Each of us, including my CAO, began to receive an influx of calls asking for our reaction to the video. With each article, each news report, and now the video, the facts seemed to change. Every solid thing we thought we knew seemed to have turned to smoke.

Every few weeks the Army had a new estimated date for the AFRI-COM brief. I held fast to the belief that the investigation would bring us peace. That hope became like an oasis in the desert for me. Every time I thought we'd reached water, I'd find it was a mirage, a trick of the sun's rays bouncing off the sand.

Along the way, Henry and I had learned a lot about the ambush on our own. By the end of March we knew for sure that the team initially set out for a one-day mission to a village called Tiloa. Some reports claimed the team was in Tiloa on a kill-or-capture mission looking for a known terrorist by the name of Doundou Chefou. Other reports claimed the team was in Tiloa simply to gather intelligence and meet with local military leaders by doing a KLE (key leader engagement). During these KLE meetings, the teams seek to gain the trust of local leaders so they can work together in the future. The Americans get a sense of the area, observe how safe the people in the area appear to be, and check to see if those people need anything, such as medical care.

After finishing their KLE in Tiloa on October 3, the team assumed their mission was complete and headed back toward their base in Ouallam. They were contacted by officials at the AOB (advanced operations base) in Niamey and ordered to turn back toward the border of Mali to act as backup for another team. According to initial media reports, they were going to an enemy encampment that intelligence showed as Doundou Chefou's new location. The team was to explore the camp and collect any intelligence they could glean that might eventually help locate the terrorist.

On the night of October 3, Bryan's team arrived at the coordinates given to them and waited for the lead team to arrive at the Mali border. The lead team was a heliborne unit stationed in Arlit, an industrial town in north-central Niger. On their way to meet Team 3212, Team Arlit encountered a large dust storm and was turned around. This left Bryan's unit alone to lead the mission to explore the enemy camp the following morning and collect intelligence. Team 3212 traveled through the night, arriving to explore and clear the camp early on the morning of October 4. While at the encampment, the team found a motorcycle and some provisions, all of which they burned before leaving the terrorist camp. Then they drove to a village to get water before heading back toward Ouallam, their home base. It was outside the village of Tongo Tongo that the team was ambushed.

We had heard media reports that the leaders in the village of Tongo Tongo had delayed the team and set them up to be ambushed by militants—or, more specifically, Doundou Chefou, a known leader of ISIS-GS. An article in *The New York Times* had quoted a Nigerien official who said the village chief of Tongo Tongo had Doundou's phone number stored in his cell phone. But we had not read that anywhere else and there was nothing concrete that made us feel certain the villagers had been involved. There had also been conflicting reports about Captain Perozeni—whether he pushed back against the second and third mission commands or had acted like a cowboy, going after a terrorist with a mission he didn't have approval for. Leaks from various "officials involved in the investigation" blamed Captain Perozeni for misleading those above him in order to go out on a mission without gaining proper approvals. Other sources said that another captain at headquarters in Niamey had ordered the mission to the border, which was above his level to command. And yet another report said none of the authorities higher up the chain of command in Chad—including the lieutenant colonel—knew anything of this mission to the border of Mali and had not given their required approvals for it. Some media was abuzz with a new story that the team cut and pasted together a bogus CONOP (concept of operations) report and was on a kill-or-capture mission that they were trying to hide from those higher up the chain of command. CONOPs are made by the teams to tell those higher up what their mission plan is so they can be certain to get proper approvals, support, and equipment for the mission. Essentially, those reports were saying the team had gone rogue.

There were still so many differing accounts in the media, we didn't know what to believe or who to blame. The only consistent theme was that the team had acted inappropriately.

An April article on the *Stars and Stripes* news site began like so many articles at that time: "A culture of excessive risk-taking, poor training and complacency were factors in the deaths of four U.S. soldiers killed in an October ambush in the West African country of Niger."

As the months wore on, each man on the team was questioned and their actions on the ground scrutinized by the investigators, the media, and the families of the dead. Being the team's lead medic, Bryan would certainly have been under investigation for any medical care he might have provided had he survived. I realized that even if Bryan had survived the ambush, we would still be living some version of this nightmare. People would have made assumptions that the unit could have done things better and it would have worked out differently. What would I have wanted the surviving family members to do if Bryan had survived? How would I want them to treat my husband? I decided I would believe every team member was innocent unless AFRICOM could prove otherwise.

By April the timeline for the family to be briefed had changed so many times that it had become a joke. "Okay, Michelle," my CAO would say. "It looks like it's going to be maybe another week or two and they will have the brief ready."

To which I would respond, "So, around January 2020?" or, "I will be sure to hold my breath."

Finally, in April 2018, the investigation was complete. As we prepared to hear the report, I thought about what I wanted. For months, I'd read conflicting media reports, articles that got basic facts wrong about my husband or the Green Berets, then claimed to know the truth about the ambush and quoted officials who were involved in the investigation. So I knew what felt wrong about all of this, but what did I *hope* for?

What I expected was complete transparency on the part of AFRICOM during our brief. I wanted the inconsistencies we'd heard in news reports clarified. And then I hoped to find out what mistakes were made and how the military would fix them so an ambush like this never happened again. I also wanted to understand what had happened with the initial CONOP written by Captain Perozeni and if there was any validity to the accusations that the team had gone against orders.

I wanted the truth: a clear layout of the chain of command, their thought process, and the orders that resulted.

Further, I believed we'd see a minute-by-minute analysis of what had happened on the ground between October 3 and October 4. The AFRICOM investigators had unlimited resources at their disposal, and I believed what they had been saying publicly—that they wanted nothing more than to bring those truths to the families of the deceased in order to ease our minds and bring us what peace they could.

I was wrong.

10

The Brief

On the morning of April 28, a dark blue military-issued sedan pulled up to the curb outside my home in Fayetteville, North Carolina, to pick up Henry, Karen, and me. AFRICOM had decided to brief each family separately.

The humidity hit us like a wave when we stepped out of the house and walked to the car waiting by the curb. At Fort Bragg, we were escorted into a large government building where the AFRICOM investigative team was waiting for us on the second floor in a large gray conference room. At an oval table sat General Roger L. Cloutier, the chief of staff to Marine General Thomas Waldhauser, commander of AFRICOM. Cloutier had been chosen as the lead investigating officer for the Niger ambush by General Waldhauser because, as Waldhauser would state later at the media brief, he believed that, given AFRICOM's responsibility for what goes on in their area of responsibility (AOR), it was their obligation to do the investigation.

Across from General Cloutier were several men and women in uniform, and beside them a large screen was set up with a slide show and video presentation for us to follow along. The large investigative team rose to their feet when we entered; there had to be at least ten people along just the one wall. General Cloutier greeted us, then introduced the others. I recall that one man in uniform was a Marine originally from Africa who spoke several of the native languages, including Hausa and Zulu; two others were lawyers in business suits; and one woman was a forensics specialist. The rest remain a blur, but it appeared the entire investigative team was present.

The room felt tense, and I felt drained of all my energy before the first words were even spoken. As he told us what we could expect from the brief, General Cloutier struck me as genuine. His eyes were kind and seemed to brim with tears as he spoke about Bryan, telling me how sorry he was for my loss. Bryan had always told me that I'm a terrible judge of character because I am too trusting. So, although I instantly wanted to trust that General Cloutier would do all he could for us, I decided to be skeptical of my first impression of him. Bryan would have reminded me it was the general's job to be nice to the families of fallen soldiers, and even if he truly regretted their deaths, he wasn't necessarily going to tell me everything I wanted to know. He was there to do a job.

General Cloutier began his speech. "We care deeply about this investigation and have done our very best to gather all of the information we could. We have combed through every detail as best as possible so we can bring to you the most accurate account of events on the ground on and around October fourth. Now, before we get started, please know that we have coffee and water available to you if you so desire."

After all this time, I couldn't imagine stopping for anything. We'd waited six months for this moment, and I was not about to waste another second on drinks. *I would drink later,* I thought to myself heavily. I wanted information and I wanted it fast.

General Cloutier continued: "I want you to know that this is your meeting. We will take as long as you need to have all your questions answered, even if that means staying significantly overtime. You are free to fast-forward through any part of it if you so choose, stop at any part to ask questions, go back over any section that you would like to, and go into further detail if that is what you desire."

The presentation began when the screen in front of us lit up with a picture of the Nigerien desert. Slowly, dots appeared.

"Each of these dots," said General Cloutier, "represents a truck in the convoy as they headed out of Ouallam and made their way to Tiloa on the morning of October third. For this mission, Captain Mike Perozeni had created a CONOP for a civ/mil reconnaissance mission, but it was actually a kill/capture mission that was improperly characterized in the CONOP." Without hesitating, General Cloutier continued walking us through the first hours of the mission. "They had finished in Tiloa and were almost an hour from home base when they were stopped just outside of the village of Mangaize after receiving a call from the headquarters in Niamey."

Not wanting to get too far beyond the first CONOP, I decided to stop the general. "Um," I said, a little too quietly.

General Cloutier clearly didn't hear me as he continued: "Higher headquarters had received word . . ."

I could feel my stomach clench as I tried to get up the courage to sound more authoritative. I stuck my hand up and said, "I am curious about something."

This time General Cloutier stopped and turned his eyes on me. The room was suddenly deafeningly quiet.

I paused. I wanted my question to be clear. I didn't want to ask a dumb question in a room full of military professionals.

"From my understanding, there were three separate CONOPs that were created between October third and October fourth, correct?"

The general smiled. "Yes, there were three. The concept of operations reports, or CONOPs, are made by the teams to tell us their mission plans so that we know what level of approvals they need. That way we can be certain they have the necessary support and equipment for the mission they are on."

I continued. "Captain Perozeni wrote the first CONOP, correct?"

Again, he smiled at me. "Yes, he did. He wrote the CONOP for the first mission to Tiloa on October third." The general looked ready to continue with the brief, but I stopped him.

"Which they conducted as a civ/mil reconnaissance mission and carried out a KLE by meeting with local officials in Tiloa. That mission was completed and successful when they headed back toward Ouallam. Correct?"

General Cloutier gave me a serious look as he said, "Yes, but it's not as simple as that. Ms. Black, a civil reconnaissance is defined as a mission that is intended to be a targeted, planned, and coordinated observation and evaluation of specific civil aspects of the environment such as areas, structures, capabilities, organizations, people, or events. The intended purpose of the mission was not consistent with this doctrinal definition."

I again pushed. "That is the definition for a civil reconnaissance mission, but the CONOP was written for a civ/mil reconnaissance mission, was it not? Wouldn't the military part have been when they conducted the KLE at the military base outside of Tiloa?"

"Ms. Black, there is no doctrinal definition for a civ/mil reconnaissance mission. They were using a term that is not clearly defined to avoid getting the proper approvals. Their original intent was different, we believe, and so the mission was mischaracterized from its outset—meaning Captain Perozeni did not gather all the proper approvals. If the first mission had been properly characterized, they would have been required to have it approved at a higher level. And by being approved at a higher level, it would have received more oversight from the chain of command. You will see once everything is released that this was a very serious mischaracterization of their mission. Their civ/mil recon mission was a kill/capture mission, and was wrongly portrayed in the CONOP Captain Perozeni created. They went to Tiloa with the express intent of finding a known terrorist by the name of Doundou Chefou. When they did not find Doundou, they conducted a KLE hoping to collect information on his whereabouts. That is a very serious mistake."

"Hmmm," I said, thinking that surely the general had some information to support this narrative and he was going to share that with us. When he said nothing further, it became clear that he either didn't have that information or wasn't going to share it. I decided to continue with another line of thought. "So, Captain Perozeni wrote that first CONOP, which covered the mission carried out on the third of October in Tiloa. They carried out a civ/mil recon mission and followed that up with a KLE, which is what the CONOP said they were going to do. That CONOP covered the first and only successful part of a three-part mission, from what I understand. When the team was headed back to Tiloa, they stopped in Mangaize after receiving a call over the radio to be rerouted up toward the Mali border. Was that then covered in the original CONOP put together by Captain Perozeni?"

"No, it was not. A new CONOP was created for the next leg of the mission," the general replied.

"Did Captain Perozeni also create that new CONOP?" I asked.

"Well, no, he could not have. He would have needed a computer and access to many things he did not have access to out there in order to create that. So that was created back at base by someone else."

"Okay. Then there was also a third CONOP created when Team Arlit got turned around due to weather, correct?"

General Cloutier forced a smile and nodded. "Yes. There was a third CONOP created."

"I'm assuming Captain Perozeni did not make that third CONOP, either," I stated.

"No, he did not. Again, he did not have the equipment available to him that he would have needed to create a CONOP, so that third CONOP was also created back at base for the team. The last two CONOPs were created properly, though, with the proper authorizations."

"And yet they are the ones that ultimately led to the ambush?" I asked.

By now General Cloutier seemed frustrated. "Trust me, Ms. Black, once you see all of the evidence presented and the report is completely released, it will become very clear to you that the way Captain Perozeni put together that first CONOP and the way he mischaracterized the mission is very serious."

Having gotten to know Captain Perozeni a little over the course of the past few months, I simply could not see him purposefully misleading his superiors.

"General Cloutier," I said, "do you think Captain Perozeni was deliberately trying to mislead those higher up the chain of command with the CONOP he wrote?"

The general hesitated. Then, slowly, he said, "No. I would not necessarily say it was deliberate. But to mischaracterize a mission is very serious and cannot be dismissed." With that, General Cloutier turned back to the screen and moved on with the presentation.

I would later find out from the team that each time a new CONOP is made it equates to an entirely separate mission. So, essentially, three CONOPs meant they did three separate missions. With each CONOP, the team's equipment and support would be reassessed. With the proper approvals, the last two missions would have had proper oversight from all levels of command. In the first mission, which AFRICOM says was mischaracterized, the team traveled to Tiloa, where they met with local leaders for a KLE before heading back toward their base in Ouallam. Once that mission was complete, that CONOP was no longer relevant to any subsequent missions, including the one carried out the following day, which ended in an ambush.

General Cloutier pushed ahead, describing the terrain near the Mali border in detail. "There was a single tree that we had eyes on through an unmanned drone. The drone had been up in that area for about six hours and had seen no movement, indicating that the area was deserted. Besides the vast desert stretching for miles in all directions, there was only the one tree where the camp was located. We could easily monitor the area for movement and be certain there was no enemy still located at the camp. At that time, on October third, it was determined that the team should turn around and head up to the Mali border to explore the camp and gather intelligence if possible, rather than return to their base in Ouallam."

Henry then asked, "General, I have read in different articles that Captain Mike Perozeni pushed back against the movement up to the Mali border. There were some news reports that said he made it clear that he didn't feel they were equipped to do such an operation. Is there any truth to that?"

A lawyer in a black suit stood up to speak. "Captain Perozeni questioned if they would be acting as backup or the lead team when it was suggested that Team Arlit be brought in. He didn't push back, but did question the idea of being the lead team. He was reassured once he was given the full picture of the enemy situation along the border and was told that they would be acting in a support role."

Henry nodded and the general continued describing the campsite: "Team Arlit was halfway into their flight toward the Mali border when they ran into a heavy sandstorm that they could not fly through safely and had to be turned around. At this time, it was determined that Team 3212 would proceed alone as the main force on the next day's mission. A third CONOP was made as directed by Lieutenant Colonel David Painter, the battalion commander who was stationed in Chad. Lieutenant Colonel Painter conferred with Colonel Bradley Moses and other experienced officers, all of whom supported his decision and reasoning for the mission. But ultimately the final decision rested with Lieutenant Colonel Painter and he gave the order for the team to proceed."

Henry again interrupted. "I'm curious, General. Clearly the second CONOP that was created showed that Bryan's team, ODA 3212, was to be a support element. Essentially working as a backup team to assist the better-equipped team, Team Arlit, who was to come in on helicopters to head up the mission laid out in the second CONOP. Am I understanding that correctly?"

The general nodded. "Yes, sir, that is correct."

"After encountering a heavy sandstorm, that team—Team Arlit—was turned around on their way to the Mali border and was forced to abort their mission as the lead team?"

Once again General Cloutier responded, "Yes, sir, that is correct."

I turned to look at Henry while he continued. I could see the same lawyer seated behind Henry looking a bit on edge. "After Team Arlit, the lead team, was turned around, ODA 3212 was then ordered to proceed alone. They were ordered to head up the mission and to do so with no support or backup, and that is when a third CONOP was created." Henry paused for a moment.

The room was so quiet, I could hear my blood buzzing as my ears began to ring.

"General Cloutier," said Henry, "my question is, was a second threat assessment conducted and had the intelligence picture changed to show the threat at the border had diminished significantly enough in the three hours between the second CONOP and the third CONOP to suggest that there was no longer need for a backup or support team?"

No one said a word. No one moved except the lawyer seated behind Henry. Only the general and I could see him as he stood and nodded.

General Cloutier looked frozen for a moment, his eyes shifting from Henry to the lawyer, then to me, before stammering slightly as he said, "Uh, y-yes."

I could also hear the lawyer standing behind Henry say "Yes."

An awkward pause followed their answers. It seemed as though the investigative team hadn't been prepared to answer Henry's question. Perhaps they had not even thought through the fact that the team had been sent without backup into a scenario that only a few hours before had shown a clear need for backup—or perhaps they were hoping none of the families would notice this discrepancy.

General Cloutier continued going over the mission to include what the team found at the abandoned campsite. "Once there, the team found a motorcycle, some rice, and some ammunition belts. They burned what they found. Before leaving, the team commander, Captain Mike Perozeni, ordered their only ISR drone up to the Mali border in order to gather intelligence on possible enemy routes leading into Mali." He continued to describe the rest of the mission and the drive the team made down to Tongo Tongo that next morning. He mentioned the village chief of Tongo Tongo. "He was very cooperative and friendly. So was everyone we spoke to from the village."

Various media outlets had reported that the village chief and others within the village were possibly involved in setting up the ambush.

I again raised my hand. "How is it that you are certain the village chief was not involved? I have read in various articles that they stalled the team and possibly were in contact with the same terrorists who ambushed the convoy."

General Cloutier gave me the same warm smile as before, and I began to wonder if he was truly kind or condescending. "Ms. Black, these villages are very remote and the people who live in them often come in contact with extremists. The village chiefs are simply trying to protect their people; that is their priority. Yes, sometimes that means they are forced to interact with these extremists in order to keep their village safe. But we feel that the chief was forthcoming and more than willing to work with us and answer all of our questions."

Remembering a *New York Times* article I read, another question popped into my mind. "General, did the village chief in Tongo Tongo have Doundou Chefou's phone number saved as a contact in his phone?"

"Well, yes, Ms. Black, but as I stated, these villagers are often forced to come in contact with terrorists due to their location, and the village chief's job is to first protect his people. We found no definitive proof there was any ill intent toward your husband's team and the village chief was very forthcoming, so there is no reason for us to suspect he was involved."

He wouldn't say that the villagers of Tongo Tongo had helped the terrorists, but he couldn't tell me that they hadn't, either—just that there was no proof.

We then went over the next two hours of the ambush and ensuing firefight. The general spoke of there being perhaps fifty to eighty attackers. He spoke of the movements of the vehicles and how well armed the attackers were.

I remembered an article I had read back in late October about militant attacks in the region. "You are saying there were at least fifty to eighty very well-armed militants who seemed to gather out of the desert to ambush the team," I said.

"Yes, there were."

"I'm curious, has there ever been an amassing of that many terrorists, that well armed, in this same region before?"

"Yes, there has," he replied.

My breath caught in my throat. I reiterated the same question but slower. "So . . . there had been attacks in that same region with an enemy of this size who had this same level of firepower?"

I could see the same lawyer stand up, then sit back down.

"Uh, yes. Yes, there had. But they had never attacked Americans before, only Nigerien units," General Cloutier responded.

"But numbers this large, with this same level of firepower, had amassed out of the desert and attacked military units before?" I asked one last time.

"Well, yes. But never Americans. We assume that they did not realize these were Americans when they attacked."

Up until this moment, I had always thought the men had been ambushed after stumbling upon a group of terrorists. A wrong-place, wrong-time scenario. But now it turned out that large-scale planned attacks by well-armed militants were happening in the region, but the military automatically assumed they would never attack Americans. Maybe the team had no idea when they went to the border that attacks had happened before or maybe that is why Captain Perozeni did not want to go on the mission. Even if the team members did know of the attacks, perhaps it wasn't the team who had become overconfident and complacent; perhaps it was their leadership.

I was still reeling from his answer to my question, as General Cloutier continued. The formation of the convoy was laid out on the screen as Team 3212 left the village. Then a video began to play, depicting the vehicles moving into the kill zone and stopping as the first shots were fired.

I stopped the presentation again and asked, "Was there a certain reason why the convoy stopped?"

"Captain Perozeni chose to stop the convoy because he wanted to get out and do a bold flanking maneuver. He did so in order to assess and engage the enemy," General Cloutier answered in a tone that made it clear he disagreed with Captain Perozeni's choice. I had to admit it seemed strange that Captain Perozeni would stop the convoy rather than continue driving until the entire convoy was out of the line of fire.

The video continued showing a reenactment as the general explained what had happened to each vehicle and truck. "Here is where the red smoke was thrown and the vehicles then did a large bound of seven hundred meters [less than half a mile]. It was when they stopped at seven hundred meters that they realized the vehicle carrying Bryan, Dustin, and Jeremiah was no longer with them. It was at this time some of the men decided to go back in search of the missing vehicle."

After showing that the men who survived the attack had run into the woods, the video revealed that one of the vehicles moved over near the bodies of Bryan, Dustin, and Jeremiah.

"Here," said General Cloutier, "you can see that someone, we are guessing one of the terrorists, has moved a truck near the bodies of the fallen American soldiers." With her voice breaking, Karen asked a question I'm certain she already knew the answer to. "Why would they do that?"

General Cloutier looked at Karen, his eyes softening as he said delicately, "We think they were planning on taking the bodies with them. That is often something terrorist groups will try to do. Two men's remains had already been loaded into the back of the truck. We believe that the French Mirage jets showed up just in time, causing this truck to be abandoned along with the bodies of the fallen Americans."

I was afraid to look at Karen but forced myself to make eye contact. Her eyes were brimming with tears. Seeing her like this drained me of all my strength and we both began to weep. They had tried to steal him. The militants had murdered him, then tried to rob us of the most important thing we had left, the peace of knowing where he was and what had happened to him. Proof that Bryan had died quickly, that he had not been captured and tortured.

"I think we need a break," I said as I rose from my seat. I felt incredibly weak as I made my way out of the room with Karen beside me. When the door shut, we turned and hugged each other in the narrow hallway.

I don't know how long we were out there, but eventually we let go and walked down the hallway to the restroom in silence. On our way back Karen said, "It's okay. We have him and I'm so grateful for that."

At the end of the briefing, General Cloutier announced, "Before we leave, the team and I would like to invite you to each give us suggestions of any improvements that you feel could be made. It is our objective to prevent another tragedy like this from occurring in the future, so we would like to hear your thoughts on anything that might help us to do that. I want you to know that any suggestion, no matter how small or how large, will be taken to heart and seriously considered."

I had a suggestion but was still intimidated to speak up in front of such a large panel of military specialists, lawyers, and generals. My voice shook as I said: "Green Berets do extensive training on languages and brush up on those skills every year before deploying. Instead of doing pre-deployment training on a language like Spanish, which they wouldn't use in Africa, why not have them train using a phrase book of ten to twenty common words needed during military movements based on the languages spoken in the regions they are deploying to? Basic Hausa or Zulu words for *aim, shoot, stop, go, get into the vehicles, get out of the vehicles*, and so on? Why not train on those?"

The room was quiet again, and I realized my hands were trembling. I tried to calm myself when the same lawyer behind Henry stood and gave me what I think was meant to be a friendly smile but seemed closer to a condescending smirk. He felt sorry for me.

"Ms. Black," he said in a fatherly tone. "Your husband was extraordinarily intelligent and had an impressive aptitude for languages. Believe me when I say we all wish we could be so skilled. With him we truly lost one of the best. But that is unusual and cannot be expected of every man on a Green Beret team. Most men cannot learn a new language every time they deploy to a new place."

All of which I took as a backhanded compliment: My husband was smart, but my suggestion was stupid. Understood.

Suddenly my nervousness turned into something else entirely. I am Irish, after all, and this man had just asked for a fight. This time I turned and faced him. "I am not suggesting they learn a whole new language. I am suggesting a rudimentary phrase book. They would have only needed ten phrases that could be understood by all the men, both American and Nigerien. *Aim, shoot, drive, stop, go, truck*, and so on. My own children could learn ten phrases in a couple of days. If AFRICOM is making a push due to lack of training, perhaps they should consider more effective training, particularly in the area of communication."

The lawyer brushed me off with another smirk. "Ms. Black, these men spend months on training and languages. They have interpreters who work with them on the ground. There is no need for them to add extra languages on top of their already extensive training."

I made one last effort to get him to understand me. "If the men on the team cannot communicate with their partner forces, the partner forces would have a hard time 'partnering' with them in a battle scenario. One interpreter for forty Nigeriens and eleven Americans in a battle doesn't exactly work out well when trying to communicate in the midst of a firefight. What happens if the interpreter is killed or runs from the battle?"

The room was uncomfortably quiet as the lawyer once again smiled tightly. "As I said, more training on more languages just doesn't make sense, Ms. Black. Your husband had a rare talent, an aptitude for languages, so it may seem easy to you, but for most people it is not."

I sat there frustrated. My husband did not have an aptitude for languages. He would have been the first to tell anyone that. He had worked his butt off to learn the languages he did because it helped him do his job better if he could communicate. Countless hours of family time had been sacrificed so Bryan could communicate with the partner forces in Niger. Now that was being thrown in my face.

Feeling dismissed for my suggestion by the military lawyer, I realized that while they may have been taking suggestions from others, they were not taking them from me. They were not looking for solutions, they were looking for quick and easy fixes and possibly someone to punish.

Leaving the brief that day, I still had some nagging concerns about the Tongo Tongo village chief's involvement in the whole attack, but realized I would probably never know the truth about that. I also wondered why more detail wasn't given on the chain of command and how the orders were handed down. Those details seemed vague, but we'd been given one more name: Lieutenant Colonel Painter, who was located in Chad, had ordered the mission to the Mali border.

My biggest question, though, was what Captain Mike Perozeni had done that was so terrible. Whatever was wrong with the initial CONOP that Captain Perozeni created seemed to be a cardinal sin to those on the investigative team, one that he needed to be held accountable for. It was clear that his CONOP had not led to the ambush, but I assumed Captain Perozeni's mistakes must have been significant and facts in the final report would make it clear why. What I didn't understand was why they were not capable of making it clear now. The only thing that was clear to me was that AFRICOM had already found Captain Perozeni guilty, yet had failed to show us anything substantial. AFRICOM had failed to prove to me that Captain Perozeni was guilty of anything worthy of punishment.

At the end of the day, I was most surprised that on one hand, the village chief having a known terrorist's number in his phone was so easily dismissed by AFRICOM, and on the other, Captain Perozeni was going to hang for improper paperwork. None of it made any sense.

11

The Shift

Bryan and I always said that the odds of him dying in a car accident driving to and from work were far greater than that of him dying while deployed in Niger. I guess that is the thing about death that we often forget: It occurs constantly and in unexpected ways. In the United States, with our tidy funeral services and our tucked-away cemeteries, we forget. Those who grieve are expected to do so quietly and quickly so as not to disturb those who are not comfortable with it. Death is easily forgotten here, so we are shocked when it demands answers. Death is not something I had feared in a while, and neither had Bryan. Since being diagnosed with epilepsy at eighteen and having to face my own mortality many times, I have found myself at peace with the idea of death. It is simply another part of my life. We often forget how short life is, and how for some it is even shorter than they had the right to expect.

And when something terrible happens, we look for mistakes. We want an explanation and someone to blame. How could this ambush have happened unless there were major blunders? We demand to know everything, down to the very last detail. We need to know why people died and who is at fault. Our novels and movies and television dramas tell us that every death has an explanation: Someone always makes a mistake, you just have to be smart enough to see it. Once those mistakes are discovered and the cover-up is exposed, the evil conspirators are held accountable.

The truth of the matter is that some deaths truly are accidental, and ambushes are simply successful attacks predicated on surprise. As a military wife, I knew there was always the possibility of sacrifice, of hearing that dreaded knock on the door. By the end of the briefing, I felt that what had happened on October 4, 2017, in Niger was simply the result of that element of surprise coupled with intelligence failures and a lack of backup. A tragedy, of course, but one I had always known was possible.

These men had trained for what is known as "by, with, and through missions." In such missions, American soldiers advise and assist local Nigerien troops and train them to do their own missions. Their pre-deployment training was not focused on combat because they were not deploying to a combat zone. While AFRICOM and the officers pushing out the missions to 3212 were aware of the fact that large groups of well-armed extremists had amassed in the border area between Niger and Mali and had attacked local Nigerien units, as they admitted in the brief, I couldn't help but wonder if Captain Perozeni and the men on his team had that same knowledge. How could the team have trained for the possibility of being ambushed or attacked by extremists if they had not been forewarned about that threat?

For reasons I couldn't figure out, Captain Perozeni became the fall guy for the entire operation—and he was left with no way to fight for himself without risking his career. He was still under gag orders and could not speak to anyone about what had happened. Captain Perozeni did the honorable thing, the thing that true leaders do: He accepted full blame, whether or not that burden should have been his to bear. While those above him seemingly tried to avoid punishment in order to salvage their careers, Captain Perozeni had called the families of the fallen from his hospital bed in Germany. With a bullet wound in his back and a severe TBI (traumatic brain injury), Captain Perozeni had called me to apologize for failing to bring everyone home. The captain was the first person I heard from who was in Niger during the ambush.

Major Alan Van Saun came to express his condolences within a day of my husband's death, as well as Colonel Moses and his wife. None of these people could tell me much about the ambush, but they understood the importance of expressing their sorrow for the sacrifice my husband and my family had made.

The week after the brief by AFRICOM, seven months after my husband's death, the man who had ordered the second and third missions in Niger came to my door for the first time to pay his respects. Until May 6, 2018, I had never seen Lieutenant Colonel (LTC) David Painter and he had never called. I was surprised to find that he was a slight man, not much taller than me, with kind eyes. His light blond hair was almost red and the smattering of freckles across his face gave him a boyish look.

"Ms. Black," he said, "I wanted to stop by and tell you how truly sorry I am for your loss. Bryan was well respected and well loved by everyone in our community."

"Thank you," I said, trying to convince myself that he was sincere. His words were kind but had come so remarkably late that they denoted little respect.

LTC Painter was the commanding officer located in Chad who had ordered Bryan's team to proceed alone to the Mali border. Unlike Captain Perozeni and Brent Bartels, the special operators on the ground, LTC Painter's name had never been leaked to the press or shown up in a single news report. It was as though he was a ghost hidden under a sheet of protection throughout the investigation. I first heard his name during the brief when General Cloutier told me LTC Painter had been the officer to order the mission. If he hadn't shown up at my door a week later, I might never have put a face to the name. How was that possible? My only guess was that he was a very well-connected man.

LTC Painter spent his visit trying to convince Henry and me why the choice to send the men up to the Mali border was a good one. "The area seemed to be deserted by all accounts. We had an ISR [surveillance drone] watching the area for a long period of time, and it had shown no movement at the camp. We had received intelligence that a known terrorist had been up in that area and we were searching for an American, Jeffery Woodke, a kidnapping victim that we believed may have been held at that site. I felt it was imperative that they go and collect any information or intelligence they could from the area."

He continued telling Henry and me that he felt it was such an important mission that he stood by his decision to send the team to the border and would make the same decision still. Which was when it occurred to me that he wasn't saying he was sorry for making that decision or even taking responsibility for it; he was justifying himself to us. If LTC Painter was truly sorry for the loss of those men, it wouldn't have taken him seven months to show up at my door. If he felt any responsibility, he would not have allowed the men on the team to be publicly lambasted for a mission he had ordered.

"I'm sorry I didn't stop by to speak with you all before now, but I couldn't," LTC Painter said. "I was under orders not to speak about the ambush, but now that the investigation is complete and I am no longer under scrutiny, I finally am able to come and tell you all how sorry I am."

I wasn't grateful, but I also wasn't angry. I was indifferent. Condolences given that long after the fact seemed inconsequential and insincere. He had waited to come by until he knew he was cleared of all wrongdoing, that much was evident.

I was also confused that this man was in a leadership position. Even the most junior-level men on the team had found the strength to offer condolences within days of Bryan's death despite being under a cloud of suspicion. They understood that saying "sorry for your loss" did not violate the gag orders on discussing the ambush. My husband's life was of more value to them than their careers. They had come to my home as soon as they could, and they said they were sorry and they wept with me on my darkest days.

Listening to LTC Painter that day, I came to the conclusion that he was either unwise or insincere. In either case, that did not bode well for a leader who had people's lives dependent on his decisions. If you cannot correctly make the most basic decisions, like a properly timed condolence call, then how can you be trusted with life-and-death decisions? The mission that killed my husband, Jeremiah, LaDavid, Dustin, and five Nigeriens belonged to LTC Painter, but he certainly didn't own it. It seemed to me that he had protected his career above all else, above doing what was right.

I spent the next two weeks wrestling with my feelings over LTC Painter's visit and my feelings about the brief. I wanted to give him the benefit of the doubt, but my gut feeling kept bringing me back to a cold, hard truth. His behavior had not matched his words, and I was growing weary of that being a common thread among the higher-ranking officers involved in the mission and the investigation. Was it all about preserving their careers? Colonel Moses had not bothered to mention that he'd known about the mission from its inception, and LTC Painter had been entirely absent until the week after the families were briefed. He had avoided any press while allowing the team members to be dragged through accusations for months on end. Then General Cloutier and his room full of investigators and lawyers carefully crafted their words and pointed fingers at the lowest-ranking men.

There were many things from the brief that had unsettled me, but there were a few questions that continuously turned over in my mind. Was the village chief truly innocent? Was Captain Perozeni really guilty of something worthy of punishment? If he was guilty when his CONOP had not directly led to the ambush, how was it that LTC Painter wasn't guilty of anything when he ordered the missions that directly led to the ambush? Why did it seem like previous attacks in the region from terrorists in similar numbers with similar weaponry were being down-played? I thought of Henry's question about the intelligence picture changing for CONOP 3 and wondered if we had gotten the full truth in response, as General Cloutier and the lawyer had reacted so strangely. I had a hard time believing they would lie to us, but slowly that was changing.

Bryan's parents and I agreed that, despite our many concerns, pun-ishing people would not bring anyone back. And AFRICOM had nei-ther proven the team had made any mistakes worthy of punishment nor shown how Captain Perozeni had fallen short in his duties. We believed the authorities at AFRICOM would recognize that fact and make it known publicly when it was time to brief the media.

Even so, I began to do a little research on CONOPs, beginning by asking Henry about his experience with them. I found out that most CONOPs are cut and pasted and then the information that is pertinent to that exact mission is changed.

A SOFREP (Special Operations Forces Report) news site published an article about the investigation and CONOP that read: "The report indi-cates that an officer copy and pasted information from a previously au-thorized concept of the operation (CONOP) document into the CONOP which was submitted for the October 4th mission in which ODA 3212 was ambushed. Why this surprises anyone defies explanation at this point. Such activities have been happening for years. At this moment, soldiers are no doubt conducting combat operations in which informa-tion in their CONOP was cut and pasted from somewhere else. In fact, junior officers are essentially forced to do this due to the amount of mandatory paperwork and bureaucracy that is forced upon them."

The initial document for Captain Perozeni's CONOP was cut and pasted and a minor mistake was found. Because of this mistake, those looking to pass blame began using the line "cut and pasted document" as though he had intentionally done something terribly wrong in order to mislead higher authorities.

After reviewing all of the material I had access to and timelines from the day leading up to and during the ambush, I became convinced that the initial concept of operations paperwork had nothing to do with the resulting ambush. The cut-and-pasted paperwork outlining a civ/mil recon mission in Tiloa was for the first part of the mission, which was completed successfully before the men began to make their way back to their base camp in Ouallam. The following missions and resulting ambush were directly related to the CONOPs created thereafter and had nothing to do with Captain Perozeni or any other man on the team.

At a Pentagon news conference in May, AFRICOM briefed the media on the same report the families had been given the week before. It was covered by all the major news networks. I had decided beforehand not to watch it, assuming it would be similar to what we had heard in April. Henry watched it but didn't say much about it other than that watching it might upset me. When I asked him why it might upset me, Henry sighed and said, "General Waldhauser said something . . . well . . . I'm ashamed to call a man like him a Marine." With that, Henry went silent and I understood I needed to watch the media brief myself. Whatever had been said had touched a nerve with Henry and with the other families as news reports began to surface about a new controversy.

I waited until the house was empty the next day while the kids were at school and Henry was at work. I stood in my kitchen with a cup of coffee in one hand and my phone in the other, looking for the full video of the AFRICOM briefing. There on the screen, General Thomas D. Waldhauser, the commander of U.S. Africa Command, introduced Robert Karem, assistant secretary of defense for international security affairs, and General Roger L. Cloutier. General Waldhauser went through all the investigative findings and what needed to be improved upon. Ten minutes in, I was out of coffee and losing interest in the brief, which so far mirrored our family brief.

He mentioned the CONOPs and focused on the one that Captain Perozeni had created, putting emphasis on it not having the proper approvals. *Even if that CONOP had higher-level approvals,* I thought, *that CONOP is not the one that led to the ambush.*

Then reporters from various organizations, including *The New York Times, Military Times,* the AP, CBS, ABC, and many others, asked questions. One reporter asked whether operations would be scaled back and General Waldhauser said no, they would continue. An older male reporter asked, "General Waldhauser, when you look at this report, you read contradicting and ambiguous operational process—approval process, lack of attention to detail, quality control, lack of situational awareness, planning problems, training shortcomings across the board with the special operators in Africa. So, in layman's terms, how would you characterize this? Are they sloppy, are they cowboys, are they taking too much risk? What would you tell the American people about this?"

I laughed out loud, thinking, *Yes, General, what should we know about this?*

"I think that the general—generally, from my observations and the evidence that this investigation found, is that special operators are doing a fantastic job across the continent," General Waldhauser began. "They work under some extreme conditions in the African continent. They have to be able to make decisions about whether to or not to take— to go into certain operations. Because if the—the assets that they need are not there today, they need to be able to come back tomorrow when they have them."

Interesting, I thought. *Then why is it that when Captain Perozeni questioned being properly equipped, higher-ranking officials at headquarters told him to go anyway? Then, when people died, it fell on Captain Perozeni's head? ODA 3212 was not allowed to "come back tomorrow" when their support team got turned around, leaving them alone. Why is that, General Waldhauser?*

General Waldhauser continued. "So, the bottom line is, the special operators on the continent are serving well. They're—they—they do high-risk missions and, based on my observations, this particular—this particular team is not indicative of what they do."

I sat in shock, listening to General Waldhauser insult my husband and all of those who fought with him and died with him. I wondered what the team had done to receive that. Or was the general only protecting his own interests? It's an absolute tragedy when the real heroes are treated like the enemy and blamed for things they did not cause.

Watching what had gone on in the past few months, it now seemed to me that more and more of our military authorities worry about appeasing the media and giving them the villain they want, whether or not it's the right thing to do, whether or not there is ample evidence. Guilty until proven innocent, that's how it works now. Some of those highest up the chain of command worry more about their images and career aspirations than their souls, so they offer up the innocent to the media to be made an example of. Many of today's highest military officials often more closely resemble politicians; they are surrounded by lawyers and they choose their words carefully. Well, here is the truth being spoken by someone who isn't afraid to speak it: Shit happens and real leaders take the blame, not just in word but in action. They defend the soldiers who took their orders and they honor the dead. That's not what I witnessed in the aftermath of the ambush in Niger, and that is not what I saw on television May 10, 2018, during the press brief on Niger. There was no valor or truth in the actions of our military leaders at AFRICOM.

My husband was the epitome of a Green Beret soldier until the day he died with a green beret on his head, and now he was being disrespected and dishonored on national television. I felt a familiar anger building up inside of me over the injustice of what was being leveled at the team. It was the same anger I had felt when I'd been told that my son's doctors' mistakes would cost him. I thought, *This is not right. These men will not be blamed for others' mistakes. I can't let this happen.*

———

As I listened to General Waldhauser that day, I hoped that he was not indicative of military generals in powerful positions. I wanted to think that there is still honor at higher levels in this country's military—but that is not what I saw that day. I decided that one thing was certain: I knew men who still acted with honor, and they would help me get the truth.

12

The Truth

I paced in my kitchen after watching the AFRICOM media brief, trying to calm down. General Waldhauser's words echoed in my ears, and running through my mind was everything I knew about the ambush. What I had learned was that our men in Niger did everything right, but under the circumstances they were overwhelmed by nearly one hundred militants against a team of eleven. Those men of ODA 3212 were outmanned and outgunned, surrounded on all sides by five of the enemy for every one of them. Still, the team had managed to kill at least thirty of the enemy forces before escaping with the seven surviving American team members. The fact that anyone survived that attack, which lasted for five hours, is a miracle and a testament to how capable that team was and how well they fought together.

If there is one thing I had learned about myself over the years, it is that my most effective actions are born in the wake of great injustice. It is in those moments that all my fear washes away and the path before me seems clear. What I had witnessed that day watching the general brief the media was a level of injustice that I could not tolerate. I would right this wrong, no matter the cost.

What could anyone do to bring the truth to the public and to show these men on the team for what they really were? They were heroic.

These men were a team, and they loved one another. These men were victims, too. They had been under orders to carry out a mission, then walked straight into an ambush, and every single one of them had nearly died. Now they were being publicly disparaged by the leader of the very organization that was meant to protect them.

For the last seven years of his life, Bryan had spent countless hours in training, in schools, and on deployments far from home in order to become an elite Green Beret soldier, just as every man on his team had done. I was willing to support him and sacrifice precious time together because it made him happy. I knew the families of all the men on his team had done the same. My husband was one of the most intelligent men I knew. He had a business degree, spoke four languages, was skilled at chess, medicine, and hand-to-hand combat, and could have had any job he chose. He chose to be a Green Beret and he was good at it. General Waldhauser had chosen to diminish that and to insult every other man on that team. That was inexcusable, and I was no longer going to sit idly by and wait for justice.

If I couldn't trust General Waldhauser to bring me the truth, how could I trust there wouldn't be punishments unjustly meted out? Something was off, and the only group I still trusted were the very men who AFRICOM had been blaming for the mistakes they claimed led to my husband's death. I believed the only place to find the real truth was with the members of ODA 3212.

It was late May 2018 when I figured out what I wanted to do. I didn't just want the truth; I wanted the truth to be made public. I decided to ask the men on Bryan's team, the survivors of the ambush, if they would allow me to interview them. These men needed someone to hear them, and then to tell their story. Someone who would not twist their words or further victimize them. Someone who could tell the truth without the worry of losing a career. Someone who had nothing to gain and nothing to lose.

The week of Memorial Day 2018, Brent had been assigned to escort our family to events honoring the men who had died that year. Bryan, Dustin, LaDavid, Jeremiah, and many more would be honored at Fort Bragg. One bright spring day, Brent picked us up in a white military-issued van. As we pulled away from my house on our way to the day's events, I cautiously said to Brent: "I've been writing a book about Bryan and I was thinking that I would like to write the whole story. Not just about his life, but, if you would allow me and if the guys are okay with it, about the ambush. I still feel like I know nothing of what actually happened to you guys during the battle, and I'm confused on many of the details leading up to it."

I paused to see whether the response would be positive or negative.

"Oh, yeah, Michelle! That would be awesome," Brent replied.

"Really? You would be okay with me writing about that?"

"Yes, I definitely would," he said.

"Do you think the other guys would be okay with that?" I asked tentatively.

"I will message them as soon as we get to the event, but I am sure they would love to have you do this."

"Thank you, Brent," I replied, surprised by how enthusiastic he was about the idea.

"Honestly, Michelle," he said, smiling at me in the rearview mirror. "I think all the guys are going to love this idea. The only thing that makes me nervous is I don't want you to get into trouble for anything."

"What are they going to do, Brent? Kill my husband? End his career? I don't think there's much more that can be done to hurt me at this point. I've already watched my husband die and then be insulted by a general on national TV."

Brent and I laughed darkly.

"You make a good point," he said.

All of my greatest fears had been realized the past eight months. Somehow I had survived, and now there was no fear left in me. All I wanted now was the whole truth, and the only person who could help me was me. I concluded that the best way to do that was to meet with each man individually to get the most accurate account of what had happened from each man's perspective. What I expected to get was a firsthand account of the same basic story I'd been told by AFRICOM. The only thing I expected to be a little different was the explanation behind the various CONOP reports, and I imagined I would get more details of what happened during the battle.

Initially the men were reluctant, not because they feared getting in trouble for speaking to me—as by then they were no longer under gag orders—but because they feared me getting into trouble on their behalf. In order to protect me, they were willing to take the full blame, whether or not they deserved it.

A week after Memorial Day the team was having dinner at my house. We were sitting around my dining room table after everyone had finished eating when Brent called for a shot of scotch to salute the fallen. I pulled out some glasses and poured a round.

Ondo lifted his glass and said, "To Dustin."

"To Dustin!" echoed around the room as we all raised our glasses and took a sip.

Next, Hanson said, "To Moody."

"To Moody!" boomed every voice in the room as we raised our glasses a second time.

"To Bryan!" went up a third echo, followed by a fourth. "To Jeremiah!" As I looked around the room my eyes were blurry as tears spilled down.

Then I asked them all, "Would you guys please let me interview each of you?" The room went quiet until I heard the first yes. Then I continued, "I could interview you one at a time. Afterward, I can compile a complete picture of the timeline from the night before you all set out to Tiloa all the way through your rescue in Tongo Tongo. I will wait as long as you want to release anything you've told me in order to make sure you are protected. What do you guys think?"

Captain Perozeni spoke up first. "Michelle, if we were to speak with anyone, it would be you. But there is no way we would want to involve you in this mess."

"Mike," I said, "it's too late. The day Bryan died I became involved. I'm one of the only people who can get away with doing what I want to do."

That night, that very moment, was the last time the members of ODA 3212 would simply be my husband's brothers-in-arms. From that moment forward, I let those men into my home and into my heart. They would soon share their stories with me and become my family, my brothers, my sons.

It was early June 2018 when I did my first interview with my husband's best friend, Brent. I had invited him over for dinner and an interview. I have always felt that a man is more willing to talk when he has eaten well, so I grilled some beautiful steaks and made a salad and a little fresh guacamole with tortilla chips. The perfect interview food to loosen a guy up. I hustled around the house getting the kids settled in front of the TV with some food, double-checking my recording device, and putting the finishing touches on the salad.

I was nervous because I had never interviewed anybody before and wasn't quite sure what I was supposed to do. I tried to think of important-sounding questions, but realized I knew very little and would be dependent on each of these guys to walk me through some of the basic stuff, including explaining acronyms. Later, I would also find out that in order to follow our discussions and interviews, I would have to do a lot of research on military tactics, techniques, procedures, and terminology. As I worried about my inexperience, something Bryan had told me once came to mind: *It's okay to be a beginner. Every expert started as one.* I smiled to myself, knowing I would be just fine, and was suddenly looking forward to my first interview.

It was around 6:00 p.m. when I heard a knock and descended a flight of stairs to open the door for Brent—all 6'4" and 250 pounds of him. As he came through the door, he seemed slightly nervous as he bent down and gave me a hug. Then he smiled and said, "All right! You ready to do this?"

I thought I was.

The truth of what happened on the ground in Niger on October 4, 2017, is one of the hardest things I have ever had to face, and I didn't have to face it only once. Over the course of the next several months, I had to face that truth over and over as I walked through the final hours of my husband's life with different men from his team, each with his own perspective on events, but all with the same story. Woven together, that story told me that AFRICOM had left huge gaps in their family brief. It also told me that these men went through hell and still lived it in their heads.

I spent months interviewing these men, laughing and crying with them over what had happened between October 3 and October 4. Each interview had moments that left either the man I was interviewing or myself completely devastated. The hardest things were the questions that still plagued the men on the team, such as why Bryan, Dustin, and Jeremiah had stopped in the kill zone when the rest of the trucks had moved out. Then there were the things that just left me completely baffled because they were contradictory to what I had learned in the AFRICOM brief or seemed inexplicably absent from that brief.

After sitting with these men and going through each heartbreaking second with them, I was alarmed at the disparities between their stories and the brief. It had taken me months to interview all of the men and then to go back with follow-up questions as I pieced together their stories. To see the chain of events from the very beginning of what led up to the ambush and then what happened on the ground. Having survived the ambush, the team was brought home only to be ambushed by their own leadership. They were looking at being punished for surviving a nightmare that their leadership was responsible for.

Suddenly I was faced with an overwhelming task: I needed to tell their story, but I needed to do what the media had not. To show the American public that these men were the victims, not the enemy. They did not abandon their friends on the battlefield—instead, *they* were abandoned by all those they thought they could depend on. All of the men, those who died and those who survived, walked right into a trap.

When I sat down to write the story of the men of ODA 3212, the weight of the task that lay before me began to sink in. These men would depend on me not only to tell their story accurately but to acquit them before the eyes of the world. To prove them innocent despite the power of their accusers. A few of those accusers were men who had made me feel marginalized, and that had lit a fire in me.

Deep inside of me, a naysayer was telling me I couldn't write a book and I couldn't set out to find the truth on my own. After all, I was just a silly housewife and didn't know what I was doing. I would be going up against multiple well-established authorities. How would my voice ever be heard? Yet louder and stronger was a voice saying that I was the wife of Bryan Black. I was not an idiot and I would not be dismissed as one. I would be heard, and I would make certain the men of ODA 3212 were heard, no matter the cost. Besides, what was the worst anyone could do to me? Kill my husband and lie to me? Already done.

I began to gear up for my own battle as I put pen to paper.

PART THREE

On the Ground

Team OUALLAM

ODA-Operational Detachment Alpha 3212

3-3rd Special Forces Group. This group operates out of Fort Bragg, North Carolina.

2-2nd Battalion. 3rd Group has four battalions.

1-A Company. Each battalion has three companies: A, B, and C, listed numerically as 1, 2, and 3.

2-Team 2. Each company has six twelve-man Special Forces Alpha Teams. At 3rd Group's 2nd battalion A company, these are 3211, 3212, 3213, 3214, 3215, and 3216.

Rank and Job, Highest Ranking to Lowest

AFRICOM (Africa Command)

General Thomas D. Waldhauser

SOCAFRICA (Special Operations Command Africa)

Major General Marcus Hicks

SOCOM (Special Operations Command)

General Raymond "Tony" Thomas

USASOC (U.S. Army Special Operations Command)

Colonel Bradley Moses—3rd Group commander, based out of
  Germany

Lieutenant Colonel David Painter—battalion commander,
  based out of Chad

AOB (Advanced Operations Base) located in Niamey, Niger, Africa

Major Alan Van Saun—on paternity leave when ambush occurred

Captain Newburn—the XO (executive officer) in command of
  the company during Major Alan Van Saun's absence; brand
  new to Special Forces

Chief Warrant Officer Marshall—noncommissioned officer with
  approximately twenty years of experience

Sergeant Major Kingman—high-ranking enlisted, with approximately twenty years of experience

Staff Sergeant Casey Wilbur—a Green Beret communications
  sergeant working with B Company in Niamey during the 2017
  deployment; a former ODA 3212 member

Operational Detachment A (ODA) team ground operators

For the mission, ODA Team 3212 would have eleven American
ground operators: eight Green Berets, two Special Forces support
members, and one contractor.

Green Berets

Captain Mike Perozeni—officer and highest ranking on team

NCOIC Smith—noncommissioned officer in charge, second-
  highest ranking. The team sergeant of an ODA has been

operational within the Special Forces community for ten to fifteen years on average. They are also referred to as the master sergeant (MSG) and are expected to lead from the front. The master sergeant is the quick decision-maker when stress levels are high. The lives of the men on the team are largely in the hands of the master sergeant, particularly during a battle.

Sergeant First Class Brent Bartels—communications sergeant. His job during the course of a battle is to shoot, move, and communicate with headquarters.

Staff Sergeant Hanson—weapons sergeant

Staff Sergeant Brooks—weapons sergeant

Staff Sergeant Ondo—weapons sergeant

Staff Sergeant Bryan Black—medical sergeant

Staff Sergeant Dustin Wright—engineer sergeant. He is an explosives expert, and his job is demolition on enemy targets.

Special Forces Support

Sergeant First Class Jeremiah W. Johnson—chemical, biological, radiological, and nuclear specialist

Sergeant LaDavid Johnson—mechanic

Contractor

Chester—non-combat-trained JIDO (Joint Improvised-Threat Defeat Organization) analyst

Acronyms

AOB: Advanced Operations Base

The AOB in Niger is located in the capital city of Niamey. The AOB provides support to the Special Forces teams on the ground through intelligence gathering, communications, and coordinating multiple elements.

CIV/MIL: Civilian/Military

Civil-Military Operations (CMO) are the activities performed by military forces to establish, maintain, influence, or exploit relationships between military forces and indigenous populations and insitutions.

CONEX

Large steel storage and shipping containers used on ships, trains, and trucks. In the outposts such as Ouallam, American teams use them as offices, storage for supplies, and sleeping quarters.

CONOP: Concept of Operations Report

For each mission, teams must create a report that details what is to be done during that mission. These reports are called CONOPs.

DShK: Degtyarev Shpagin Krupnokalibernyi

A Soviet-era heavy machine gun that uses 12.7×108mm cartridges.

EFoN: Expeditionary Forces of Niger

A highly trained and highly capable Nigerien Special Forces unit.

HUMINT: Human Intelligence

Any information that can be gathered from human sources.

ISR: Intelligence, Surveillance, and Reconnaissance

A basic aerial component of modern militaries today—offering real-time battlefield tracking of ongoing actions and enemy positions. The ISR used by the military are basically drones with far more sophisticated capabilities.

JSOC: Joint Special Operations Command

Under the umbrella of JSOC fall such elite units as Delta Force, 75th Ranger Regiment, Seal Team 6, and more.

KLE: Key Leader Engagement

A meeting held between the leaders of the military and leaders of a village or other military installment.

MRE: Meal Ready to Eat

Individual food rations that can be heated without a fire or a stove.

ODA: Operational Detachment A

Also known as an A-Team or Green Beret team, such as ODA 3212.

QRF: Quick Reaction Force

An armed military unit capable of rapidly responding to developing situations.

ROE: Rules of Engagement

ROE are instructions issued by military authorities that outline the limitations and circumstances in which soldiers will initiate and continue fighting with other forces encountered. ROE are read to soldiers if authorities are expecting contact with an enemy.

RTB: Return to Base

SIGINT: Signals Intelligence

Intelligence gathering by the interception of signals.

SOCOM: Special Operations Command

SOCCE: Special Operations Command and Control Elements

SOCCE-LCB: Special Operations Command and Control Elements-Lake Chad Basin

Lake Chad is where battalion headquarters is located. Being the battalion commander, LTC Painter was based in Chad as the SOCCE-LCB commander during the 2017 deployment.

SOCFWD-NWA-Special Operations Command Forward-North & West Africa

Baumholder, Germany, is where the command for SOCFWD-NWA is located. During the 2017 deployment, Colonel Bradley Moses was the SOCFWD-NWA commander.

TBI: Traumatic Brain Injury

TIC: Troops in Contact
Usually means there is a firefight.

USASOC: U.S. Army Special Operations Command

VDO: Vehicle Drop-off

VEO: Violent Extremist Organization

VTC: Video Teleconference

ZPU
Soviet-era heavy mounted antiaircraft gun.

13

Hurry Up and Wait

Bani Bangou, Niger, on a mission after getting word that there may be an attack planned on the district center. *(Nigerien villager)*

Since arriving in Niger on August 30, 2017, ODA 3212 had conducted three missions in-country with their local partner teams: young Nigerien soldiers with little training coming from villages throughout the country.

Together they visited surrounding villages and military outposts to gather intelligence and see if the villagers needed anything. With instability in the region and a growing militant presence, it was important for the local population to see the military checking in on them.

The team had noticed a worrying pattern: All the missions they went on following orders from the advanced operations base (AOB) were consistently based on the same single source of signals-based intelligence. Signals-based intelligence is also known as SIGINT. Typically, there are two types of intelligence on which the military bases their rationale for missions: HUMINT and SIGINT. HUMINT is human intelligence, the gathering of real information from human sources. SIGINT is the method of intercepting signals or communications transmitted electronically through radios, radar, or weapons systems.

Dustin Wright and Brent Bartels. *(Ondo)*

The night of October 2, 2017, the men of ODA 3212 were sitting around the team office filling out paperwork from the previous day's mission.

Bryan and Jeremiah Johnson waiting outside the military camp in Tiloa, Niger. *(Ondo)*

Ondo—who looked like he just stepped off a California beach with a surfboard—turned in his chair and asked Dustin, "Hey, how are you and Jenna doing?"

"I'm thinking about taking a vacation down to Jamaica with her once we get home from this trip," Dustin replied in his thick Georgia accent.

"What makes you want to go to Jamaica?" Ondo asked.

Dustin moved the computer screen toward Ondo to show him all the places he planned to visit on his future Jamaican vacation.

Ondo walked over to take a closer look. "Seriously, man? Not going to lie, that looks like a fun time. You must really like this girl if you're already planning trips outside of the U.S. together."

"Yeah, man. I'm pretty sure she's the one."

"Well, brother, I'm happy for you." Ondo gave Dustin a pat on his back, then walked back to his chair to get ready for their nightly meeting.

Ondo pulled his chair next to Hanson, who was leaning back and chatting to Bryan.

"Hey, Black," said Hanson, "can you hand me that cup, man?" He pointed to a cup just to Bryan's right where he had left it earlier in the day. Since he arrived in-country, Hanson's curly brown hair had started filling out and he had grown a small mustache that made him look closer to his twenty-five years.

Bryan ignored Hanson as he continued to do his paperwork.

"Hey, Black," Hanson said again.

Bryan didn't respond.

"Seriously, man?" Hanson said.

Slowly, a smile spread across Bryan's face.

"You're so annoying, man!" Hanson said, shaking his head but laughing a little, too.

Still smiling, Bryan responded with a high-pitched "Thanks!" Hanson started to talk, but Bryan cut him off. "Maybe you should have picked it up earlier. Then you would have it with you now." Falling silent, Bryan continued to work.

"Wow, great advice. Thanks, Bryan," Hanson said, finally reaching around Bryan for his cup.

The other men started laughing. Brent said, "Yeah, Black's right. Pick up all your shit. It's everywhere!"

The men were still laughing when the phone rang. Chief Warrant Officer Marshall was calling from the AOB in Niamey.

"Captain Perozeni," he said, "we just received intelligence from the embassy that Doundou Chefou is to be in the area of Tiloa tonight. The intelligence has come with a time limit of two hours. We would like your team to go up there tonight on a find-and-fix mission in order to verify if the terrorist is in the area and more accurately identify his exact location."

Having been in Niger only five weeks and having seen a bad intelligence pattern form, with the same SIGINT being used for every mission, Captain Perozeni was not eager to jump on this information. In fact, the whole team felt uneasy about the missions that were being handed down to them.

Captain Perozeni replied, "Chief, I am not comfortable with this mission. I think there are better ways to go about using this intelligence. If we continue to use the same single-source reporting and action it every time, the enemy could be alerted to our tactics, techniques, and procedures. Instead, we should continue to watch and collect intelligence on Doundou Chefou's movements into and out of the area around Tiloa before going in. Let's make him feel comfortable and believe he is not being watched so we will have the element of surprise."

Captain Perozeni tried to point out that when the terrorist's movements in and out of that village became a pattern, they would know when to target him. The captain asked if he could have a few minutes to talk the mission over with his team and then call the chief back.

"Of course," the chief replied, "but make it quick. I'd like you guys to head up there as soon as possible."

Captain Perozeni had two previous combat deployments to Afghanistan under his belt. He had run multiple combat missions during a 2012 deployment to Afghanistan with the 82nd Airborne Division as the platoon leader of forty while working with a partner force of Afghans. In a 2014 deployment to Afghanistan, Captain Perozeni worked as the company executive officer with logistics as his focus. He was tasked with shipping items by way of convoys through dangerous territory. Experience had taught Captain Perozeni that using caution and allowing the intelligence to build before acting made for a better and more successful mission.

In our interview, Captain Perozeni told me that the best missions are built on two sources of intelligence, so that the reliability of the information can be checked. And if only one source is being used, it is better, at the very least, not to consistently use the same source over and over again and to act on it in every instance. He was also deeply concerned about time. He felt the AOB was calling regularly with single-source intelligence to suggest a short-suspense mission, meaning it had to happen fast. By the time of the Tongo Tongo mission, he was upset with the pace the AOB was demanding.

In the aftermath of the ambush, I read articles stating that Doundou Chefou—this terrorist the team was supposed to find—had a cell phone, as did most of his cohorts. Much later, this was confirmed by multiple news sources and military members who briefed our family. It led me to wonder if the embassy was using cell phone signals to track Chefou and how dangerous it would be to consistently go after him every time his cell phone sent out a ping. I was reminded of a story about how for years ISIS has used online tutorials explaining how to choose the best software to evade detection in war zones. If the terrorists use software to avoid detection, they are tech-savvy enough to figure out that their cell phones are being used to track them. If a terrorist sees the military showing up every time they visit a village or use their phone, surely the terrorists can figure out how to use that to their advantage.

After hanging up the phone with the chief in Niamey, Captain Perozeni called the entire team into the office and filled them in.

"Well, there's no way we're going to make it up there in that two-hour time window. So what's the point?" asked Hanson.

"There *is* no point," said Bryan.

In his deep southern drawl, Dustin said, "This is stupid. We're just going to be wasting our time going up there again. It's dumb—that's what I think."

Jeremiah Johnson assessed the mission and said, "The AOB knows that the time limit is two hours and it'll take us at least five to get up there. Sounds like a waste of a mission to me."

Captain Perozeni sighed as he told the men: "All of you are right and I tried to put up resistance. I know it's a dumb mission, but, bottom line, they give us orders, we execute, and I have a feeling we are going to have to do this one. I'll give more push back, but I think we are going up there tonight anyway."

Captain Perozeni had two options: to accept and execute the mission, or to refuse with the understanding that he would be fired for disobeying a direct order. So that night Captain Perozeni put up a reasonable amount of resistance to the AOB in Niamey but knew it might be futile.

Normally, Major Alan Van Saun would command the company and direct all missions from the AOB in Niamey, but he had just left for the United States on paternity leave after receiving word that his wife had gone into labor. Major Van Saun, who had been the commanding authority at the AOB during the 2017 deployment to Niger, was a tall, slender man of thirty-five. He graduated from the United States Military Academy at West Point, then attended the Naval War College in Newport, Rhode Island, where he was named Honor Grad. In his absence, the leadership positions at the AOB were filled by Captain Newburn, Chief Warrant Officer Marshall, and Sergeant Major Kingman. Captain Newburn, the executive officer (XO) for the company, became the acting commander. Newburn was brand new to Special Forces, having just graduated from the Special Forces Qualification Course, but after five years in the conventional Army he was trained for this kind of experience. It wasn't unusual for an officer like him to be in this position.

It is a requirement in the Army to have a commissioned officer in charge, since there are legal authorities that come with being commissioned. A commissioned officer has had authority conferred on them by the president of the United States, which means they can command those who rank lower. So, officially, Captain Newburn was in command at the AOB in Major Van Saun's absence, but over the next few days he would rely heavily on the guidance of the two more senior members of the AOB: Chief Warrant Officer Marshall and Sergeant Major Kingman, each of whom had more than twenty years of experience in Special

Forces. They had both spent years in Afghanistan, which meant they not only had experience but a more aggressive mindset than Captain Newburn did.

Crucially, however, Marshall and Kingman were used to having unlimited assets and backup at their disposal when they sent out a team for missions. In Afghanistan, there are numerous drones, military bases situated throughout the country, and assets like Black Hawk and Pave Hawk helicopters that might be in the air to rescue and pull out a team as soon as they get a call. The goal in Afghanistan is to provide backup and evacuation for injured soldiers within what is called "the golden hour," the first hour after injury, since a person is most likely to survive if they can quickly get to a place with surgical capabilities.

In western Africa, things work very differently. There are few drones or helicopters, and medical evacuation times are estimated at six hours.

When Captain Perozeni made his next call, his men sat in the office tensely listening to him push back to the AOB leadership.

"Chief, I really don't think we should do this. I think we should wait. With the two-hour time window, by the time we pack up the trucks and make the nearly four-hour drive up there, he'll be gone. I am not comfortable with this mission and feel that we should be more cautious. I believe there are better ways of approaching the target. If we continue to action the intelligence we get every time we receive it, we are less likely to have impactful results."

Chief Warrant Officer Marshall responded, "I understand what you are saying but do not agree with you, Captain. Your team will do this mission anyway. Remember, you do not get to pick your missions. You are not in a unit with such privileges, you're not JSOC. Your team will only be in-country for six months and you are expected to be as busy as possible. You will go on any and all missions chosen for you."

Frustrated by the situation but feeling he could argue no further,

Captain Perozeni responded, "Understood, Chief. We will leave for Tiloa as soon as possible."

As Captain Perozeni hung up the phone, the team looked at him warily.

"So they still want us to do this stupid mission?" Dustin Wright asked.

"Why?" Bryan asked, clearly annoyed.

"So we can take a lovely evening drive through this beautiful fu-fucking country," said Brent, "and maybe get shot at by some terrorist assholes in the dark who can see and hear us coming from a mile away." He rubbed his temples and laughed darkly to himself.

"Whatever, man. Not like we have a choice, right?" Ondo asked.

"No, we don't," said Captain Perozeni. "We have to get ready fast and get up there if we are going to make it up somewhat near this two-hour window of time. So let's get the trucks ready to roll."

Master Sergeant Smith cut in. "All right, y'all, no choice here, you know? We gotta do this. We got our two-hour time window and you know, so we gotta just make it happen. Let's do this, baby."

Brooks, in a rare moment of breaking his silence, let out a deep sigh.

Ondo grabbed his Altec Lansing wireless speaker and set it outside near the trucks. He cranked the dial as "Kickstart My Heart" by Mötley Crüe came screaming from the speaker, cutting through the silent Nigerien night. Instantly Dustin Wright, a large-framed southern boy, started playing air guitar and lip-syncing. Wearing headlamps, the men began to yell back and forth as they prepared the trucks.

"Hey, Hanson! You got water? Did we put water in the cooler yet?" Brent yelled over at Truck #1.

"No, man, like, I just put twelve bottles in the chest freezer."

"All right. What about the playlist? You got the pl-pl-playlist good to go for tomorrow yet?"

Hanson responded, "Yeah, man, I'm working on it right now!"

The men worked into the night, filling the trucks with fuel and storing in freezers huge bottles of water that would be loaded onto the truck in ice chests. They wanted to ensure they had enough water for two days out in the sweltering heat and humidity of the African desert. Soaring temperatures meant the men often drank more water than they anticipated, and drinking from African wells was not an option for the Americans, since they ran the risk of picking up dangerous bacteria and viruses.

By Truck #3, Ondo and Jeremiah were working together. "Hey, Ondo, what kind of ammo do you need up there?" Jeremiah shouted.

"I'm going to need two more cases of 762 up here, bro," Ondo yelled back as a new song—"Dr. Feelgood"—shook the camp.

Jeremiah grabbed ammo out of the large metal CONEX shipping container, then handed it up to Ondo.

"Let's get some water bottles frozen and we will throw them in the truck's cooler right before we leave," Ondo shouted down to Jeremiah as Master Sergeant Smith walked up to them.

"Yeah, man, we got to get some water going," Master Sergeant Smith agreed. He stood for a moment watching the other men work before disappearing into the office.

At Truck #2, Bryan, Dustin, and Brooks worked in silence. Bryan prepared his medical equipment and loaded extra ammunition for his grenade launcher. Dustin and Brooks filled the water and loaded ammunition for their weapons. Each team member checked batteries and radios to make sure their communications systems were up. Machinegunners Ondo and Hanson made sure their weapons were good to go, that their ammo was clean and set up. LaDavid Johnson, a support mechanic who was on his second deployment to Niger with ODA 3212 by special request of the team, checked the trucks' oil levels and that the vehicles' tires were ready to roll for the next morning. LaDavid looked so young that the native Nigeriens had started calling him the Hausa word for *young*, which sounds similar to the English word "moody." The name caught on and by the end of the 2016 deployment LaDavid was known as Moody by all the members of Team 3212.

Walking up to Truck #1, LaDavid asked Brent, "Hey, yo, Sergeant B! You wanna pop the hood?"

Checking fluids, then checking air pressure with the tire gauge, La-David thoroughly inspected the vehicle. "Ah, you good to go, aight? Your car A/C working good on this thing?"

"Absolutely, Moody, but you know we don't ever turn that thing on," Brent said. "We like to keep the windows down because we don't like to make Hanson feel like he's the only one out there in the h-h-heat."

Hanson, as the gunner, sat on top of the vehicle, so those inside the vehicle wanted to be able to hear Hanson and kept their windows down so he wasn't the only one sweating.

While the team in Ouallam prepared their trucks and ammo, the three leaders at the AOB discussed how to make this mission work. Marshall and Kingman advised Captain Newburn until he, being the only commissioned officer, gave the final approval. Newburn read through the CONOP, which was his responsibility to sign. Chief Warrant Officer Marshall made the calls over the radio to Team 3212 at their base in Ouallam. But upon realizing that the team would miss the two-hour time window no matter how quickly they left, the leaders at the AOB changed course.

ODA 3212 knew they were under pressure to get prepared fast and leave their base as soon as possible. Nearly three hours had passed since they'd received the phone call from the chief at the AOB ordering them on the mission to Tiloa. Captain Perozeni was just about to put the finishing touches on the CONOP for the mission when the office phone rang again.

Chief Warrant Officer Marshall got on, saying, "Captain Perozeni, we have had a change of plan. We would like you to leave in the morning instead. We will be sending up a Nigerien reconnaissance unit to join you on the mission. They will need time to prepare to leave so will not make it up to Ouallam until nearly six a.m. tomorrow. I would like you to adjust your CONOP accordingly and prepare for a mission in the morning instead."

The change of plan frustrated Captain Perozeni, as nothing about it made sense to him. "Chief, I mean no disrespect, but with the intelligence having a time limit of two hours, what is the purpose of the mission? By the time we arrive the intelligence will have long since expired."

The chief pointed out, "I'm aware of that, Captain Perozeni, but you'll do the mission anyway. We are sending the reconnaissance vehicle up there, which will have the equipment necessary to locate the target if he is still in the area. So despite missing the window of intel we have, if he is there they will know. I understand that it is unlikely Doundou Chefou will still be in the area, but what I would like your team to do is have your partner force go into the village and conduct a civilian military reconnaissance and see if any of the people in that village heard or saw anything. Let them know we are aware of the situation and make them feel safe knowing we are on top of it."

At that point the intelligence that Doundou Chefou was in the area was so old that Captain Perozeni doubted the mission was worthwhile. He also knew that on the off chance the terrorist was found to still be in the area there would need to be further coordination and approvals. Having been to Tiloa on a previous mission, Captain Perozeni felt that stopping in and conducting a KLE with the leader of the Nigerien military at the base in Tiloa would make for a good mission, so he decided to set the mission up as a civ/mil reconnaissance.

"Okay, Chief, I'll get my guys prepared. Have a good night."

Captain Perozeni stoically walked out to the staging area, where the team was steadily working on their preparations for that night's mission.

"Hey, guys, change of plans!" Captain Perozeni shouted to get everyone's attention.

"Of course there is." Ondo laughed as he wiped sweat from his brow.

A murmur of frustration and incredulity swept through the group of men.

The captain continued. "We are now leaving tomorrow morning around six and will be joined by a reconnaissance team coming out of Niamey. So I need you guys to pull all of the water back out of the trucks and throw it into the freezers and repack for the morning rather than tonight. I'm going to redo the CONOP and head over to the partner force camp and meet with Lieutenant Boubacar to let him know what's going on."

Not happy that they were now ordered to go up to Tiloa in the morning with a reconnaissance team from Niamey on the off chance the terrorist was still there, the team grumbled to one another.

"Once again, stupid," Dustin Wright said, making clear his opinion.

Bryan agreed with Dustin. "Yep. But what else should we expect? At least they're consistent."

"True. But hey, going on a stupid m-m-mission is more interesting than sitting around here training all day," Brent said in an upbeat tone.

Back in the office, Captain Perozeni created a CONOP for the civ/mil reconnaissance patrol and sent it to Captain Newburn at the AOB in Niamey for approval. It was policy for those higher up the chain of command to be notified of the mission, too. The men at the AOB passed the CONOP up, notifying LTC Painter in Chad of the following day's mission, as well as those at the embassy. The official report would later state that LTC Painter was not briefed on the "true nature" of the operation.

Late in the afternoon of October 2, I received a call from Bryan. I noticed his voice sounded a little strange. He told me he was calling from the team office in Ouallam. They were getting ready to go out on a mission the next morning, which he was not happy about; he went so far as to label it "stupid." He asked me to talk, to tell him about what was going on with me and the boys. He had only five minutes and needed to be working, but he just wanted to hear my voice. I spent the next five minutes talking about absolutely nothing, just day-to-day things like picking the kids up from school and my funny conversations with them.

Suddenly Bryan interrupted me: He had to go. He told me he loved me and would call me when he got back. I could tell he was upset and he let slip they had just returned from a mission and were going back toward the area of Mali the next morning; he didn't like those missions, because they were dangerous. I told him I loved him and to be careful, I'd talk to him soon. The conversation had been so short and meaningless that I felt guilty as I hung up. I felt like I gave him a five-minute monologue about my day and trivial things and hardly got to hear his voice. That call would haunt me in the days and weeks to come.

The night of October 2, a Nigerien reconnaissance team of two soldiers drove their truck from the capital city of Niamey to meet ODA 3212 at their base in Ouallam. Captain Perozeni and Lieutenant Boubacar, the leader of the Nigerien partner force, met that evening and discussed the plan. They knew they could run rehearsals all that night, but that would mean giving the men no sleep. They had been running the same rehearsals repeatedly the past several weeks, so they agreed it was a bad choice to run the men into the ground the night before a mission. They agreed that the Nigerien partner forces and American team members would benefit more from a few hours of rest. The next day's mission was straightforward; they would be back at base in less than fifteen hours.

The mission would comprise eleven Americans: eight Green Berets, two Special Forces support members, and Chester, who was a JIDO analyst. The JIDO analyst was a non-combat-trained contractor representing the Joint Improvised-Threat Defeat Organization, whose primary purpose was to map out the area. The Americans would split up among three trucks. American Truck #1, a white Toyota, would carry Captain Perozeni while the communications sergeant, Bartels, would drive. Jacob, the team's interpreter, would sit in the back of the truck with Chester, and Hanson, as weapons sergeant, would sit on top of the vehicle at the mounted machine gun. American Truck #2, a gray SUV, would be driven by the engineer sergeant, Dustin Wright, while Bryan, as the medical sergeant, would ride shotgun, and Brooks, as weapons sergeant, would ride along. American Truck #3, another white Toyota pickup, would be driven by LaDavid Johnson, the team's support mechanic; Master Sergeant Smith, the team sergeant, would ride shotgun; Jeremiah Johnson, a support personnel, would sit in the back; and Ondo, a weapons sergeant, would man the mounted machine gun.

It was late at night when the team began to prepare their gear and vehicles for a second time. They finished prepping the vehicles around 11:00 and settled in for the night. The men were left with only a few hours' rest before rising around 4:30 and moving out that fateful Tuesday morning.

14

Mission Confusion

The team woke up at 4:30 a.m. to eat a quick breakfast. Walking out of his tent, Brent passed by Bryan, who was carrying his toothbrush and wearing his usual brown silk long underwear, long-sleeved camouflage shirt, boonie hat, and red-and-black Merrill shoes. "Looking good, Black," Brent said and laughed.

When they were dressed for their mission, the men converged at the chow hall, where the television blasted news of the Las Vegas mass shooting. Though the shooting had occurred two days earlier, this was the first time word of it reached them.

Sitting down next to Ondo, Dustin Wright shook his head, saying, "What's wrong with people in this world? I mean, this could've happened when we were at that Carolina country music festival this summer. Why would anyone do this shit?"

Ondo agreed. "I don't know, man. There's just some fucked-up people in this world." He shook his head. "Seriously. You want to fucking kill people, go to war. Don't go to a fucking country music concert. That's some serious messed-up bullshit."

LaDavid said, "I feel really bad for all their families."

Smith said, "Yeah, man, that shit's just wrong, you know?"

They filled the trucks with the frozen water bottles, weapons, and their kits of body armor and ran last-minute checks on their radios and vehicles. The partner force of Nigeriens arrived, followed by the reconnaissance vehicle from Niamey. Captain Perozeni conducted a roll call and did an "actions on," which meant going over what to do if various scenarios occurred. Vehicle crashes were usually the biggest threat to troops in Niger, so Captain Perozeni reminded them all about keeping enough distance between vehicles, warning the trucks behind when your vehicle is going to stop, and being aware of speed on the dirt roads that ran throughout the region. The captain finished roll call and actions on around 6:00 a.m., and together they set out for the village of Tiloa.

The convoy rolled out of the gate, heading north from Ouallam on the main road, led by two partner-force trucks, each truck carrying six to eight Nigerien troops. The partner-force vehicles were followed by American Truck #1, which was followed by the reconnaissance vehicle from Niamey. Next came American Truck #2, followed by two more partner-force vehicles carrying another six to eight passengers apiece. Finally, American Truck #3 brought up the rear.

All three American trucks had built-in secured communications systems with a cryptographic key worked into them so no one could overhear their conversations. The radio systems worked in a way where they could be dialed into the same frequency as anyone else in the region and those in the trucks could hear anyone military or nonmilitary talking on that frequency, but no one else could hear the trucks. Since the American trucks could speak to one another without being listened in on, they scattered themselves throughout the convoy.

The rule is for partner-force vehicles to go first in their own countries, because the American teams are there to support and train the Nigeriens, not to lead the missions. Each Nigerien vehicle had a small walkie-talkie so the trucks could communicate with one another. Jacob, the interpreter in Truck #1, had a walkie-talkie as well, so he could act as the go-between with the partner-force vehicles and relay any information coming from them.

Communication was complicated because Niger has eleven official languages and as many as twenty indigenous languages, including Hausa, Zarma, Manga, Fulani, and various Tuareg dialects. Jacob was Nigerien and had learned all the languages of the partner-force soldiers, making him a crucial link. Even soldiers in one Nigerien truck did not speak the same language; some spoke Hausa and some spoke languages specific to the regions or villages they were from. Even Lieutenant Boubacar, the leader of the partner force, did not speak all of the languages; he only spoke French, Zarma, and Hausa. Without Jacob, there was no easy way for the groups to communicate with one another.

The convoy made good time that day as they headed north toward Tiloa. As they drove, red dust billowed all around them and covered the men sitting atop the vehicles with a layer of dirt until they looked like children who had spent the day digging in sand. Once the convoy was about ten kilometers outside of the village of Tiloa, they stopped and

Dustin Wright on the road outside of Tiloa waiting for the partner force to return. *(Brent Bartels)*

waited while the Nigerien partner force thoroughly explored the small desert village of Tiloa and spoke with the local inhabitants. An hour later the partner force returned, having found no sign of the terrorist they had been searching for.

Once the convoy arrived in the town, Captain Perozeni, Master Sergeant Smith, and Lieutenant Boubacar held a KLE (key leader engagement) with the local Nigerien military leaders at a camp near the village. Using Jacob to translate, Captain Perozeni told the Nigerien major of the military camp that they were up in Tiloa attempting to locate the terrorist Doundou Chefou.

"We have not seen him here," the major told them. "But every Monday in the village of Tiloa they have their market day. Perhaps he came down on that day and someone went in for him." The major told Captain Perozeni, "If the bad guys do come and they're important enough, they probably wouldn't come over to the east side of the river. They would stay on the west side of the river in the forested area. They would send in someone they paid or a low-profile guy to run in and get the supplies they need and come back. Doundou Chefou probably wouldn't have come into Tiloa himself to do that kind of stuff."

Tiloa and the market sit on the east side of the river, as does the military base, but the forested area is on the west side, so it made sense that a high-profile terrorist such as Chefou would not put himself in danger by crossing over—especially if he was operating in the no-man's-land of northern Niger and southern Mali. Since Tiloa is near the border, he probably came with one or two men, sent one to the market, and then left.

After discussing the whereabouts of Doundou Chefou, the Nigerien major invited Captain Perozeni, Lieutenant Boubacar, and Master Sergeant Smith to stay for lunch. Sitting cross-legged on a mat in the shade, they enjoyed goat and rice, which had been cooking over an open flame nearby. The major told them about the various challenges that came with operating in the area. He spoke at length about the hard time they had operating from the east side of the river. Getting over the river to patrol the west side was difficult that time of year because the river was still very full and marshy from the rains. Whenever they would try to cross over, their trucks would get stuck.

While the leaders conducted the KLE, the rest of the team and partner force spent a couple hours near the river on the edge of Tiloa eating lunch in whatever shade they could find. Brent had declared himself the team photographer for the 2017 deployment to Niger. While the soldiers waited for their captain to return, Brent got out his cell phone and began taking videos and pictures. In one video, a Nigerien soldier joking around with Dustin Wright explains to the camera in French that Dustin is a very good driver while Dustin pretends to drive and hold a steering wheel. In another video most of the men can be seen sitting around the trucks in fold-up camping chairs, a wide muddy river flowing in the background. As Brent walks by, LaDavid turns and smiles at him while others wave from the roofs of the vehicles where they are seated at their mounted guns. The men look relaxed and are enjoying themselves. It's hard to watch the video knowing that for four of those young men sitting at the water's edge, time was running out.

Around 2:00 p.m., the KLE finished and the American team members along with their Nigerien partner forces climbed into their vehicles, heading back toward their camp in Ouallam. They all felt it had been a successful mission even though they didn't locate Chefou. The convoy headed south along the hot and dusty red desert roads back toward the team outpost in Ouallam. Brent and Captain Perozeni in Truck #1 were looking forward to making quick time on the journey back and had made a wager on how fast they could make it back to camp.

"We are going to make it to Ouallam by six." Brent was certain.

"No way," the captain argued. "There is no way we are going to make that kind of time."

"You want to bet? I'll bet you one case of lukewarm African Coke that we will make it."

Captain Perozeni looked at Brent and said, "All right, you're on. But there's no way we're making it back that fast."

"Oh, we're going to make it," Brent said with enthusiasm. "I'm going to push this truck to its fucking l-l-l-limit."

They were right outside the village of Mangaize, approximately forty kilometers from their base in Ouallam, when they received a message over the radio from the operations base in Niamey.

"Beast one two, this is beast one zero. Do you copy?"

"Beast one zero, this is beast one two. We copy. Go ahead."

"Beast one two, please halt convoy and wait for a call."

"Copy that, beast one zero."

Slowly rolling to a stop in the middle of the dirt road, the convoy waited while Captain Perozeni listened to Chief Warrant Officer Marshall on his satellite phone. "We have a possible new location for Doundou Chefou. The embassy contacted us with SIGINT suggesting he may now be up near the Mali border at what we suspect is an enemy camp. We want you to turn your team around and head up there."

It was 4:36 in the afternoon in Mangaize, and while Captain Perozeni talked on the phone, the men exited their trucks to drink some water and stretch their legs. The chief gave Captain Perozeni details and coordinates, then hung up the phone.

The Niger-Mali border region has no real marker where one country ends and the other begins. Militants move freely throughout this no-man's-land, crossing into and out of Mali unheeded. Most of the area in the region is devoid of human movement except for that of militant leaders such as Doundou Chefou and their followers. While U.S. forces worked with the Nigerien army, the Americans did not legally have authority to cross into Mali and the terrorists knew it.

Tongo Tongo is one of the villages closest to the Mali border. The only people found close to the border who are not terrorists are the nomadic herders, who are few and far between. Captain Perozeni sat down to look over the information and grid coordinates. It would be difficult for any slow-moving vehicles and men on foot to approach the target from the south and establish an effective northern blocking position to prevent militants from fleeing across the border safely into Mali.

The men of ODA 3212 gathered around Truck #2, attempting to find shade and escape the hundred-degree heat. Some sat on the tailgate of the truck; others stood with their arms crossed while the sun beat down on them.

"What do y'all think those fuckers want us to do now?" Dustin Wright asked as he tried to fold his large frame into a small bit of shade near the rear of the truck.

"Probably chase that piece of shit Doundou all over Niger, man," Ondo responded while raking his fingers across his head, trying to shake the red dirt from his sandy blond hair.

Brent walked over from Truck #1 toward the men while pulling off his ball cap to push his black hair back, trying to cool down, saying, "Sounds like they want us to go on another mission. Head up to the fucking Mali border."

Brooks tilted his head back into the sun and let out a short blast of annoyed-sounding air.

Dustin Wright asked, "What the hell do they want us up there for?"

"I don't know. Sounds like they think they found D-D-Dondon or whatever the fuck his name is again," Brent said.

Leaning in silence against the truck with his arms folded and the sun gleaming in his sweat-laced red hair, Jeremiah Johnson just shook his head.

Standing against the truck, a head taller than Jeremiah but still noticeably shorter than Brent, Bryan peered out from under his camouflaged boonie hat with an intense gaze. "This is stupid. This whole mission has been a waste of time. Turning around and going all the way up to the border is the worst possible idea." He fell silent and no one else spoke; his words seemed to carry what all the men were feeling. The group sat in silence, staring out across the desert at the scrub brush and occasional thorny tree that marked Niger's arid landscape.

Captain Perozeni walked over to the men, calling over the partner force and Lieutenant Boubacar. "With few villages and no roads," he said, "traveling with a large convoy of eight vehicles at night is going to make it impossible to move quickly or go undetected if there's an enemy out in that region."

Hanson pointed out, "Yeah, man, between the noise of the trucks and the number of all of us, we are going to stick out."

Ondo added, "How are we going to navigate an entire convoy up there with no roads in the dark? That's risky and stupid."

"What do *you* think?" Captain Perozeni pointedly asked the Nigerien leader.

Speaking to the captain in French, Lieutenant Boubacar replied, "No. You don't go up there. That's not a place we go. It's the wild west up there. No, that is not a good place."

The men on the team and the partner force all knew that the sparsely populated border area was dangerous. So dangerous, in fact, that the Nigerien army had named it a "free-fire zone," which meant that if they saw anyone out at night, the Nigerien army could shoot. Even during the day, the Nigerien army could shoot at anyone on motorcycles. The few nomadic herdsmen who lived in the region had been warned not to come out at night unless it was worth risking their lives.

Niger is one of the poorest and most underdeveloped countries in the world. Outside the capital of Niamey, there are no paved roads and the average Nigerien cannot afford personal transportation. There are no railways in the country, either; riding animals or walking are the most common methods of transportation in Niger. When the American and Nigerien military see men in the remote Mali border region driving motorcycles that require money to buy and fuel, it was safe to assume that they were funded by criminal activity or terrorist organizations and therefore dangerous.

The team was also concerned that the Nigeriens were sleep-deprived and low on food. While Green Berets with their extensive training in the Special Forces Qualification Course were used to running on little to no sleep, the Nigerien partner forces were not used to going without sleep and had never been trained under the stresses that the lack of it can cause. The American team members knew their food supply of MREs would last them long enough to do this mission, but their partner forces had not planned on the extra day of the mission, so they would be going without sleep and with little to no food. The Nigeriens would soon run out of water. The American team was also a bit short on water; they felt they could make it stretch, but it just wouldn't be comfortable.

The American vehicles were another problem. They were not armored and had weak engines, which often led the trucks to get stuck in the desert sand and mud. The American vehicles could not carry more than four men and their equipment without straining the engines. The trucks driven by their Nigerien counterparts, by contrast, could carry ten or more men and all of their equipment without any issues. Often the Americans had to have the Nigerien partner forces pull them from the sand or mud after getting stuck. This was an issue that teams working in Niger had brought up with their leadership for years, but the problem had been ignored. The older-model unarmored Toyota Hiluxes with no off-road modifications meant slow moving and an unprotected team with a good chance of getting stuck.

Lieutenant Boubacar again voiced his skepticism. "Captain Perozeni, your leaders have said we will find Doundou many times, but we never find him. Why should we think we will find the terrorist this time? I don't know. I don't think he will be there. But if you think we should go on this mission, Captain, then we will go with you. But I do not agree with this mission at all." As the commander of the partner force,

Lieutenant Boubacar had the authority to decline using his force on missions—but that day he did not.

When the phone rang again, Captain Perozeni expressed his concern and those of the partner force to leadership at the operations base in Niamey. "Chief," Captain Perozeni protested, "I don't think this is a good idea. I don't see how we can effectively establish a blocking position. Not to mention that we are once again basing this off the same single-source reporting intel. Acting on it instantly just like we did last night may alert the enemy."

Captain Perozeni continued: "Chief, I just don't see this mission making any sense. The minute we leave Mangaize, we will run out of roads and will have to navigate with compasses approximately fifty kilometers through rough desert terrain. On top of that, it will soon be dark, and moving in such a large convoy, we will need to travel without our headlights using our night-vision goggles in an effort to avoid enemy detection. Which, honestly, if there is any enemy out there, they will still spot us because we will be sticking out like a sore thumb. To get up to the border will take us about ten hours, and that's a rough estimate. Also, if the terrorists are up there they will be on motorcycles and there is nothing we can do to catch them or outmaneuver them in our vehicles. They can travel twenty-five miles per hour in the sand when we will only be able to move at ten miles per hour at best. Nothing about this makes any sense. Chief, I request we be allowed to return to our base in Ouallam and wait for a better opportunity."

The chief responded, "I certainly understand your concerns, Captain. But as of right now this is an operation I'd like you to go on. I'm going to give you some time to talk it over with your team and look over the map to see how you might be able to make this operation work. I will call you back in a few minutes."

Well known up and down the chain of command—and even in the highest echelons at AFRICOM—was the fact that on the continent of Africa, military assets were severely lacking. Listening to the men on the ground who knew the terrain and the risks was the best way to avoid a potentially catastrophic situation. During previous years while Special Operations Command Africa (SOCAFRICA) was still under the leadership of General Don Bolduc, it was written policy that the men on the ground determined the risk. If they were uncomfortable with a mission, the men on the ground had the ability to cancel the mission, because everyone knew if something went wrong it would take a significant amount of time to rescue a team.

The Special Operations Command framework under Bolduc specifically stated that the organization is bottom-up and their decisions are driven by subordinate unit assessments. Experienced Special Operations Forces (SOF) operators and supporters will continue to do their assigned missions as directed until they assess that the risk is too high. Subordinate commands will be given full latitude to make these determinations of risk to mission, risk to force, and risk to do nothing with full support of SOCAFRICA headquarters.

During the media brief after the ambush, General Waldhauser, the leader of AFRICOM from July 2016 to July 2019, agreed with General Bolduc about Green Berets operating in the region: "They work under some extreme conditions in the African continent. They have to be able to make decisions about whether to or not to take—to go into certain operations. Because if the . . . the assets that they need are not there today, they need to be able to come back tomorrow when they have them."

All of which is to say that if a team said they were uncomfortable with a mission and wanted to return to base, that decision was to be respected. A mission was supposed to be canceled if the men on the ground found that the assets they needed were not available to them.

General Bolduc turned control of SOCAFRICA over to Major General Marcus Hicks on June 29, 2017. Whether it was because the new commander ignored the rule or was just carrying on business as usual and SOCAFRICA had never followed their own rule, ODA Team 3212 was not afforded an opinion. Just months after General Bolduc's retirement, the policy of listening to the men on the ground clearly didn't apply as Captain Perozeni voiced his concerns clearly to the acting AOB commander and the chief warrant officer at the AOB that October day. Their concerns would continue to be ignored when the AOB handed the operation over to LTC Painter in Chad later that day.

Sitting on the side of the red-dirt road outside Mangaize waiting for a call back, Captain Perozeni found himself frustrated with the situation his leadership was putting him in. He stood sweating in the blistering heat, talking to Brent and Hanson about the situation. The men had been looking at a map of the area and trying to decide how best to approach the operation.

"What we need," said Hanson, "is a better way to block the northern position. Coming from the south, that will be nearly impossible to accomplish with any sense of surprise."

"What other assets do we have in-country?" Brent asked. "Isn't Team Arlit nearby with helicopters? It would make more sense for them to fly in from the north and set up a northern blocking position instead of us d-d-driving from south to north and trying to block the northern areas. There's no way we can keep these terrorists from running across the border into Mali coming from this direction in our slow-ass trucks."

Team 3216—known as Team Arlit—was the heliborne unit stationed in Arlit, an industrial town in north-central Niger.

"That's a really good idea, Brent," said Captain Perozeni. "Team Arlit could act as close air support and casualty evacuation in the event we run into trouble up near the border. I know some guys on the Arlit team. I'll call my buddy real quick and see if they are up for doing this mission."

When Captain Perozeni called, the commander of Team Arlit answered. "Hey, Mikey! What's up, man?"

"Hey, man," said Captain Perozeni. "Listen, I'm out on the ground in Mangaize with my team. Headquarters in Niamey wants to send us up on a raid to the Mali border, but we won't be able to pull off a northern blocking position in our trucks. Any chance you'd be down for taking part in the mission?"

"Yeah, man, for sure."

"Great. Hey, let me just hang up and call the AOB in Niamey, then we'll get this thing rolling. Thanks, man."

Captain Perozeni called the AOB and brought up the idea of bringing in another Green Beret team better suited to be the lead on the mission. "The only way I would feel comfortable doing this mission is if we have a unit with built-in air support that has the ability to set up a realistic blocking position. Arlit would be perfect for that. With just my team, the mission would make no sense. I contacted Arlit and they are up for doing the operation with us."

"Okay, Captain," responded Chief Marshall. "Go ahead and let them know it's a go."

Once Captain Perozeni contacted Team Arlit and confirmed the mission, the Team Arlit lead then called the AOB about doing a multi-team mission with 3212. Those at the AOB immediately deferred to LTC Painter. "If we are going to have two ODAs on an operation assisting each other, it is outside the authority of the leadership here at the AOB. We'll have to contact Lieutenant Colonel Painter, and we'll get back to you."

After a short wait, LTC David Painter, the battalion commander located in Chad, called Team Arlit's team lead to ask, "Captain, is this an operation your team and your partner forces are comfortable with?"

"Yes, sir. Absolutely."

"Okay. I want you to be ready to brief me in one hour on your plan for this operation."

"Understood, sir."

Team Arlit's Nigerien partner force, known as EFoN, had been trained by Special Operations Forces throughout the U.S. Army since 2014. They were a highly trained and capable Nigerien Special Forces unit that Team Arlit knew could be used for more than just patrols around their local area. They were excited to get the team and partner force out together on a joint operation utilizing their full capabilities.

Coordinating all the plans was going to take some time, so the AOB in Niamey called Team 3212 out on the road again.

"Captain Perozeni, take your team and start driving toward objective north. Arlit is now going to be the lead team and your ODA will drive in and offer backup for the mission. Let's get you guys covering some of that distance before it gets too late."

"Sounds good, Chief. We will leave right now."

For every mission, a commander writes up a concept of operations (CONOP), just as Captain Perozeni had done for the first mission to Ti-loa. Now that the mission to Tiloa was complete, the new mission required a new CONOP. For the new mission to the Mali border, a CONOP would be created by all those working with Team Arlit. In this case, the second CONOP would be overseen and reviewed by both LTC David Painter and Colonel Bradley Moses, the 3rd Special Forces Group commander located in Germany, since it required two teams and their partner forces. From that point forward, all CONOPs would be made by those in leadership above ODA 3212. LTC Painter would be signing all final approvals for the CONOP and assigning ODA 3212 their missions.

This fact is important. In our family brief following the investigation into the ambush, we would be told that the CONOP Captain Perozeni had made for the mission to Tiloa was not approved at the proper level. General Cloutier would tell us that improper characterization of the first mission to Tiloa caused confusion and left the team improperly prepared for the mission to the border the night of October 3. But the reality was that LTC Painter had been notified of the mission to Tiloa and that ODA 3212 had been on a civ/mil reconnaissance mission. Knowing this, he should have assumed the team was underprepared to go to the dangerous Mali border on short notice. The team didn't have time to run rehearsals with their partner force, prepare their trucks with more weaponry and ammunition, or resupply their food and water.

The plan from LTC Painter was for ODA 3212 to drive through rough terrain with no roads until they were twenty-five kilometers south of the campsite. The team was told they would sleep at that position, then get up early and drive closer to the border to act as a quick reaction force (QRF) for Team Arlit. Team Arlit was supposed to arrive before sunrise at the Mali border location. The problem for Team 3212 was that to act as a QRF they would still need to navigate four to six hours in the dark before sunrise to be in place to offer assistance if Arlit needed them. But with the vehicles in the convoy moving at a slow speed through difficult terrain, there was little chance they would be any help to the heliborne unit. As the men said that day and have said multiple times since, it was a stupid mission for them to be on. They did not have the mobility to effectively block the enemy from slipping over a border that the Americans could not cross.

The area was also very dangerous. General Cloutier would later tell me at the family briefing that there had been attacks in the past similar to the ambush, with similar numbers of attackers and weaponry. After doing some research, I would find out that in the year leading up to the ambush, there had been sixteen attacks in the area surrounding the ambush. Five of those attacks had occurred within one hundred miles of Tongo Tongo—and of those five attacks, two were ambushes. At least one of those attacks were reportedly carried out by groups with a hundred or more attackers armed with mortars, guns, grenade launchers, and mounted ZPUs (a Soviet-era heavy mounted antiaircraft gun). Exhausted and with the potential threat looming, ODA 3212 followed orders for the second time in two days and headed north.

15

The Long Drive

Around 5:15 on the afternoon of October 3, only an hour away from their camp in Ouallam, the convoy regretfully turned around and headed back out for a new mission. They drove north toward the border of Mali as night fell, and not long into the expedition the roads disappeared and the trucks were forced onto small trails that slowly faded into nothing. When they could no longer risk keeping the truck lights on, one of the American trucks pulled into the lead to guide the rest of the trucks along using their night vision.

Green Berets train extensively in the dark with their night vision, and many on the team had been on countless deployments where they had to employ it for long periods of time during operations in darkness. They were much more comfortable and skilled leading the convoy with just night vision than were the Nigeriens. Once Truck #1 pulled to the front and started navigating using night-vision goggles, the convoy slowly moved forward. The men sat in their vehicles, listening in the dark as the ground moved slowly under them, jarring the trucks as they struck rocks and rolled into divots in the desert sand. Straining to hear any odd noises that would tell them the enemy might be near, the men's hearts beat loudly in their ears. They managed to move along at this slow pace until the road fell away into tall grass that was so thick they couldn't see what was in front of them.

The grass stretched high above the hoods of the vehicles and made it impossible to see if there were drop-offs ahead or any other major terrain changes. The rainy season had just ended, so the riverbeds were now dry and cracking. The convoy ran the risk of driving off a riverbank and either rolling a truck or getting stuck high-centered while the tires spun away the sand under them. Getting stuck was a risk they could not afford to take as they drove through hostile territory. Their only option was to have a man get out of the vehicle and walk ahead through the hostile terrain to help the trucks navigate. Captain Perozeni walked more than ten miles that night through deep grass and dry sand in the heat and humidity to navigate the convoy through the wild west of Niger, listening intently for anything out of the ordinary in the deep desert night. The bugs sang a low tune and the wind occasionally whispered by. Even the sound of too much grass moving set off alarm bells in Captain Perozeni's head as they moved deeper into unknown territory.

As Team 3212 made its slow trek toward their first stop, back in Chad LTC Painter was coordinating with Colonel Moses in Germany and Team 3216 out of Arlit for the mission near the Mali border. Team Arlit had put together a concept of operation for the mission. According to Team Arlit: "We knew we were going to fly in from about a ten-kilometer offset to the east and kind of walk in along the border and we had to paint that picture for Lieutenant Colonel Painter. What did he want from us? He understood that the AOB and battalion command were taking care of some of the supporting aspects of this, like when the ISR (drone) was going to be up. Outside of our two organic helicopters he told us what assets we had for that night and what medevac we had, which wasn't much. We put together some slides of what we thought we could do. We talked about the capability of the EFoN and assets. There was one rotary wing asset out of Niamey. Our two helicopters after insertion would drop us at ten kilometers away from the campsite, then fly to Ouallam to stage for anything they might be needed for. The helicopters' response time from Ouallam to the border of Mali was less than thirty minutes by air. What Lieutenant Colonel Painter didn't ask was if we had rehearsed."

Team Arlit and their partner force hadn't rehearsed as they normally would have, due to the time constraints placed upon them by the battalion commander, LTC Painter. The team was ordered on the mission by LTC Painter with the full knowledge of Colonel Moses, despite the lack of pre-mission training rehearsals, the very thing ODA 3212 would later be lambasted for and for which Captain Perozeni would be punished. Fortunately for Team Arlit, the god of winds and dust storms was with them that night.

After several hours of planning and conversation, Team Arlit was given the go-ahead by LTC Painter and Colonel Moses, and all approvals for the second CONOP were given. But by now it was much later than originally planned for the flight time and Team Arlit was looking at 10:00 p.m. rather than 7:00 p.m. for going wheels-up in their helicopters. The contracted aviation company pilots had the helicopters ready and waiting to go. Once Team Arlit was finally in the air for the four-hour flight, they flew into strong headwinds, reducing their speed from 136 knots to only 108 knots. Realizing they were going to burn through more fuel than normal due to the wind and wouldn't make it to the border without refueling, the team planned to fly to Niamey to refuel—a four-hour flight. After a short period flying toward Niamey, Team Arlit was hit by a heavy sandstorm and the heliborne unit was forced to return to their base in Arlit. This meant the convoy of ODA 3212 and their partner forces were waiting alone out along the border of Niger and Mali.

Around 10:50 p.m., after more than five hours of treacherous driving, Team 3212 and their partner forces arrived at the designated stopping point given by those in charge at the advanced operations base in Niamey to await the arrival of Team Arlit twenty-five kilometers north. They had been instructed to spend the night there before setting up their blocking move to prevent a possible enemy from escaping to the south as Team Arlit cleared from the north the following morning. They were waiting for Team Arlit to act as the lead team and to conduct the main mission. ODA 3212 knew that Team Arlit was to be in the air by 7:00 p.m., but during their drive had heard on the radio that Team Arlit was delayed until 10:00 p.m. Team 3212 knew that they would be lucky to get in a fifteen-minute nap before they began the final leg of the journey to the border, but they were anxious to hear that Arlit was going to make it before getting some rest.

Sitting at their staging point, Team 3212 could hear the radio calls being exchanged between Team Arlit and the AOB. On Arlit's end the conversation was somewhat broken up. Sitting in their trucks with the windows down, the men felt exposed breathing in the thick, hot air as the stillness of the desert engulfed them. The only noise to be heard for miles was the sound of their humming trucks, the only light was the glow emanating from their dashboards. Looking out the truck windows, they saw that the blackness stretched out endlessly. In the desert wasteland hours beyond the last hut it was too quiet out and they knew it. The men felt conspicuous.

Crackling through the radio came: "Beast one zero . . . one six. We need . . . around . . . storm . . . to Arlit."

It was in that moment, sitting in the treacherous Mali border region hours from their base, that ODA 3212 came to the grim realization that Team Arlit was probably not coming. Feeling extremely uneasy, and knowing the distance and rough terrain that lay between them and any help if they were to need it, Team 3212 waited to hear confirmation of what was happening with Team Arlit. In the stillness Brent turned to Captain Perozeni and whispered the question that was on everyone's minds: "What the hell are we doing out here?" The captain just shook his head. There was nothing to say; it was a bad situation and a bad mission, they shouldn't be out here, and they all knew it.

The crackling of the radio broke the eerie silence. "Beast one two, this is beast one zero. Do you copy?"

Captain Perozeni replied, "Beast one zero, this is beast one two. Go ahead."

"Beast one two, Team Arlit has been turned around. You are no longer the backup team. You will continue to move to exploit the objective. Do you copy? Over."

Captain Perozeni responded, "Beast one zero, this is beast one two, we have been moving since six this morning other than a couple hours' stop off in Tiloa. Are you telling me that Arlit is not coming in now and you want us to be the main effort? This is a bad idea. We haven't had sleep, we are running out of water, we don't know anything about where we are going. We still have approximately twenty-five kilometers to go to the campsite, and creating a blocking position with our slow-moving vehicles will be nearly impossible. We do not have the assets to properly execute the mission. This makes absolutely no sense. Requesting to abort mission and return to base. Out."

Staff Sergeant Casey Wilbur was sitting in the office at the AOB that night, messaging the men on the ground as they had been making their slow trek north. He had been a member of Team 3212 for several years, and he had twice deployed with them and recruited many of the men to the team. He had recently made a career change, putting him at the AOB in Niamey, running communications for the 2017 deployment to Niger. Casey was in the AOB listening to Captain Perozeni's radio call and thought, *Of course.* Having the convoy return to base made the most sense, given how the plans had shifted in the night. The initial intelligence they had been working off of was now too old to be useful. The team was also staged a long distance south of the target, meaning the team would have a considerable amount of distance to cover to reach the terrorist camp before morning.

Chief Warrant Officer Marshall looked at Casey, Captain Newburn, and Sergeant Major Kingman and said: "Yeah, okay. That makes sense."

The chief said: "Sounds good to me, man. Fuck it, tell them to come home."

"I'll contact Lieutenant Colonel Painter and let him know we're giving them permission to return to base," said Captain Newburn.

Knowing that would probably be a long conversation, Casey went to bed assuming Team 3212 would soon be on their way back to the base in Ouallam.

Those at the AOB had to contact LTC Painter, because now it was up to him. He had given final approval for the mission, so he had to give final approval to cancel it. Contacting LTC Painter in Chad, AOB commander Captain Newburn informed him that the men on the ground had requested to abort the mission and return to their base in Ouallam and that he had approved it. LTC Painter asked Captain Newburn why he thought it was okay for Team 3212 to abort the mission and return to base. The captain laid out the reasoning Captain Perozeni had given as to why the mission should be aborted and why those at the AOB agreed with him. In the end, LTC Painter disregarded the ground commander's perspective and Captain Perozeni's request to return to base was denied. LTC Painter overrode the AOB and ordered the mission to continue. The AOB was instructed by LTC Painter that Team 3212 was not to return to base but to be ordered to move ahead on clearance of the campsite near the Mali border.

Despite the changes to the team's mission, neither the AOB nor LTC Painter developed a CONOP detailing the team's modified concept of operation. LTC Painter's command notified Colonel Moses's command, which in turn notified SOCAFRICA via email of the revised plan through a short description of what is known as the five *w*'s (who, what, when, where, why). The five *w*'s are used to define a mission before developing a CONOP to detail how a mission will then be carried out. Missing from the description of the five *w*'s on October 3, 2017, was a second threat assessment evaluating the situation, given that the team would now be proceeding to the border alone.

During our family brief following the investigation into the ambush, all of this would be glossed over. We would simply be told that there were three CONOPs but it was the first one created by Captain Perozeni that lacked detail. Thanks to information buried deep in the final redacted report, I found out just how lacking in detail the third CONOP was. There was only one paragraph full of redactions and confusing military acronyms that made clear how much danger the men were in. It took me hours of piecing together interviews and researching military terms to figure out just how the final CONOP had been created. Not only had the third CONOP been glossed over in my family brief, but when Henry had asked about a second threat assessment, General Cloutier assured him one had been done. In the end I would find out that was not true. No second threat assessment had been done before ordering the team to proceed alone to the Mali border.

To leave a team alone and potentially exposed to a high-risk target without running a threat assessment is careless at best. At the beginning of this mission, it was determined that the risk required two teams, a heliborne unit and a QRF, or quick reaction force. Now that the heliborne Team Arlit couldn't arrive, it should have been critical to reassess that risk and see if it had significantly diminished. But on October 3, 2017, that never happened.

What should have been included and carefully considered in a second risk assessment was the fact that the team and their partner force had slept four hours the night of the October 2, then had gone the next twenty-four hours with no sleep; there were no quick reaction forces assigned; the execution timeline would put the team near the Mali border at daylight, making them easily visible to potential threats; there was no CASEVAC (casualty evacuation) plan; and their ISR drone did not have enough fuel to cover the team's return trip to their base in Ouallam.

LTC Painter notified an operations officer in Colonel Moses's command that the mission to the Mali border had been changed and only one team would now be going. The operations officer, however, did not notify Colonel Moses during the night of the change to the mission. Nor was the SOCAFRICA commander, Major General Marcus Hicks, notified of this change to the mission.

Sitting in the darkness along the border between Niger and Mali, the team was preparing to turn the convoy around when the most ominous call came over the radio around 11:15 p.m. The acting advanced operations base commander, Captain Newburn, came on and said that LTC Painter had overridden the request to abort and ODA 3212 and their partner forces were now cleared to execute clearance of the campsite where the suspected terrorists were thought to be. Even though Captain Perozeni was not comfortable with the decision that had been made to send the men forward on their mission, the acting operations base commander read them the entire Rules of Engagement, giving them the go-ahead to move on the targeted terrorist campsite.

Rules of Engagement, or ROE, are read to a team only when contact is expected. The men of ODA 3212 were not read the ROE for any other mission they had conducted in Niger; this was the first. Later in our family brief we would be told by General Cloutier that there had been no movement in the area for many hours and LTC Painter was certain the area was deserted before sending the team in. AFRICOM claimed the team was simply there to gather intelligence and destroy the deserted camp. But if the camp was deserted, why would LTC Painter feel it necessary to have the Rules of Engagement read to the team that General Cloutier later claimed was not expected to be coming into contact with the enemy?

For the third time in three days, the men on the ground were ignored when they warned that the mission was not a good one and they were not comfortable with the risk and lack of assets. Over and over again they were put into a compromising position on orders from those who outranked them. Now they would have no backup and no safety net if anything went wrong as they were ordered to drive deeper into hostile territory and farther from help. "You will not engage unless engaged upon. You will stay at the last cover-and-conceal position and allow the partner force to move in ahead of you," Captain Newburn began, as he read the Rules of Engagement for the region. That is when the team learned that not only was Arlit not coming on the next day's mission, but Team 3212 would be going ahead *alone* as the order from LTC Painter was handed down for them to continue the mission. Without Team Arlit, they would have no backup and the nearest assets would be six hours away if the team needed help.

One thing I would come to learn later was that if the timetable had been pushed back just a few hours into the morning, Team Arlit could have flown into Ouallam and staged once the dust storm passed. This would have allowed them to be within a thirty-minute flight to the Mali border when Team 3212 conducted the mission, then moved back south, passing through Tongo Tongo. This was the first mission of its kind that had been conducted in that area near the border where terrorist activity had significantly picked up over the past several months. Why a battalion commander would send an ill-prepared team with no sleep through hours of driving, with no assets in place and no backup, into enemy territory on the first mission of its kind I do not understand.

As one of the men involved in the mission would ask: *Why are you going to commit to something you've never done before, before you've got all your chess pieces where you want them to be?* I certainly wish all of the chess pieces had been put into place that day for my soldier. Bryan spent his life dominating chessboards, only to become a pawn in someone else's game, someone who hadn't thought more than one move ahead.

That night LTC Painter ordered ODA 3212 ahead to the Mali border alone, while back in Chad he filled out the paperwork and approved it. Once he did that, there existed a *third* CONOP, made by and approved through the highest levels in the chain of command.

The team heard the order come over the radio from the acting advanced operations base commander telling them to plan for the next day's mission. An ISR (intelligence, surveillance, and reconnaissance) drone had been sitting above the terrorist camp, watching it for the past six hours, and had reported no movement. But with dense tree cover in the area, the team couldn't be certain that the camp was really empty. The trees in the area were known for having large, dense canopies that hung all the way to the ground, which militants used to their advantage by riding from tree cover to tree cover to move undetected. For all the team knew, terrorists could have been under the trees, hiding. There could have been no enemy waiting for them—or a hundred.

The men decided on a plan: In order to effectively use their advise-and-assist method, the Americans would drop off their vehicles at one site just south of the camp, leaving a few team members there to keep an eye out in case any terrorists escaped in that direction. The rest of the team members and the Nigerien partner force would break into two groups and walk different routes up to the enemy camp. One group would move farther west in order to sweep across the camp from west to east, and the second group would provide support by fire by positioning themselves at the south with fire going to the north. Together, the two groups would use an L-shaped formation to clear the area of the campsite. Once the Nigerien partner force had cleared the area successfully, the American ODA team members would come and join their partner force to finish assessing the site.

The American team gathered with the Nigerien forces that night and went over the plan for the following morning. They had only seven hours left before daylight and twenty-five kilometers to travel before reaching the enemy campsite. They wanted to be there before sunrise to have some element of surprise. That left the team and the Nigeriens with only one hour to sleep. The ODA team members pulled a security patrol in shifts of fifteen minutes so each American could get in a brief nap before pulling their turn on security. As the Americans kept watch, they allowed their partner forces to sleep through the hour. The exhausted men fell asleep in whatever gear they had on, many just lying down on the hard dirt next to the vehicles they had driven. Some men slept in the hard, uneven metal truck beds, while others sprawled out across the seats inside.

Though the desert was enveloped in a deep silence, the hour of sleep was miserable. The mosquitoes were large and voracious, the heat an unbearable one hundred degrees, the humidity around eighty-five percent. A full moon shone brightly down on them from a sky dense with stars. Every now and then a hot breeze blew through, blasting everyone on the ground with sand. The only way to avoid it was to curl up near a clump of grass. The Americans were now starting to run low on water, so they tried to conserve it by drinking less and less. The Nigerien partner forces had run out of food and their water supply was nearly gone. The sleep-deprived men had barely shut their eyes when it was time to move again.

Around midnight, the call went out to wake up and begin heading north. An hour into the mission, the moon disappeared from the sky, plunging the convoy into utter darkness even as the terrain became exceedingly difficult to navigate. Captain Perozeni got out of his vehicle and donned his night-vision goggles as he helped navigate the rest of the way to the designated vehicle drop-off site. The seemingly flat ground would often drop off sharply into dry riverbeds, and these two- to four-foot drop-offs could not be seen in the dark by those driving the vehicles. The ground constantly changed from dry, windswept hardpan to deep desert sand. Navigating through and around the difficult terrain made for hours of frustratingly slow progress.

Walking ahead of the vehicles, Captain Perozeni followed a grid given to him by the AOB. Attempting to drive in a straight line, he, Brent, and Hanson in the lead vehicle noticed a large plateau rising up ahead of them. The plateau was in the direction they were heading, so the men decided to use it as a landmark for navigation toward the border. Slowly they picked their way closer through the rough terrain and toward the plateau. Getting closer, though, the men could see that the rains had come through and near the plateau had created enormous ravines similar to the wadis found in Afghanistan, but deeper than any truck could drive through. They were now faced with the challenge of navigating around sizable ravines.

Walking cautiously ahead, Captain Perozeni directed the vehicles around the edges of each ravine until he found shallow points where they could cross. The movement was painstakingly slow for the exhausted men as they strained their eyes in the dark, trying to keep the vehicles in line and safe from any sudden drop-offs. As they moved along in the void of light and sound, Captain Perozeni could hear his heartbeat with each step as he strained to discern any movement or unusual noises in the surrounding desert. It all felt too quiet.

After hours of crawling slowly through the desert and feeling no closer to the target, the buzz of Captain Perozeni's phone sent a shiver through his body. He grabbed it and looked at the screen, shaking off his nerves. It was a secured message from Casey, checking in on the team. "Hey, man. How's it going out there?"

———

Back at the AOB, Casey got out of bed around 1:00 a.m. to check on the team's progress and was alarmed to find out the convoy had not gone back to base. He found out LTC Painter had ordered the team to continue the mission, overriding Captain Perozeni and the men back at the AOB who had opposed it. Casey sent a message asking the team how it was going.

"Hey, man," typed Captain Perozeni. "Not so good out here. This is stupid. We can't navigate up here."

"What do you mean?" Casey messaged back.

"I am physically walking in front of my truck trying to find a route that we can drive on. This is no good, we are hardly moving. I am not on board with this. We should turn around. We should have turned around and returned to base hours ago."

Casey grabbed his uniform off the floor and quickly pulled it on. He stooped as he stepped through the door of his living quarters and out into the night. A warm breeze blew across his bare head as he quickly crossed the base in Niamey, heading up to the AOB to see what was going on.

Casey showed the chief at the AOB the conversation he was having with Captain Perozeni, who had just sent another message: "We're not making any time. There are no roads and we are looking at attempting to make this movement by sunrise. But we are not even moving 1 kilometer an hour right now and we have 20 kilometers to go. This makes no sense. There is no way we will make it in the desired time frame."

Chief Marshall looked around the room. "Captain Perozeni is right. What he's saying makes sense. They should head back to base. Why are we even doing this?"

Casey agreed, as did the sergeant major and Captain Newburn.

The chief said, "Unfortunately, at this point what we think doesn't matter. Lieutenant Colonel Painter is ordering this, so we have no choice."

The feeling of frustration was palpable.

Casey's deep voice resounded through the room as he said: "This whole thing is fucked up. Those guys shouldn't be out there."

———

South of the militant camp the morning of the 4th at the vehicle drop-off site. Brent and Hanson were with the trucks and Brent took this picture as the rest of the group walked north to conduct the sweep of the camp. *(Brent Bartels)*

Captain Perozeni fought exhaustion as he continued to walk, leading his convoy through the dark. He was still angry and frustrated, but now he was resigned to his team's fate. It was clear that his opinion as the ground commander held no weight with those higher up the chain of command who continued to order him to proceed. For the next five hours, his team and their partner force worked painstakingly to keep the vehicles from rolling or breaking down as they made their way far-ther north.

At 5:30 in the morning, far behind schedule, the convoy finally reached the vehicle drop-off site. The group of American and Nigerien soldiers sat together one last time and went over the plan for the mission while checking equipment. They scanned the area, noticing with con-cern that the dense vegetation created the ideal place to set up a camp that would be undetectable to ISR drones. Trees were scattered through-out the area, with large canopies of leaves stretching down nearly to the ground. Like mountain laurel found in many regions of the U.S., the Nigerien landscape is covered in a thick brush that is thorny and diffi-cult to see through. The brush surrounded the trees, making it impos-sible for someone to see what lay under the trees unless he was standing next to them.

Captain Perozeni told the group gathered around him to be cautious and aware of their surroundings. "We're going into hostile territory. Keep your head on a swivel. Everyone, be smart."

Master Sergeant Smith broke in. "Hey, y'all, uh-um. You know this is three-two, baby. Three-two is . . . this . . . this is what we do! Um, yeah, you know you gotta keep your head on a swivel up there and be ready."

As the sun came up around 6:30, everyone was finally getting into position near the enemy campsite and the Nigerien partner forces started to clear the land across the camp, followed by the American team. The team didn't find any militants at the camp, but as they pushed through the tree-covered landscape, a motorcycle engine started up be-hind them to the northwest. They spotted two men pushing a motor-cycle out from under a tree, hopping on, then speeding off in a cloud of red dust across the desert. The motorcycle headed north toward the Mali border going about twenty-five miles per hour. And while that informa-tion was quickly relayed back to the team waiting with the vehicles at the drop-off site, after the difficulty they'd had navigating the terrain in the trucks the past few days, the men knew they would never be able to catch a dirt bike before it crossed into Mali. Instead, the ISR drone was sent after the motorcycle in the hope that they could continue to track the motorcyclists to see where they crossed the border—and to make sure the militants didn't circle back to attack the team. Seeing the two men on the motorcycle shook some of the men.

As ODA 3212 continued to clear the enemy camp, it became apparent they had stumbled upon a very heavily trafficked area. They were in the middle of sub-Saharan Africa, but there were hundreds of motorcycle tracks crisscrossing all over the deserted encampment. They also found an abandoned motorcycle, which they later burned.

They found clear cutouts made under the canopies of surrounding trees where it was obvious that militants had pulled their bikes to hide and then climbed up into the trees. It was eerie, and the U.S. team members—realizing what they had walked into—began to instruct everyone to stay alert, to look out for movement from all surrounding trees and shrubs. The place covered a far larger expanse than what they had expected.

As they worked to gather items around the campsite, they got word from the drone operator. The motorcycle with the two men that had sped away from the campsite was seen meeting up with several other motorcycles. The drone operator informed the captain that a group had gathered for a few minutes then separated. Captain Perozeni was asked what he wanted the ISR drone to do.

"Continue to follow and watch the motorcycles," he said. He did not want to be caught unawares if the men on the motorcycles were following them.

The drone was sent to follow the motorcycles and continued to relay information down to the team. Eventually the team would hear that they had crossed into Mali and continued in a northerly direction.

After gathering all the items they found, the Nigerien partner force burned the abandoned motorcycle in an effort to destroy it. They saw a nomadic herdsman with several cattle, so they questioned him, then began preparations to leave, glad to be heading back to their base and safety. Everyone operating in Niger understands how dangerous it is up near the Mali border, and the soldiers of ODA 3212 were looking forward to putting some distance between themselves and that treacherous area once again.

The morning of October 4, the team left the terrorist encampment and began driving back. Captain Perozeni again walked ahead through the tall grass, helping to direct the vehicles safely through the rough terrain. After ten miles, the terrain finally opened back up and the convoy was able to navigate without having Captain Perozeni directing the vehicles on foot. The Nigerien partner force wasn't sure where they were, so the American team with their maps and compasses directed the convoy back to a road. They headed for a tree off to the southwest, as their maps pointed to a road that way. Though the area had opened up enough for Captain Perozeni to be back in the truck, it was still like driving the trucks over a broken washboard. The men were tossed about as the vehicles lurched and lunged across the desert sand and rocks.

Eventually the convoy reached an area that was like a dried-up lakebed. The hardpan allowed them to pick up some speed, and for the first time since leaving Mangaize the day before, the trucks were out of first gear. At 10:00 that morning, they finally saw a small hut—the first building they had seen since the evening before—and were all elated to be back to civilization.

As they followed a road, the Nigerien trucks got back in the lead and again took over the mission. There was a village ahead to the southwest, and the Nigeriens needed food and water, so they headed toward it. As they pulled into the village, everyone seemed friendly. There were no "demeanor hits," such as nervousness, lack of eye contact, or perceivable animosity that would lead the team to feel alarmed, so they asked about food and water. That particular village did not have a well, so the village elder directed them to drive down a road so small it looked more like a goat trail, then off to the left another five or six kilometers to the village of Tongo Tongo, where they would find a well.

As the convoy entered Tongo Tongo from the northwest, Ondo and Hanson saw a small child, maybe three years old. The little boy sprinted as fast as he could toward his mother, who was running out to meet him. She grabbed him up into her arms and dashed into her hut and out of sight. Normally children in a village run out to greet the Americans, knowing they might get candy or a toy. Hanson and Ondo decided perhaps these villagers had never seen Americans before, so they were frightened. The Americans drove through and parked in an open area on the north end of the village of Tongo Tongo, pulling under the shade of some large trees in a 360-degree security formation with the machine-gunners facing out. Everyone got out of their vehicles and stretched their legs, drank water, and opened up some MREs while the Nigerien partner forces went to collect water and food supplies.

The team members of ODA 3212, now relieved to be in a village and away from the militant camp, talked and enjoyed their meal standing under the shade of a large tree on the edge of Tongo Tongo. They were laughing with one another when Captain Perozeni watched twenty-seven village elders approaching them. It had been about fifteen minutes since their arrival there. Captain Perozeni, Brooks, and Lieutenant Boubacar walked out to the elders, who clearly wanted to meet with the leaders of the American and Nigerien teams. Usually, the team coming into a village initiates a meeting, but in Tongo Tongo, in an unusual move, the village elders did so. Captain Perozeni spoke with the village chief through Jacob, the interpreter, but became alarmed when the chief pointed at him in an agitated manner and raised his voice to tell him that the Army never came up to their area anymore and he, the chief, never got any help from them. The village chief said that recently he had been arrested by the Nigerien authorities and taken to Niamey for questioning but then had been released. He accused Captain Perozeni of being the one who turned him in—which alarmed the captain. While Captain Perozeni had never visited Tongo Tongo before, he knew the previous ODA that was stationed in Ouallam might have.

A few minutes into the meeting, the chief and other village elders began to calm down and became very friendly with the team, making jokes and seeming to appreciate the Americans being there.

Meeting with the village elders right before the ambush. The Americans' vehicles are in background. *(Hanson)*

The meeting continued on a friendly note long enough that soon the Nigerien partner forces and the Americans had all finished their meals and were ready to leave. It had been thirty minutes since they arrived, and plenty of time to devote to the village elders who had requested a meeting.

Captain Perozeni informed the village chief that they needed to leave and head back to their base in Ouallam, but the village chief continued talking, making it hard to break away. The captain listened for a few more minutes before interrupting to say they could stay no longer. The village chief asked him to please wait and ran off into a hut. He was gone for about five minutes before emerging with a child.

The child had a mild form of scoliosis and the chief hoped a medic would examine him. Bryan was called over to examine the boy. He recommended they take the child to Niamey for treatment if they could, but for the time being to focus on keeping the boy strong, especially exercising his back muscles. As Bryan wrapped up, the team began to say their goodbyes—but again they were stopped when the village chief asked them to wait as he ran into the village to get something.

After several minutes he emerged with a goat. The village chief wanted to slaughter and cook the goat and have the Americans eat lunch with him and his elders, but Captain Perozeni told him no. They appreciated the gesture, but they needed to get going so they could get back to Ouallam before dark. When it became clear the team was not going to stay, the village elder gifted the goat to the Nigerien partner forces and they thanked him and said goodbye as they loaded it into their truck.

The trucks all got back in line, with the two Nigerien partner-force vehicles heading up the convoy. Driving slowly along the forty-five-mile route that would take them back to Ouallam, the men were elated. As they rolled out of town, the team was blasting Justin Bieber and having some laughs. Passing the last hut on their way out of Tongo Tongo, Ondo, who was sitting at his gun on top of Truck #3 at the rear of the convoy, suddenly heard four shots pop off.

16

The Kill Zone

Four gunshots echo through the hot desert air.

Brent, driving Truck #1 toward the front of the convoy, assumes that one of the partner forces has accidentally shot a gun while loading up the vehicles. According to military briefings the men received when they first arrived in-country, it was rare for enemy combatants to attack a military target in Niger. In the rare instance when militants attacked a military target, they popped off a couple rounds, then retreated to the safety of the desert if fire was returned. Brent keeps driving ahead along the narrow red-dirt road situated between desert scape covered in clumps of grass, thorny bushes, and an occasional small scrub tree. Approximately one hundred meters from the road on the right and forty meters from the road on the left, trees dotting the land slowly become thicker and lead into forests with marshes left by the rainy season that has just ended.

The convoy continues down the dusty path until they hear more shots ring out. Realizing it is not their partner forces and thinking it's one or two guys feeling lucky and viewing the convoy as a target of opportunity, the team continues to ignore the small-arms fire coming in from the left as they make their way down the road. The men in Truck

#1 figure the attackers will soon turn around and head back up north, as they have been told is typical militant behavior in the region.

Brent comments to Captain Perozeni, "Well, here's some asshole on a motorcycle who probably just wants to, like, get his ji-ji-jihad on. You know? Fire a couple rounds at us and he's probably going to hightail it and run now back north and we're not going to be able to catch him. Or maybe he wants to meet his m-m-maker today and go see his seventy-two virgins."

Both men laugh.

Driving down the red-dirt path, Brent glances out the driver's-side window to his left, trying to spot a motorcycle. Ahead of him, he sees the two lead partner-force vehicles stop short, apparently alarmed by the gunfire. Brent hits the brakes to avoid crashing into the Nigerien trucks. Then one of the Nigerien drivers begins backing up, trying to go around the rest of the convoy, attempting to flee. The Nigerien partner-force truck clips Brent's truck, then stops right next to it—so close that Brent cannot exit his vehicle using the driver's-side door. The second Nigerien vehicle in the line now begins backing up, also in panic, and slams into the front of Truck #1. Now Truck #1 is immovable, stopping the entire convoy in what will soon become the kill zone.

The team is a flock of sitting ducks, boxed in and unable to move. Captain Perozeni jumps out of Truck #1 to the sound of more shots being fired. At the back of the convoy, on top of Truck #3, Ondo swings his M240 mounted machine gun around as he begins to charge it, preparing to shoot. On top of Truck #1, Hanson also charges his M240 and begins looking for targets.

With the convoy at a stop, Captain Perozeni decides to go see what the enemy situation looks like. "Brent, I'm going to take some Nigeriens with me and flank around the side of that forested area. See if we can get a read on these guys and put them down fast. You stay here and direct fire."

Captain Perozeni, who speaks French, grabs four French-speaking Nigerien partner-force soldiers to go with him. They run off ahead and then go left into the trees. The captain is confident that with four men he can flank the enemy on the right-hand side and eliminate them easily. From the sound of the incoming fire, it appears there are only a few militants. Captain Perozeni and the Nigeriens can kill them quickly before getting back to the convoy to continue the drive toward their base in Ouallam.

Brent, the team's communications sergeant, takes a moment to call up a warning over the trucks' secured radio. "Beast one zero, this is beast one two. Troops in contact." Brent then gives the grid location. The time is 11:43 a.m. His call alerts those at the advanced operations base in Niamey of shots being fired and where. Grabbing his M4 assault rifle, Brent scoots across to the passenger side of his vehicle and jumps from Truck #1. He sprints back to the other trucks, alerting everyone to what Captain Perozeni is doing. Directing the men to aim away from where the captain is flanking, he shouts, "Hey, Mike's going to the right of that forest. You guys need to shift fire left! Shift fire left!"

While Brent directs fire, a Nigerien vehicle behind Truck #2 begins moving to the right and going around the other vehicles attempting to flee to the south. The Nigerien reconnaissance vehicle between Trucks #1 and #2 also pulls to the right, attempting to escape. Just then the volume of fire increases significantly, making it clear that this is more than just a couple of guys shooting at the convoy hoping to get lucky.

"Oh, shit! Everyone, grab your kits, get your armor on!" Brent yells as he jogs back toward Truck #1.

The men have what are called kits. Their kits contain all their gear, which is attached to their bulletproof vests. The vests have plates of armor that are inserted into pouches. There are other pouches and pieces on the vests to which they can attach and store other things, such as knives, tourniquets, and magazines. It is all attached so that if they find themselves in an unexpected combat situation like this, they have everything they need ready to go.

The men of ODA 3212 have been driving vehicles—most with no

air-conditioning—across the desert with their water supply running low, so it made more sense to travel without their heavy kits on rather than needlessly risk heat stroke. Niger is not a combat zone, so teams are not expected to wear body armor. Brooks, LaDavid, Hanson, and the other men now hastily throw on their body armor as they prepare for a firefight.

What at first seemed like a small attack directed toward the back of the convoy is now intensifying and shifting directions. Sitting at his gun on top of Truck #3, Ondo can see militants moving forward through the tree line opposite the team as they begin aiming most of their fire toward the middle of the convoy. Machine guns and small-arms thunder through the air, slowly at first, then building as the enemy fire steadily grows into a torrent. Back at Truck #1, Brent lies over the hood of his vehicle, his body armor now on, and begins returning fire.

The men who've been in combat in the past quickly realize this attack is much worse than anything they've experienced before. It's a serious and organized ambush by a powerful and well-trained hostile force. Their ingrained fight-or-flight instinct kicks in and their adrenaline amps up. This is their worst-case scenario.

Back at Truck #3, Smith, too, feels the increasing intensity of the fight, but is surprised by his reaction. After a long career in Special Forces, he's been in combat before, but this time is different. This is his last deployment before he retires and all he can think about are his wife and young son back at home. He knows what to do and how his body is supposed to focus in on shooting the enemy, controlling the men, and directing the battle. Hearing a bullet bounce off the truck nearby, his body doesn't respond quickly like it always has in the past. He forces himself to move. *What is going on with me?* he wonders. Smith tries to shake off his nerves, but his mind is drifting. He pushes himself to ignore his fear so he can fight effectively, but he is struggling to do so for the first time in his career. He manages to get things under control, pulling out his weapon and taking aim at the enemy from behind his vehicle.

With the gunfire increasing, Jacob, the interpreter, who has been cowering in Truck #1, jumps from the vehicle and sprints away, abandoning the team and partner force in the greatest act of cowardice any of them have ever witnessed. Worse, he takes the walkie-talkie with him, leaving the Americans with no way of communicating with the Nigeriens on the ground or in their trucks.

Faced with the loss of their interpreter, Brent, Hanson, and Ondo continue to direct fire at the enemy while many of the thirty-two Nigeriens cower behind trucks and are spread out widely among the bushes, holding their weapons but not shooting. Green Berets go through three years of training on top of what the normal soldier goes through, then they attend other specialty schools to teach them tactics and how to remain cool under pressure. The Nigerien partner forces, however, are between the ages of seventeen and twenty-two, come from small villages throughout Niger, each speaking their own language, and have little training. Most Nigerien soldiers have no battle experience, either, but have heard stories of militant attacks and are filled with fear as the noise of war grows around them.

The Nigeriens are shooting their weapons while keeping most of their bodies hidden behind the vehicles. They throw out an arm every now and again, without looking or aiming, and shoot a few rounds in the general direction of the enemy. Some Nigeriens are also shooting from underneath their vehicles in the direction of the trees. Watching this, Brent is concerned for Captain Perozeni's safety. Normally the team sergeant would be directing fire, but Smith is near the rear of the convoy and Brent can't see him. Leaving the protection of his fighting position by the truck, Brent rushes among the Nigeriens, yelling in broken French over the deafening gunfire. "Aim! Aim! *Regarde! Votre Amies en* the *Arbre!* You have to aim!" Using hand motions, Brent tries to show the Nigeriens where to aim.

With the language barrier, and the interpreter gone, there is no way to calm down the panicked Nigeriens, no way to direct them where to shoot or to tell them to stay. Many begin to run, abandoning their fellow soldiers to the fight. All Lieutenant Boubacar and the other men can do is focus on their efforts as the violence intensifies all around them. Lieutenant Boubacar gathers the men he can using the languages he knows—French, Hausa, Zarma. Then he directs the handful of Nigerien soldiers to stay and keep shooting.

At Truck #2 Bryan has in his hands the M320 grenade launcher he spent the first several weeks in-country zeroing in the sights on. He knows how deadly accurate it is and is ready to put the weapon to work. He lobs his first grenade and the weapon makes a hollow, tinny *thunk* as it tears from the short tube. Bryan smiles, watching the first impact explode in the trees. Next to him, Dustin and Brooks have out their M4 assault rifles. Dustin spreads himself over the hood of the truck, pulling the trigger as he releases short bursts of fire in the direction of the enemy. "Take that, fuckers!" he yells in his southern drawl. Brooks, near the rear of the vehicle, laughs at Dustin as he unleashes a barrage.

At the back of the convoy, LaDavid, Smith, Jeremiah, and Ondo in Truck #3 decide to move their truck forward. With machine-gunner Ondo sitting atop the truck, LaDavid knows the mounted weapon will be more effective in the middle of the area with the heaviest fighting—the kill zone. LaDavid hops into the driver's seat and drives straight into the kill zone to create a tighter formation with the trucks.

LaDavid stops between Truck #2 and Truck #1 while Jeremiah Johnson jumps from Truck #3 and runs into the kill zone. LaDavid grabs his assault rifle, then tears off after Jeremiah. Choosing to stay exposed to incoming fire, LaDavid and Jeremiah steadfastly discharge round after round on the enemy, thundering out bursts from their M4s. Ondo, meanwhile, lets out a series of earsplitting cracks from his mounted machine gun, attempting to suppress the enemy and to stop them from moving closer to the convoy. Together, LaDavid, Jeremiah, and Ondo knock back the militants who are trying to move out from the trees.

At Truck #2, Bryan, Dustin, and Brooks lay down gunfire and hurl grenades into the center of the growing enemy. At Truck #1, Hanson sits at the mounted machine gun, laying out rail after rail of thunderous cracks. Brent is settled over the hood and lets out short bursts from his M4. Smith and Chester have out their M4s as well, lying prone near the wheels of Truck #1 and Truck #3. At the front of the convoy, the Nigerien vehicles that led the convoy out of Tongo Tongo are still blocking Truck #1. Together with Lieutenant Boubacar, several Nigeriens—some lying prone in the dirt around the Nigerien trucks, others taking cover by the wheel wells—shoot round after round toward the advancing enemy in the tree line.

The dusty desert air is thick with the stench of sweat and gunpowder and the deafening sounds of war. The earsplitting volume of the battle makes it clear the enemy force is growing exponentially and the convoy is in trouble. This is nothing like the two to four enemy combatants that the team was warned about. This is something else entirely. Sweating under their heavy armor, the men continue to battle for the upper hand in a situation that has escalated alarmingly fast.

With Truck #3 sandwiched between the other two, Jeremiah steps out, exposing himself to a wall of incoming fire as he runs ammunition to Ondo. Sprinting back, he pulls out his M4 and lays out a couple blasts in the direction of the enemy. He fights alongside LaDavid, a kid from Miami Gardens, Florida. As they shoot at the sides of the enemy attacking them the young soldier displays surprising skill and fearlessness. Together they rain fire down on the militants' motorcycles and enemy vehicles, which are mounted with machine guns, as the enemy continues trying to close the distance between them.

Jeremiah hears a call come over the handheld radio that the men at Truck #2 need a resupply of ammunition, so he grabs what they need and runs back to Truck #2. Once there, Jeremiah decides to stay and switch places with Staff Sergeant Brooks. Brooks grabs his weapon and ammo, turns his back, and is jogging toward Truck #3 when the partner-force vehicle sitting behind Truck #2 turns around and drives northwest, abandoning the fight and kicking up a cloud of dust as it tears away down the dirt road. Truck #2 is now at the back of the convoy in the kill zone, with Jeremiah, Dustin, and Bryan laying down heavy suppressive fire. The red dirt is thick in the air, the taste of it chalky as it lingers in the soldiers' mouths, which are sticky with thirst.

The staggering number of incoming rounds tears through the metal and glass of their truck, kicking up dirt all around them. Their own return fire roars in their ears. Jeremiah, now near the back panel of Truck #2, aims and shoots his weapon over and over. Dustin, lying over the hood of the same, takes aim and fires in the direction of the enemy by the trees, providing cover fire for Bryan. Bryan is down on one knee by the front of the truck, holding the M320 grenade launcher and grinning wildly as he propels grenade after grenade in the direction of the attackers.

Ahead is Truck #3, and a little to the left Truck #1 remains boxed in by the two partner-force vehicles. At the front of the convoy and to their right sits the reconnaissance vehicle. As Ondo, Smith, LaDavid, and Brooks lay down burst after burst, the tactical prowess of the militants begins to alarm them. The militants understand tactics and have clearly had training.

As the convoy battles the growing horde of militants, Captain Perozeni and the four Nigeriens with him continue to flank along the right just outside of the wood line where the enemy is situated. Arriving at the edge of a large marsh by the trees, Captain Perozeni spots more militants with guns attacking the convoy. There are far more of them than the captain initially estimated, but not enough that he is worried. Captain Perozeni and the Nigerien soldiers shoot and kill the militant targets, picking them off one by one. The captain notices, though, that the number of militants doesn't appear to be diminishing and hostile fire is increasing. Suddenly alarmed, he realizes there must be more militants streaming in from someplace nearby.

Captain Perozeni is watching the enemy fighters closely now, seeing that they are beginning to change direction, moving around the marsh from the left of the wooded area to the right, coming toward him and the Nigeriens. Several militants on motorcycles and vehicles mounted with heavy machine guns move in a manner that makes it clear they are trying to outflank the convoy by getting ahead of them on the road and trapping them there. Seeing this maneuver, Captain Perozeni knows he needs to get back to the road fast and give the team a heads-up. He gathers the four Nigeriens and they run quickly back around the forested area, to link up with the convoy.

On the road at Truck #2, Bryan continues to use his M320 grenade launcher, hitting targets with astonishing precision. He charges out into the open under intense fire and accurately fires a 40-millimeter grenade round at the oncoming horde, trying to halt their attack. Covering Bryan, who has made himself a target, Dustin lets out several short burst of bullets in the direction of the enemy. At the rear of the vehicle, Jeremiah pops off several rounds, once again exposing himself to heavy incoming fire. The volume of fire is so high that soon Dustin, Bryan, and Jeremiah have exhausted their ammunition and need another resupply.

Ondo's radio crackles to life with word that Jeremiah, Dustin, and Bryan need more ammo. Ondo hops off the machine gun and gathers what he needs to make a quick run. Dustin refuses to leave his friends and move out of the heavy fighting as he uses up his last rounds while waiting for Ondo. Through a barrage of incoming fire, Ondo runs, ducking, to take his teammates a resupply of ammunition. Arriving at Truck #2, he hands Dustin ammo. Dustin smiles and yells, "Hey, man, tell everyone I love 'em!" Ondo looks at Jeremiah, who nods as he takes the ammo and goes to reload. Ondo begins to jog away, watching Bryan grin bigger than he has ever seen him grin before; he is already back down on one knee, lobbing one perfectly placed grenade after another.

A strange feeling washes over Ondo. It is as though the men at Truck

#2 are saying goodbye, as if they know they won't be making it out. Trying to shake the feeling, Ondo focuses on what he needs to do next.

Sprinting back to Truck #3, Ondo climbs up behind the M240 mounted machine gun as a hail of gunfire falls all around him. Looking to his left, he sees a seventeen-year-old Nigerien kid named Inza who is fighting with all his heart. Ondo smiles at Inza, glad to have him there as he once again spins his weapon around and begins to fire.

Ondo then sees Captain Perozeni running up to Truck #1, returning from his flanking maneuver. The captain is screaming, but it's barely audible over the noise of battle. Then Ondo hears him: "They're amassing! They are amassing to our east, they're trying to outmaneuver us!" Captain Perozeni yells that the enemy's numbers are growing by the minute as the militants are circling the convoy to trap them on the road. Jumping up on Truck #1 next to Hanson, the captain points to the spot where he saw the enemy moving closer.

Hanson immediately starts pounding out long lines of fire from his mounted M240, as the volume of incoming enemy fire begins to escalate. There are still militants firing at them from the left side of the forested area, but now they are also firing at the convoy from the center of the trees. Other militants who moved around to the right of the forest are picking up fire as they attempt to reach and then overtake the team on the road. The volume of gunfire is rising.

It is 11:55 a.m. when Smith sprints to Truck #1, using the radio to call in overwhelming fire. He is trying to come up with a plan to get them out of there, to no avail. Still fighting himself with each breath so he can remain in the battle, Smith closes his eyes, takes a deep breath to clear his head, then runs back to Truck #3 and gets back in the fight.

Hanson is trying to cut the enemy flank down by rapidly blasting out string after string of bullets from his machine gun. But knowing that he needs to change barrels soon in order not to burn out his gun, Hanson is trying not to push his barrel too hard. From the tops of different trucks, Hanson and Ondo begin "talking the guns," one man resting his gun barrel for a moment while the other shoots, and then trading back. This method is used to keep the guns from getting too hot, and so far it is working well for them, as they continue to hold the enemy at bay. Ondo lets his weapon go quiet as Hanson turns his weapon in the direction Captain Perozeni is pointing to. Hanson pulls the trigger but nothing happens. There is no sound, no shaking, and no rounds being fired. The gun is jammed.

Reaching down, Hanson searches and finds a new barrel. He pulls the feed tray up on his gun and a loud crack erupts as a round explodes and the case shoots out backward, zipping right past his face as it exits the chamber. Hanson's heart races as he realizes what happened: The hot case barely missed hitting him in the face and possibly doing severe damage. Knowing his machine gun needs to cool down, Hanson pulls out his M4 and continues shooting at the enemy, desperate to keep knocking them back. He waits a few minutes, then goes back to his machine gun, changing out the barrel while the battle rages around him. In a hurry to get his vital weapon up and running, he charges the gun and tries to shoot, but again it jams. When he opens the feed tray a second time, another casing explodes out backward. He is now forced to methodically go through a list of possible gun malfunctions and fixes. With his machine gun down, Hanson knows his team will be in serious trouble.

Captain Perozeni begins organizing the men to prepare to move out of the kill zone. He decides they will use two three-hundred-meter bounds to reach an area approximately six hundred meters away to avoid being outflanked and trapped. Once they get there, they will reassess the situation. Captain Perozeni knows that there is no good area for the convoy's next position, but to remain where they are would be catastrophic. The area they are in is like a bottleneck, with the village behind them, a forest to the right, and an enemy closing in to their left and circling around to their front.

Captain Perozeni turns to Brent and tells him to come up with a plan to get out of there while he tries to gather the partner force. Brent grabs his radio and lets the rest of the team know they need to move. Back at Truck #3, Brooks picks up his radio and calls Brent. "Let's throw a smoke grenade, then move once it billows." Brent agrees it's a good plan. Jeremiah Johnson, who is listening in at Truck #2, gets on his radio to say he's for the plan, too. Brent dashes to Captain Perozeni and begins yelling over the noise the plan to throw a smoke grenade. Captain Perozeni gives Brent a thumbs-up. Brent gets back on his radio and shouts to everybody, "Keep holding the enemy off! We're going to gather the partner force, then I'll throw a smoke grenade. When you see it billow, we are going to start rolling out of here!"

Brent hurries back over to help Captain Perozeni as he runs around, trying to communicate to the Nigeriens, who are hiding in the bushes across a large expanse. He tells them they need to move. Everything is disorganized and chaotic as the men focus on the Nigeriens attempting to get everyone moving. Without the ability to communicate with the Nigeriens, getting them back to their vehicles is a nearly impossible task. The Nigeriens need to be calmed down and coaxed out of the bushes and back into their trucks while bullets zip past, kicking up the dirt and tearing at the bushes. The terrified Nigeriens slowly begin to move from their hiding places as the stench of gunpowder and the deafening pops and booms tell of the firefight raging all around them.

The rest of the team continues to fight as the battle crescendos. Captain Perozeni, Brent, and now Brooks struggle to gather the remaining disoriented and scattered partner force, unwilling to leave them behind. The time it takes to get their partner forces back to their trucks will end up costing lives. In the chaos, one of the Nigerien partners runs by Ondo, LaDavid, and Smith in Truck #3, shooting his gun into the ground. He leaps in fright after nearly shooting his own foot off and runs faster toward his truck, as though the bullet had come from the enemy and not his own gun.

As the men at all three American trucks continue to pound out rounds toward the enemy, the two partner-force vehicles at the front of the convoy that boxed in Truck #1 are now loaded up and quickly peel off to the southwest. Lieutenant Boubacar, who is in one of the partner-force trucks, directs the driver of his vehicle to seven hundred meters, where he stops to wait for the American vehicles. The second partner-force vehicle speeds off into the desert, abandoning the rest of the men, leaving them to fight the enemy on their own. Of the thirty-five Nigerien partner-force soldiers, only nine now remain with the eleven Americans battling more than one hundred enemy combatants.

Seeing the Nigeriens speed away, the American team members clamber into their vehicles while still shooting. Just ahead of the American trucks is the reconnaissance vehicle with two Nigeriens. This vehicle is now out in the open and not moving. Brent starts waving as he yells for the Nigerien driver to move, but the driver freezes in fear. Brent throws his hands up as he shouts, "Move! Move!" Not wanting to leave anyone behind, the men in Truck #1 are waiting for the reconnaissance vehicle's driver to move first.

Brent and Captain Perozeni watch as bullets rain down on the reconnaissance vehicle. Suddenly one breaks through the driver's window. The driver of the reconnaissance vehicle lurches violently as he is struck in the head by the bullet. Captain Perozeni, Brent, and Chester yell in frustration and horror as the driver crumples forward over the steering wheel. Up until this moment, most of the men felt certain this whole fiasco would make a good story later and that everyone would survive to tell it. Suddenly the threat is not only real but fatal, and the danger for the rest of them explodes exponentially.

Suddenly an enemy vehicle with a mounted machine gun rushes forward toward the convoy, unleashing a barrage of heavy gunfire straight at the American trucks. The onslaught brings a wall of fire preventing the convoy from moving forward.

At Truck #2 Bryan sets his jaw and runs into the hail of incoming bullets. Getting down on one knee, he peers down his sights as he aims his M320 grenade launcher at the advancing enemy vehicle. He pulls the trigger and with a tinny *thwunk* the grenade launches out of the tube. The grenade hangs for a moment as if suspended midflight before slamming into the target. A blast erupts as the grenade damages and disables the enemy's vehicle.

The militants turn their weapons' focus on Truck #2. Behind the truck's wheel well, Bryan loads another grenade while Jeremiah and Dustin direct fire on the gunner with their M4s. Running back out, Bryan gets into position on one knee and pulls the enemy vehicle into his sights once more, this time focusing on the gunner as several rounds whiz by. Sweat pouring down his back, Bryan takes a deep breath, then pulls the trigger. The grenade flies out of the launcher's tube and through the air, then drops onto the machine gunner, ending the vehicle's onslaught. With the enemy vehicle and its machine gun disabled, the American convoy can now move out of the kill zone.

Captain Perozeni quickly gives the order to withdraw and Brent pulls the pin, throwing the smoke grenade out the window of his truck. Captain Perozeni grabs his radio saying, "Signal to move out." Each gunner sitting on top knows to look to the vehicle behind him for a signal because the gunners' platforms block the truck's rear windows. On Truck #1, Hanson looks back to see LaDavid in Truck #3 give a thumbs-up as the vehicle begins to roll. Hanson pounds on the roof to signal to the driver that he has confirmation. On Truck #3, Ondo turns and sees Jeremiah at Truck #2 give a thumbs-up as they begin to roll, and Ondo then slams his signal on the roof. Ondo's sweat-slicked shirt clings to him under the weight of his bulletproof vest as he grits his teeth and turns away from Jeremiah. Ondo spins his gun until he again faces the enemy along the wood line, opening up a string of fire on them. As he focuses on the enemy, he doesn't see Truck #2 stop rolling forward.

The stench of sweat, dirt, and gunpowder hangs thick in the humid air, and the men feel their ears ringing with the sound of incoming fire. It feels like death is chasing them. Brent drives Truck #1 for three hundred meters, with Truck #3 following close behind. Stopping to do a quick check at three hundred meters, the men in both trucks realize that Truck #2 is no longer with them. Captain Perozeni's plan to escape the kill zone to avoid being outflanked by the enemy has worked, but Truck #2 is still in the kill zone.

Jeremiah, Dustin, and Bryan decide to make a stand at the rear of the convoy and draw the full force of the enemy's attack. The three men know that drawing the enemy's attention to them is risky, but it will allow their teammates time to exit the kill zone. When Truck #1 and Truck #3 are successfully out of the kill zone, the three remaining men will begin their own effort to move out to the three-hundred-meter mark in Truck #2.

Bryan, Dustin, and Jeremiah take heavy fire as they try to slow the enemy while attempting to cover the movement of their friends out of the kill zone. Dustin is shooting over the hood, Bryan is shooting near the front wheel well, and Jeremiah is shooting from the back quarter panel of the vehicle. Seeing that the other trucks are gone, Dustin quickly jumps off the hood and slides from the passenger side of the vehicle across to the driver's seat and begins rolling the vehicle forward. Jeremiah moves into a more perilous position that allows him to better see and shoot at the militants. His fire distracts the militants for a moment as Bryan sets a group of militants in his sights. *Thwump.* A grenade goes flying through the air and lands on target. Remaining in the exposed firing position, Bryan jogs alongside the vehicle, directing it forward, then shifts and reloads his weapon to return more fire on the enemy. Jeremiah jogs along the back side of the vehicle. Suddenly Truck #2 stops moving and Bryan moves ahead of the truck. There is a small scrub tree nearby, and Bryan takes cover to shoot as Dustin grabs his weapon and lies across the front seat of Truck #2 and takes a few shots. The vehicle rolls slowly forward while Dustin yells something, but now the volume of incoming fire is so earsplitting that nothing can be heard above the din of incoming and outgoing rounds.

Bryan looks around the small scrub tree at the front of the vehicle and sees enemy forces continuing to circle the forest and advance, trying to outflank them on the road. Jeremiah is trying to hear Dustin when he suddenly falls backward onto the ground and the truck continues to roll forward, leaving him near the back tire as he turns onto his stomach to get onto his feet. As Jeremiah falls, Bryan lunges forward, leaving his limited cover to launch another grenade at the enemy's flank. As he looks for a target, he sees the round coming straight at him. It is too late. The thirty-five-year-old staff sergeant falls to the ground.

Jeremiah rushes toward Bryan and attempts to pull him back behind the safety of the truck. He realizes he needs help and yells for Dustin. Dustin runs over and Jeremiah begins to shoot in the direction of the enemy, covering Dustin as he drags Bryan's 230-pound frame behind the truck. As the escalating fire begins to converge on him, rather than running for safety, Jeremiah ferociously fights back. Dustin inspects Bryan's wound and realizes he can do nothing for his friend.

Dustin switches places with Jeremiah. The smell of sweat in the hot, dusty air is now mixed with the distinct metallic smell of blood as it pours from Bryan's wound into the red Nigerien desert and Jeremiah realizes his friend is dead.

"He's gone!" he yells to Dustin. "Run for the trees! We need a better position!"

Looking around them, Jeremiah and Dustin know they are now too far separated from the rest of the convoy and can no longer fight beside their truck if they wish to survive. The men sprint away from their vehicle and toward the forest to the right of the road. It's about a hundred meters away. As they bound through the Nigerien sand and scrub, they expose themselves to a staggering level of incoming fire. Sweating and laboring to breathe as they are weighed down by their heavy body armor, the dehydrated men sprint for their lives. The enemy fighters, loosely clad in robes, run after the two Americans, closing in on them as they give chase both on foot and on motorcycle, unleashing everything they have. The brunt of the enemy's ferocious attack is focused on just two men.

It has only been a half-hour since the first shots rang out and Dustin and Jeremiah are now sprinting desperately in hopes of finding cover to set up a new fighting position. Then a shot strikes Jeremiah, gravely wounding him. He falls to the hot, red earth. Dustin, still running, hears the shots and turns to see Jeremiah on the ground, struggling to get up. Dustin gives up on reaching the safety of the trees and fearlessly runs from the salvation of the woods to his friend's side to face the advancing enemy, refusing to leave his friend behind. Dustin repositions to make a last stand beside his friend and teammate.

With no hope of escape, Jeremiah continues to fight with fierce determination. The thirty-nine-year-old sergeant first class lays his head down, grateful to have Dustin there when at last he succumbs to his wounds. Dustin stands his ground, fighting the oncoming horde alone. As the militants surround him, he raises his weapon and opens fire. Staring down the enemy, the twenty-nine-year-old staff sergeant fights to the death, knowing he gave all he could in a desert far from home.

17

Overrun

After bounding three hundred meters out of the kill zone, Truck #1 stops in a clearing with Truck #3 close on its heels. Looking behind them, Ondo and Hanson, on the mounted guns, realize Truck #2 is missing. Ondo reaches down and slams on the window to get LaDavid's attention. "Moody! I can't see Truck Two! Try to raise them on the radio!"

Using the truck's communications system, LaDavid shouts over the noise of the machine gun and incoming fire, "Truck Two! Truck Two! Come in!" He waits, then calls again, then once more. There is no response.

Ondo stops shooting, pulling out his radio as he also tries to contact the missing truck. "Truck Two! Come in! Truck Two!" Ondo drops from the roof of Truck #3, grabs his M4, and motions for Brooks to follow him. Looking inside the vehicle, Ondo shouts to Smith, "I'm taking Brooks back to look for Bryan, J.W., and Dusty! Don't come after us, we'll be back in a minute!" Brooks and Ondo run back toward the kill zone. They know the danger that lies in front of them.

At the same time, Truck #1 and Truck #3 move another four hundred meters away from the kill zone, meeting up with the Nigerien vehicle that had already driven seven hundred meters before stopping. The reality of just how dire the situation they are in hits hard. There are missing teammates and a ferocious enemy is fast on their heels. For the moment, though, the incoming fire is noticeably less intense. Everyone exits the vehicles to discuss strategy. Lieutenant Boubacar grabs Captain Perozeni's attention; he wants the captain to contact the lieutenant's command back in Ouallam to make them aware of the dire situation. Lieutenant Boubacar doesn't have a satellite phone, and his radio doesn't carry that far north. The lieutenant is scared for his men and hoping his next-in-command can send help faster than those stationed in Niamey can. Captain Perozeni understands Lieutenant Boubacar's dilemma. Captain Perozeni assures him that he has contacted Niamey and they will pass the information to the lieutenant's command, as well as to all their allies, including the French, reassuring him that backup will soon be on its way. With enemy rounds coming in and men missing, Captain Perozeni and Lieutenant Boubacar agree they need to focus on the firefight right now. Lieutenant Boubacar says nothing more; he runs back to his truck to direct his men and join in the firefight.

There are now only six Americans and seven Nigeriens at this position. Truck #1's machine gun is still jammed and out of the fight. Hanson gets increasingly frustrated as he runs through every remedial action he can think of, but nothing works. His gun is finished. With only one working machine gun, the team's firepower and ability to protect themselves is significantly diminished. Hanson grabs his M4 and sprints over to Smith to tell him: "We need to go! We need to help Ondo and Brooks if those guys in Truck Two are injured. Two men can't move three guys and provide cover fire! Let's go!"

Smith is hesitant to run back toward the kill zone without a clear plan to save his men, but Hanson convinces him. They run over to Captain Perozeni to tell him they want to go back toward the kill zone to assist Ondo and Brooks. As the commander on the ground, Captain Perozeni has the final word. It's his job to assess the risks and consider worst-case scenarios. Captain Perozeni decides that the quiet spell right now provides a small window of opportunity to locate the missing men and they need to take advantage of it. Captain Perozeni gives Hanson and Smith the go-ahead.

Hanson pulls out his radio to tell the men back at Truck #2, as well as Ondo and Brooks, that he and Smith are going back to offer their support. They leave LaDavid in charge of Truck #3. Running along the tree line to avoid the incoming bullets, Smith and Hanson make their way back to the spot where they last saw Truck #2.

As they depart, Brent lies over the hood of Truck #1, using his scope to call out targets as he once again directs LaDavid, Chester, and Inza in the fight. Captain Perozeni gets on the radio to contact Truck #2, but again there is no response. He tries to contact Bryan, then Jeremiah, and finally Dustin, but they don't answer. Ondo and Brooks have still not sent word back, so Captain Perozeni tries to reach Ondo and Brooks. They don't answer him, either. He is becoming more anxious with each passing minute.

While Captain Perozeni is on the radio, LaDavid climbs on top of Truck #3 to take Ondo's place in control of the machine gun. He's used a machine gun only twice before, but now he fires the weapon with surprising accuracy.

The volume of fire starts increasing again as the militants close the distance on this new position. The enemy fighters are coming from the left at approximately two hundred meters and circling wide, attempting to get around the front of the convoy. The rolling terrain makes it so the Americans can't see the enemy circling. With Brent, Inza, Chester, and LaDavid shooting consistent bursts of fire from their weapons, Lieutenant Boubacar and the five other remaining Nigerien soldiers fire on the enemy from behind the Nigerien vehicle. As they all work together to suppress the enemy, the situation seems under control for a bit longer. Captain Perozeni tries one more time to raise Truck #2, as well as Ondo and Brooks.

Running back toward the forest, Hanson hears Smith suddenly halt behind him. He turns to see Smith not moving.

"Wait. We should think about this," Smith says.

Hanson recognizes the fear in Smith's face. He gently but forcefully yells, "We can't think, we have to move! If we stop moving we die. Let's go!"

Smith nods and they start moving again.

Ondo and Brooks are jogging along the tree line back in the direction of the kill zone when they run into two Nigerien soldiers hiding in the trees. Ondo, in a rush, tries speaking Spanish to them, then realizes his mistake and tries French. The Nigeriens look at him, puzzled. Not sure which language they speak, Ondo uses the Hausa phrase for "American car" that Bryan taught him, hoping these men understand him and know where the American truck is. *"Amerikan Jirgin Mota! Amerikan Jirgin Mota!"* He shouts over and over in Hausa until one of the men points behind him to the left toward the road where the convoy had once been parked—the same direction where Truck #2 was last seen. Ondo and Brooks turn and run to the left toward the tree line. They scan the area where they believe the truck was last parked, looking for Bryan, Dustin, and Jeremiah as the Nigeriens run in the opposite direction, deeper into the forest attempting to escape the battle.

Smith and Hanson spot Brooks and Ondo moving closer to the edge of the wood line and they shout that they are there to help. Smith and Hanson provide cover fire up along the ridge line as Brooks and Ondo walk down a small incline toward a marsh. They start to cross the marsh in knee-high water as bullets begin skipping off the trees and dirt around them.

Failing to reach Truck #2 on the radio and getting no response from the men who had run back to the kill zone, Captain Perozeni pulls out his M4 and runs out to the front of Truck #1 to join the fight. He begins popping off round after round at the oncoming militants. Brent, as communications sergeant, takes a moment to again call up the team's location over the radio to those in Niamey and state that there is now a missing American vehicle and three Americans missing in action. It is 12:20 p.m. Both mounted machine guns are now entirely shot out, their barrels burned up.

Lying on the top of Truck #1, firing at the enemy, Brent spots a militant running toward him in a red-and-black one-piece tracksuit. Brent shoots, clipping the man in red and slowing him down until the militant drops, wounded, to one knee. At Truck #3, LaDavid climbs on top of the vehicle, holding a sniper rifle. LaDavid yells out to Brent, "Sergeant B!" before he points at the tracksuit guy. Brent shouts over the noise, "You going to shoot him?" LaDavid smiles, lifts the rifle, then takes the guy out with one shot. It is his first time ever shooting a sniper rifle. Brent watches and says to himself, *That's awesome! Moody, a mechanic, just killed a dude with a 300 Win Mag in Africa. That is gonna be a story! I mean, come on, our mechanic is on top of a truck shooting a sniper rifle at a guy—now* that's *badass.*

Captain Perozeni, firing at the enemy near the front of Truck #1, sees in the distance another truck speeding toward them. It has a huge gun barrel crudely laid across the bed. As the truck gets closer, there's a deep pounding and an eruption of fire as 14.5-millimeter rounds begin coming in. THUMPK! THUMPK! THUMPK! Pounding out rounds, it sounds like thunder. It feels as though the very air is coming alive as bullets blast out of the long metal cylinders at the team. A whole new level of threat has opened up before the men. The men are used to the pops, zings, and cracks of the small-arms fire, which is 5.56-millimeter in diameter, and about two inches long. But the 14.5-millimeter rounds are six inches in length and are coming from a ZPU Soviet-era antiaircraft heavy machine gun. It is terrifying.

Brent's thoughts about LaDavid's perfect shot are interrupted by the barrage of thunderous pounding and flashes of fire coming from the right. The volume of incoming rounds exploding around them changes the firefight into a war zone. Two technical vehicles, which are light improvised fighting trucks mounted with weapons, appear about one hundred meters away—one mounted with a ZPU and another mounted with another Soviet-era machine gun with a similar bullet size known as a DShK. The technical vehicles are surrounded by twenty to thirty men. The vehicles arrange themselves to block the southern side of the road. Militants start running at the team, alternately dropping to the dirt and rising to shoot as they approach.

The remaining team members continue shooting. To their right, the road stretching south shows enemy vehicles now approaching. Fire bursts from heavy machine gun barrels as large artillery falls, sounding like a metallic rain. The road to the left is filled with yet more of the oncoming enemy. And in front of the men is a horde of fighters carrying guns on motorcycles, on foot, and in vehicles. Blasts begin to explode around the convoy, and they realize grenades are being launched at them.

The fury of the fire and weaponry thundering out in their direction makes the men's blood run cold, the hair on the back of their necks stand on end. Remaining in place any longer is an act of suicide. They are running out of ammo and nearly surrounded. There's no choice any longer but to jump in the vehicles, pick up whoever they can find, and attempt to make it out by driving through a thick wooded marsh. Captain Perozeni yells over the roar of incoming fire: "We've got to go! Let's head back and pick up who we can, we've got to get out of here! Now!"

Everyone scrambles for the vehicles. LaDavid drops from the roof of Truck #3 and collects his weapons, putting them in the back of his vehicle as he prepares to load up. Lieutenant Boubacar runs with one of his soldiers to get into the Nigerien vehicle, but the driver takes off in the direction of the two technical vehicles, somehow managing to get by them. Lieutenant Boubacar and the soldier turn and run for LaDavid's truck. Using Truck #1 as cover, Captain Perozeni continues to send out bullets, trying to hold the enemy off as long as possible, while Brent, Chester, and LaDavid pack up their guns and ammo and load their trucks. Inza and three other remaining Nigerien soldiers jump into the back of Truck #1, Chester dives into the passenger seat, and Brent launches into the driver's seat. The trucks roll as Captain Perozeni dashes for the back of Truck #1 while the world explodes all around him.

With no rearview mirror and the gunner's platform blocking half the back window, Brent can't see Truck #3 once he starts moving. He puts Truck #1 in drive, turns, and takes off blazing through the desert straight toward the forested marsh. He assumes LaDavid is close behind.

Brent heads back into the marshy forest in the direction of where Ondo, Smith, Brooks, and Hanson ran. He needs to rescue them now, as two militant trucks with Soviet-era heavy machine guns, a number of motorcycle gunners, and armed men on foot shoot at them. Flashes of gunfire spark as the ZPU and DShK fire on the truck, the rounds pelting it and tearing at the metal exterior. Two bullets come through the windshield, sending glass flying over the front seat as Brent weaves back and forth, employing evasive driving maneuvers on the narrow and bumpy path. Sweat pours down his face as he curses and tries to shift gears.

Picking up speed, Brent desperately searches for his team members on the ground, when Truck #1 hits a large bump. The truck lurches violently and Captain Perozeni, riding in the back, reaches for something to hold on to. But when an object strikes him in the back, he's thrown off balance and falls out of the truck.

Truck #1 continues speeding along the dusty path until one of the Nigeriens screams from the back of the truck: "Captain! Captain Perozeni! Captain Perozeni!" Chester looks back and hollers in horror, "Brent! Captain Perozeni is gone! He's not in the back of the truck anymore!" Brent slams on the brakes and turns the truck around to get him. It's at this moment the men in Truck #1 realize that Truck #3, with LaDavid and Lieutenant Boubacar, is not behind them.

At that moment, LaDavid, Lieutenant Boubacar, and a Nigerien soldier are fighting for their lives. They've been forced to flee on foot while responding to the full force of the enemy attack. With no cover and a horde of enemy combatants swarming relentlessly, the men seek out a better fighting position.

There are fighters coming at them from multiple directions, and the three men begin to sprint in the only open direction they can see. They aim for the first cover in sight: a tree on a hill about a half-mile away. Lieutenant Boubacar runs as fast as his legs will carry him, gulping in air. He can't afford to look back or slow down. Death is on his heels. A third technical vehicle suddenly appears over the hill they are running toward, and then a muzzle flashes as it fires on them. Lieutenant Boubacar lets out a yell as he falls to the ground. Pain shoots through his lower body as he lies in the sand, bleeding. Lieutenant Boubacar shouts in French to the remaining men to run as he lifts his weapon and attempts to hold the enemy off a bit longer. He pops off several shots before another blast of incoming rounds catches him and he drops his weapon, succumbing to his wounds.

Looking back, the remaining Nigerien soldier and LaDavid know there is nothing they can do. They continue sprinting uphill. There is another flash from the vehicle speeding toward them, and the Nigerien soldier falls to the ground behind LaDavid. Fear and determination grip LaDavid; he is now alone, but close to the tree. Gasping for breath, he aims for the thorny tree weighed down under his hot military fatigues and body armor. He is nearly there and puts the last of his energy into his sprint, then dives, his lungs bursting. LaDavid rolls under the cover of the tree's canopy. He is safe for now, but foreboding sets in; it is only a matter of seconds until the enemy arrives.

LaDavid lies on his stomach with the stock of his weapon against his shoulder and takes aim at the militants he spots approaching. Their weapons are out, but they can't yet see him. He shoots one man, who falls, and then LaDavid moves, aims, and shoots another. Again, LaDavid moves, aims, and shoots, then moves again. Systematically, LaDavid picks off the enemy until he begins to run out of ammunition, and they surround the tree. He continues to spray bullets, killing several of his enemy before he is hit with the first bullet. Running on adrenaline, LaDavid ignores the searing pain and sends out another burst of rounds. He hears a vehicle arrive, crawls toward the edge of the tree's canopy,

LaDavid on a mission in Maradi, Niger, with Team
3212. *(Casey Wilbur)*

aims his weapon toward the truck's driver, pulls the trigger, and spends
his last round. A thunderous sound erupts as a muzzle flash sends fiery
rounds blasting into the thorny tree. Alone on the edge of the Sahara
desert, twenty-five-year-old LaDavid Johnson sinks to the earth, rolling
onto his back as he releases his last breath.

LaDavid's effort to spend his last moments fighting allows the team a
chance at escape. At Truck #1, the men understand the terrible situation
they are in, but two trucks are now missing, and their captain is nowhere to be seen.

Lying on the dusty red desert ground, Captain Perozeni comes to. He peels his eyes open to the bright, hot sun as he lies alone under a hail of gunfire. Stray bullets are kicking up the dirt next to him. Stunned by the fall, he looks around to see all of his gear strewn about. He sees his armor lying next to him. His pistol, still in its holster, has broken off from his belt, so he grabs it and the armor. Confused, but knowing he's in danger, Captain Perozeni tries to stand and run. As he picks himself up, he takes two steps, then falls flat on his face as a bullet flies over his head. He tries to run again, but once again stumbles and falls to the ground.

The captain realizes his legs and arms can't move together, and he has to leave his pistol and heavy armor behind. He slowly staggers up, moving awkwardly across an open section of desert. His back radiates with pain. He heads toward a single tree while a barrage of gunshots chases him, bullets flying right past. He stumbles again and lands on his hands and knees near the tree. He has no armor or weapon anymore, and he tries to sort out his thoughts and get some sense of where he is, but everything is fuzzy. Captain Perozeni watches bullets kick up the dirt all around him and take out chunks of the tree as his ears ring and his head pounds. He wonders: *How do I get out of here?*

Driving Truck #1, Brent urgently scans ahead—and notices a man on his hands and knees near a tree next to the road. As he pulls closer, he realizes he has found his captain. Brent sees a bullet wound in Captain Perozeni's back and begins yelling at him to get in the truck. Having sustained a traumatic brain injury, Captain Perozeni is confused. He looks at Brent, but can only talk about losing his gear, seemingly unaware of how much danger he is in.

"Mike, get in the truck!"

Captain Perozeni looks at the white truck, but his legs won't move. He tries to stand, but his body doesn't work.

"Mike! Get in the truck!"

"I lost my stuff," the captain mumbles dejectedly.

"Mike! Get in the fucking truck now!" Brent screams, and with rounds coming in all around them, hitting the truck and the dirt, Captain Perozeni finally manages to pull himself up. He grabs on to the side of the truck as it begins to move while bullets shoot at his back. Miraculously, the captain makes it onto the truck without sustaining any further wounds. Brent spins the truck around to head back in the direction he came from.

The truck picks up speed again, when suddenly a man behind the trees aims his AK-47 straight toward Brent. A bullet bursts through the driver's-side window, tearing through Brent's elbow, shattering the bone. Blood spurts. "Motherfucker!" Yelling out in pain and anger, Brent continues to maneuver the vehicle as best he can with only one arm. Bullets are flying all around, rounds ripping through the vehicle, glass shattering and falling. Bullets tear through the vehicle's metal exterior; the noise level is deafening as the men speed closer toward the marsh. Of the six men on the truck, only two are not wounded.

Brent spots Hanson ahead, to the left of the vehicle, on one knee, hiding along the trees. For Ondo and Brooks, seeing Brent madly driving Truck #1 toward them is like seeing the General Lee from *The Dukes of Hazzard* arriving to save the day. Along the ridge, Smith and Hanson are kneeling down and shooting off rounds at the militants, trying to make their way into the wood line and across the marsh toward them. Off to the left are Brooks and Ondo and a hill dotted with trees; on the other side, the hill dips back down into what looks like a washed-out creek that is now just mud.

Brent thinks he can run the truck through the muddy creek to escape out the other side of the woods—but then realizes he will have to get out to lock the hubcaps for the mud. That's too big a risk. Instead, he puts the truck in low gear and tries to ram his way through the creek bed as fast as he can. As the truck hits the mud, it instantly begins to sink. Brent throws the transmission into reverse, but it's too late: The truck is stuck and so are they.

"Shit!" Brent says.

"Yeah, man." Chester sighs before reaching for the door.

Ondo and Brooks are crossing the water in the marsh when they hear the truck's gears grinding and watch Brent get stuck in the mud. Miraculously, Brent isn't ejected from the vehicle, despite the speed he was traveling at before coming to an abrupt and violent halt. Captain Perozeni is not so lucky: For the second time that day, he flies from the vehicle and crashes to the hard ground.

Brent grabs the radio and calls "broken arrow" at 12:33 p.m., then zeroes the radios out, rendering it useless should they fall into enemy hands. The only true definition for "broken arrow" recognized by the military is when referring to an incident involving the loss of or damage to a nuclear weapon. But in the heat of battle, Brent shouts the phrase because he remembers it from a Hollywood movie where the term was used to reference a team that had been overrun and were calling for direct fire on themselves, sacrificing themselves in order to destroy the enemy forces. But Brent's point is clear: The team has been overrun.

After the call, Brent and Chester jump from the truck and run around back to grab their gear. Inza and another Nigerien jump from the back of the truck as the incoming fire intensifies. Brent reaches into the back of the truck and grabs the hand of a third Nigerien soldier to help pull him out when a round comes in, striking the man in the chest. Brent yells out in frustration as the Nigerien falls back into the truck, dead, and the men shout that it's time to go. They don't have time to grab the Nigerien soldier's body to take with them.

Ondo is up on the ridge, emptying magazine after magazine into the oncoming horde of militants, trying to suppress them as they approach. Hanson races past the buried truck when he sees an arm pop up from the back, waving him down. An injured Nigerien soldier is lying next to the dead Nigerien who was shot just moments earlier. Hanson pulls the injured Nigerien from the truck and helps him move up the hill toward the rest of the team. As Hanson helps the wounded Nigerien, Brent grabs his communications bag from the back of the truck but can't un-clip it with his one good arm, so he's forced to grab his gun and leave behind all hope of communicating with the outside world.

With no satellite phone and no cell service, the men know for the first time that they are one hundred percent alone. They have never felt so abandoned in their lives. Incoming rounds are picking up, and it feels like they're being shot at from every direction. All they can hope for now is to go out fighting. Maybe they can put a few more enemies down first.

Ondo, Inza, Brooks, and Hanson—dragging the injured Nigerien man—provide cover fire as Captain Perozeni, Brent, Smith, and Ches-ter retreat into the woods, seeking a more advantageous position. The two Nigeriens who gave Ondo and Brooks directions to find Truck #2 are now running with the team as well. As they jog through the woods, Ondo sees a significant amount of blood pouring from Brent's arm. Blood spills over the ground and splashes on Ondo's pants and boots as Brent comes up next to him. They need to put a tourniquet on his arm to stop the bleeding right away. Brent's already lost a significant amount of blood; if he loses more, he could pass out or go into shock.

Still moving, Ondo pulls a tourniquet off of his kit, wraps it around Brent's arm, and tightens it down as Brent tries not to yell out in agony. Brent grits his teeth as Ondo tightens the tourniquet until the bleeding stops. Ondo puts an extra half-twist in the tourniquet to lock it. He then grabs Chester, the JIDO analyst, telling him to keep heading to the west end of the forested area, and instructs him to keep an eye on Captain Perozeni and Brent. He's got to make sure they stay quiet and remain with the group as they move through the woods.

Ondo turns back to see Hanson dragging the injured Nigerien, who seems to be trying to pull away from him. Ondo also sees Inza and Brooks covering each other, using an Australian peel maneuver—a tac-tic designed to allow a smaller force to escape a larger one—as they slowly retreat into the woods. Ondo joins them, and as his turn comes to provide cover fire while the men in front peel back, Ondo sees Hanson and the injured Nigerien fall. Hanson gets up and slowly moves toward Ondo, but the Nigerien is wounded and drags himself along the ground in the opposite direction of the team as he attempts to get away from the Americans. Suddenly, four militants appear over the ridge, shooting at Ondo and Brooks. Ondo and Brooks return fire, stopping the enemy's movement forward. Hanson is uninjured, but the Nigerien has been shot in the leg, destroying his Achilles tendon. "Leave him!" the men yell at Hanson as they continue their retreat. Hanson refuses to leave the injured man, even though he is trying to crawl away. Hanson knows the man will die if left, so he runs after the Nigerien, grabbing and dragging him along, until they catch up with their remaining team members.

The men are terribly thirsty, but they ran out of water more than an hour ago, and as they jog deeper into the woods they hear the whistling sound of an incoming mortar round followed by a large boom. The rounds begin to fall to their left and right as the enemy uses a technique known as "walking on your target," where mortars are thrown far, then near, far, then near, until a direct hit is made. The impact of the rounds reverberates through their bodies as flashes of fire split trees apart on one side and then on the other, followed by billows of smoke. The men sprint through the trembling forest, dragging the wounded with them while at least five mortar rounds come at them.

All of the men emerge with no further injuries. The more ground they gain, the more the rate of incoming fire slows. The enemy is having trouble seeing them as they get deeper into the forest. The team continues toward the edge of the forest to take stock of how much ammo is left. Not much, they learn—just a hundred rounds total among all the remaining men. They still have their handheld radios, but the satellite antenna was attached to the truck, so until an aircraft arrives they have no way to communicate with the outside world. Before abandoning the truck, they were notified that an unarmed Predator aircraft was on its way, but it was at least forty-five minutes out when the truck got stuck in the mud. Every man on ODA 3212 is certain they don't have that long.

The men move out as far as they can to the edge of the wood line. They are down to five Nigeriens, six U.S. soldiers, and Chester the JIDO analyst. Once they reach the other side of the woods as far away as they can get from the militants searching for them, they stop. There is nowhere left to go. Flat, wide-open space extends as far as the eye can see—except for the village of Tongo Tongo, which is to their right, and they know they can't go back there. The team believes the elders in the village set them up for the militants. It was a trap.

Captain Perozeni, who normally would be directing the men, is incapacitated by his injury. He recognizes Smith is also struggling, so he turns to Brooks, Hanson, and Ondo, the most junior men on the team, and says: "It's up to you three now. You need to come up with a plan of what we need to do."

Their only choice is to arrange themselves in a defensive position and prepare to kill as many of the enemy as possible once they are discovered. With only so much ammunition in hand, the men know that once they are found they won't have enough to kill all of the enemy—some men save one bullet for themselves, to prevent being captured.

This is their Alamo. The place where they will make their final stand. They look at one another knowingly. They will fight to the end, and—knowing that—a feeling settles over the team that even though the other four team members are not with them physically, they are present, standing with their hands on the men's shoulders, telling them it will be okay, no matter what happens.

18

Hunted

The men decide their best option is to flatten themselves down in some tall grass at the edge of the woods. This cover offers them the best tactical position possible. If discovered, they're confident they will be able to do significant damage to the enemy before being overrun.

Hiding in a small depression of sand and shrubbery, they can see in every direction while remaining well hidden. Motorcycles and vehicles echo all around them, getting closer by the minute as the men hastily set up a perimeter and turn off some of their radios to conserve batteries and to keep any squelch to a minimum.

As Ondo, Brooks, and Hanson set up security, Captain Perozeni pulls Hanson aside. Hanson is the newest member of the team, but the only Ranger-qualified member still in the fight. The captain and Hanson went through the Special Forces Qualification Course together before being recruited onto the same Special Forces A-Team. They've known each other well for several years. His eyes wide and intense, Captain Perozeni looks steadily at Hanson and whispers, "You've got to do this. You can do this." A moment of fear washes over Hanson as he realizes that his friend is not acting like himself. He didn't see the captain fall from the truck, but it dawns on him that the captain, unable to perform his duties, is handing them over. A man he considers a warrior and has always looked up to is entrusting the fate of the team to him.

The two men stare at each other in understanding as the weight of the lives entrusted to Captain Perozeni shifts to Hanson. Hanson nods. With the enemy moving in, they are running out of time, so the two friends hug each other, possibly for the last time.

"I love you, man," says Hanson. "You're a phenomenal human being. It's been a pleasure."

"I love you, too," says Captain Perozeni. "I'll see you on the other side of this, brother."

Hanson walks to his position as Captain Perozeni slumps to the ground. They get in position to make their final stand.

The men lie in a large circle. Ondo points his gun in the direction of the swamp where they buried the truck. Next to him, the injured men lie together in an area called a casualty collection point. They give their ammo to those still able to shoot accurately, but each of them keeps a pistol ready. Some of them begin to write and store messages to their families on their cell phones. Brent hands over his phone to Captain Perozeni so he can do the same as everyone settles in silence to await the enemy.

The injured men know that despite the amount of pain they are in, they cannot make a sound. When one of them starts to move to relieve his pain, Captain Perozeni reminds them with a finger to his lips. They are in the most important game of hide-and-seek of their lives, and no matter how badly they want to groan or move, they simply cannot. One sound will cost them the element of surprise—and probably their lives.

To Ondo's left lies Hanson, with his weapon pointing into the woods behind Ondo's feet. On the other side of Hanson, Brooks lies pointing his weapon to the north, in the direction of Tongo Tongo. Lying near Brooks are Smith and Chester. To the right of Brooks, the five remaining Nigeriens lie in silence.

The seventeen-year-old Nigerien soldier named Inza is now acting as the team's interpreter. Inza is the only Nigerien there whom the team is certain is loyal to them. Speaking French and Hausa, he is able to communicate with the team and has stayed beside them throughout the ambush, fighting fiercely, not once attempting to run. They are certain he will not give up their position to the enemy in exchange for his own escape, but they are not sure of the other four Nigeriens, all of whom already tried to flee the battle a few times. The team has Inza sit with them to keep them quiet, too. The men hunker down and prepare for their final battle: They know Inza will fight to the end alongside them. He has fought bravely that day, earning his spot on the team as one of their own.

The team waits in silence as the motorcycles circle, and they can hear deliberate footsteps of men walking through the brush as the militants search for the Americans. At first the sound of the enemy talking is far away, but soon the voices draw nearer as they close in on the men lying in the grass.

With his elbow shattered and white-hot pain shooting through his arm, Brent wrestles with himself to stay quiet. He waits for the tourniquet to make his arm go numb, but it doesn't—and Bryan, the team's medic, who kept all the pain meds on his person, is lying dead somewhere in the desert. The tourniquet is causing Brent an excruciating amount of pain, and Captain Perozeni realizes it is becoming impossible for him to keep quiet. Captain Perozeni grabs a medical kit and packs Brent's wound with gauze, then slowly releases the tourniquet, making sure the bleeding completely stops. The removal of the tourniquet brings Brent almost instant relief, and he settles back into his hiding spot silently.

Satisfied that Brent is okay for the moment, Captain Perozeni pulls out his phone to send another desperate text to Casey back at the AOB: *"We are fucked. We need help now or we aren't going to make it!"* The captain waits for confirmation, but the message fails to send. Frustrated, he puts the phone away. There is no one to help them now.

Messages Captain Perozeni attempted to send to
Casey at the AOB while lying in cover at the
Alamo spot.

Ondo, Brooks, and Hanson are lying down in the grass a few feet
from one another. Using hand signals, they convey to one another how
many men they see from their positions and what direction the enemy
is heading. The terrorists can be heard moving closer to the team—then
farther away, and then closer again. The men are exhausted and desperately thirsty, they haven't slept in two days, and now they have had to
stay still and silent for nearly forty minutes. As the adrenaline from the
battle ebbs away, they fight to stay completely alert.

Near the casualty collection point, the wounded are struggling as the loss of blood further dehydrates them. Hoping against hope, Captain Perozeni pulls out his phone to try contacting Casey again. *"We need help man. Brent is in a bad way."* Again, the message fails to go through. The hopelessness of the situation sinks in as the captain puts the phone away.

"Hey! Hey, Mike," Brent whispers to him. "Hey, Mike, take a selfie." Brent is in and out of consciousness, his head resting on one arm, and he has a vacant and exhausted look on his face.

"Okay, man." Captain Perozeni laughs darkly as he flips the screen around for a group selfie and shoots a photo. They hear someone walking close by and duck just as the photo takes.

Ondo and Hanson are pulling security on the ground near each

At the Alamo spot lying in the brush as the terrorists approach. *(Captain Perozeni)*

other when Hanson gives Ondo a hand signal to say there are three men walking toward him. They are moving in a wedge directly toward what is left of ODA 3212. The men lie there in a cold sweat, shaking from head to toe with a mixture of shock and fear, adrenaline coursing through their bodies. For nearly an hour they have lain in the woods, awaiting their executioners' arrival. Now the moment is upon them.

Ondo and Hanson watch as the militants approach, as close as twenty-five feet from where Hanson remains in the grass, hiding, ready to shoot. Tracking three men with AK-47s who are wearing chest rigs to hold their extra ammunition, Hanson flips his safety selector off. When Ondo sees Hanson adjust his position a bit and move his finger over the trigger, he holds his hand up toward him, motioning for him to wait. Ondo turns to look ahead of him as he stares at the brush moving about twenty feet straight in front of his position, only fifteen feet or so to the left of where Hanson lies in the dirt.

A man appears and creeps straight toward Ondo, moving slowly, gun by his side. Two other men walk on either side of him. There are now three men approaching Ondo and three men approaching Hanson. Ondo takes his gun off safety now, too, and puts the front man into his sights. He pulls the slack from the trigger as he holds his hand over the sight so that no sunlight creates a glare by bouncing off the glass, giving up his position. Ondo then places a red dot directly in the center of the man's forehead as he begins to count his steps, swearing after each one that he is going to shoot.

One deep breath, one step—one more and he'll shoot. Another breath, another step—*just one more,* and he'll have to shoot. *Just one more and—* He inhales deeper in preparation to fire.

Suddenly, the man stops and looks directly at Ondo. Not moving, he stares coldly.

He *sees* Ondo.

The men approaching Hanson now halt as well. Ondo and Hanson both freeze, waiting for the men to raise their guns. That will be the signal to start shooting. They know they can easily kill these six men, but they also know that shooting them will instantly give up their position. They can hear the motorcycles close by, circling and circling, looking for them still. From their position they can see militants walking up and down the nearby ravines and hills, looking for them. Once they shoot, they will be surrounded and killed. All of them.

But no guns are raised.

Time seems to stop, almost moving backward for a minute. The man closest to Ondo begins to smile, cruel and threatening, as he looks Ondo directly in the eyes, holding his gaze. After a long moment, he breaks eye contact. Slowly turning to the right, he walks out of sight with the other two men following. The men near Hanson turn at the same time, but to the left, and walk away in that direction. Ondo's and Hanson's heart rates spike as the reality of what has transpired begins to sink in. Lying in silence, their heartbeats pound in their ears.

The entire team lies still for several agonizing minutes, waiting for the men to return with more fighters, but they never do. To this day Ondo and Hanson have no explanation why, but the men simply disappear and never return. As the men continue to lie quietly in the grass, they hear raucous shouting coming from the direction of the village of Tongo Tongo. Guns are being shot in the air as chants of "Allahu Akbar!" reverberate over and over.

Hearing the chants and the gunfire do nothing to calm the men's nerves. The militants know the team is hiding in the small wooded area with nowhere to run. Maybe the gunfire and chanting is a trick to get the team to come out of hiding. Surely it is only a matter of time before the enemy comes back looking for them. The men remain there, sweating, in pain, dying for a drink of water. It has been hours since the meeting in Tongo Tongo.

Out of nowhere, a deep rumbling fills the air around them. The men listen intently, their hearts pounding as they try to figure out what they are hearing, fearing it is some new onslaught from the enemy. Suddenly the trees around them bend toward the forest floor and a French Mirage jet appears, flying a hundred feet overhead and followed by another. The jets are so low the men can see the numbers on the bottom. As the jets pull back up into the sky, they let off a string of flares, and the smoke forms a pattern that looks like little angel wings.

The men feel an overpowering sense of relief. They are no longer alone; people are out there to help them, which means more will be coming. Hope is rekindled in an instant. Those jets mean they may see their wives and children again, hug their fathers and mothers, delete those hurried and anguished texts, bury those last bullets. They are almost free. The sound of those jets stir something deeper than mere words can describe.

It has been nearly fifty minutes since they left their last vehicle buried in mud and ran into the woods. Fifty of the longest, most fearful minutes of their lives. As they lay there for nearly an hour, being hunted by the enemy, they ponder what happened to Dustin, Jeremiah, LaDavid, and Bryan. They pray they might still be alive but fear the worst: that they've been taken hostage. Everyone knows that for an American soldier, to be captured by ISIS is a fate far worse than death.

And now, for them, maybe death can be avoided. Except the Mirage jets are unable to pinpoint the exact location of the team members, preventing them from dropping any bombs or shooting any weapons. They also can't pick the men up who are on the ground because the fast-moving jets require long runways to land.

Indeed, the French jets are there as a show of force to scare away the attackers; it works, and in this crucial moment it is enough. From the air, the French pilots see men running from the woods and escaping into the desert on motorcycles and trucks. They know this means the men are enemy combatants.

The team waits to be rescued, which takes another four hours. In that time they tend to the wounded, trying to make them as comfortable as they can. The team is on the edge of a wooded area just south of Tongo Tongo, and their position sits right near a footpath that runs out of the village. This path is heavily trafficked, and the men are able to observe people walking by. The people walking along the path are not necessarily fighters, and the team sees both adults and children moving past. The Nigerien villagers walking past are unaware of the men lying in their covered positions.

The men quietly relay messages, attempting to reach the Mirage jet pilots. An unarmed drone flies above them now, so the men can communicate with it using their radios. The drone communication is being sent to South Dakota, where the American drone operator is stationed. The team's communication, vital in the moment, has to run a global maze.

The drone operator in South Dakota calls the AOB in Niamey, the AOB blasts the messages out over mIRC chat, which is similar to a chat room. The mIRC messages are received by the French forces stationed in Burkina Faso, where the French Mirage jets are based. Then those at that base interpret from English into French the messages to radio the pilots of the Mirage jets.

Messages are being relayed in a similar fashion across the globe and back to the team on the ground from the pilots in the jets above them. The team on the ground is also receiving communications in a similar fashion from the U.S. Special Forces officers at the AOB in Niamey. There is so much chat going through the drone operator in South Dakota that no critical information seems to get from the team to the AOB in Niamey, but a multitude of questions are relayed to the men on the ground. They are becoming frustrated answering for the tenth time how many soldiers are missing in action, then an eleventh time and a twelfth. The hours drag by as they are asked over and over what their coordinates are and if they have been picked up. Meanwhile, Brent is slowly dying in the African marsh.

After some time, a few militants reappear, seeming to look for the team. They are no longer armed, which makes them less of a threat, but the team members are certain these men were a part of the group who attacked them. The militants can't be sure if the aircraft overhead are armed, so they could be hiding their weapons in an attempt to feign innocence. The men do their best to remain still and silent in their concealed position, understanding that they must avoid being discovered until reinforcements are on the ground.

Every time a team does a mission like the one the men are on, the military is supposed to have what is called a QRF—a quick reaction force—able to respond quickly to assist the team in a bad situation. There should also be a plan in place for PR (personnel recovery), whose purpose it is to help soldiers out of an area if they are stranded, and CASEVAC (casualty evacuation) if injured soldiers must be evacuated. In Niger, the PR and CASEVAC time is accepted at four to six hours—which is not at all helpful when men are dying. What happens when a long reaction time and faulty communication with the QRF, PR, and CASEVAC becomes an issue? What happens when they are searching for a team's location to perform a rescue or drop bombs on the enemy without hitting the team? Years after the ambush, AFRICOM still won't have an answer to these questions.

The team tries multiple times to give coordinates to the Mirage jets to drop bombs and to get the team's correct location to the helicopters that are supposed to be coming in to pick them up. One helicopter is sent out of Niamey to rescue the team and instead picks up a group of Nigerien soldiers they found in the desert—the very men who deserted the team early on in the fight. Word is sent back to the AOB that the team has been picked up even as the team is still lying in the woods outside of Tongo Tongo, anxiously waiting for help. When the helicopter arrives at the air base in Niamey, a frustrated Casey watches as several Nigeriens looking perfectly healthy pile out of the aircraft—but no Americans.

And while those Nigeriens walk out of the aircraft in Niamey, back near Tongo Tongo Captain Perozeni lies in the dirt with his head pounding and a gunshot wound in the back, Brent loses more blood as his heart rate drops to nearly forty beats per minute, and one of the Nigerien soldiers has a gunshot wound through his Achilles tendon and is unable to move. Yet none of this information is successfully communicated between the AOB in Niamey and South Dakota.

Then the Mirage jets circling above them run out of fuel and have to head back to their base in Burkina Faso.

Alone again, the team receives a communication relayed by the drone operator from the AOB in Niamey asking for confirmation that they are the ones who have been picked up by the helicopter. Frustrated and angry at being abandoned, the team again radios back to the operator to relay to Niamey that they are still on the ground and they need a medical evacuation as soon as possible. They have a casualty who is dying.

In an effort to keep Brent conscious, the men continually push on his collarbone, a painful pressure point, to keep him awake. Using this method, the men avoid shaking him, which may negatively impact his wound, but over time it stops working. Watching Brent fade as they wait for rescue fills them with a helpless and sickening feeling.

Suddenly the men hear the sound of distant helicopter blades chopping through the afternoon sky. The sound grows louder as the French show up in force. The French have sent attack helicopters from Gao in Mali and from Ouagadougou in Burkina Faso to Niamey to stage, then flown two choppers to where the men are lying in the woods. As opposed to the jets, these helicopters will be able to land and assist the team.

Even now, though, communication is a disaster. The soldiers on the ground can't talk directly to the aircraft because everything is still being relayed from the men on the ground to the drone operator in South Dakota to the AOB, then through mIRC chat. The helicopter pilots' commands in Gao and Ouagadougou then send the messages to the pilots. But with the delay the messages are confused, which makes it nearly impossible for those flying the aircraft to identify them. Hours go by while the men attempt to communicate their coordinates to the helicopters. The helicopters are hesitant to land for fear they will come under attack by the same enemy that attacked the team earlier, so they won't land until they are certain of the team's exact location.

Finally, Brooks remembers he has an American flag stuffed between the plates of his body armor. He pulls the stars-and-stripes flag out, and with Ondo carrying an M4 to provide cover fire if necessary, Brooks walks into the open holding the flag high over his head and begins waving it. To the team's relief, the French helicopters spot the flag and the information is relayed back to the team that they need to walk out into the open to meet the helicopters before the helicopters will land. Still seeing multiple men milling around, the team does not like the idea of leaving their protected position inside the forest for an area with no cover, but they are given no choice. The helicopters don't like the idea of landing in the wrong place and being ambushed by the same group that just attacked the American team.

The men nervously leave their defensive position in the woods to walk onto the completely exposed western side of the wooded marsh. Slowly, they move in a V shape, helping the injured walk while keeping their weapons drawn. They begin making their way into the wide-open desert to stand where Brooks waits, waving the large American flag. The helicopters are finally coming to land and pick them up.

They lay the injured men down onto the dirt, kicking the desert sand into a pile to prop up Brent's head and leg, hoping to promote circulation. Brent begins to black out, so Ondo bends over and tries to shake him awake. "Brent! You gotta stay awake!" he shouts. Brent doesn't hear him, so Ondo tries pushing on Brent's collarbone, then his good arm, and finally his injured arm, but nothing works. Determined, Ondo swings his arm back with his palm wide open and slaps Brent hard in the face, yelling at him to wake up. Brent's eyes flutter open. He is dazed, but to Ondo's relief he's awake.

Kneeling next to Brent, Ondo sees something moving out of the corner of his eye. There are two females—the first he has seen since they arrived in Tongo Tongo hours ago—walking on a nearby path. One is wearing a pink dress and both wear the full Muslim head garb. Though he cannot see her eyes, Ondo feels the female in the pink is staring at him. For a moment he stares back, then she raises her hand up almost as though she is waving at him. Ondo is mystified as to why she would be waving at him. Suddenly certain that she *wasn't*, he crouches down low and turns around. The village elder of Tongo Tongo is standing only thirty yards away, close enough for Ondo to recognize his face.

Ondo is filled with dread. This cannot be good. He grabs his gun and begins to stand. As he rises, two vehicles mounted with 12.7-millimeter heavy machine guns appear from the north heading toward them, the same type of vehicles that attacked them earlier. The men radio up to the unarmed drone, requesting information on the incoming vehicles. The drone hasn't seen the incoming vehicles and now scrambles to identify if they are friendly.

Without warning, the village elder points at the team, and the vehicle-mounted machine guns open up, firing on them. The sounds of battle ring out once again as bullets kick up dirt and tear at the ground all around the battered team. Round after round comes flying toward the men. Ondo and Hanson open fire on the gunners and burn the thirty rounds they have left in their weapons before dropping to the dirt beside their teammates, clinging to a few small tufts of grass for cover. Captain Perozeni is still standing, dazed, bullets blazing past him. As he runs for cover, the men on the ground yell at him. They watch as a round zips right at his head. He goes down and they are sure he's been hit again.

Using their radios, they shout up to the drone to have the helicopters engage the trucks to the north, but there is no response. For nearly a full minute, the trucks unload everything they have on the men lying in the dirt. Once again, the men and the few remaining Nigerien soldiers expect death as they try to flatten their bodies as best they can. They have no more ammunition and are relying solely on the poor aim of the gunners and the grace of God.

Inza, the Nigerien soldier who won the Americans' respect, starts shaking from head to toe. He looks at Brent and Ondo, saying the word *friend* in French over and over, then his eyes go wide as he suddenly jumps to his feet. He begins screaming *"Amis! Des amis!"* and waving his arms around wildly.

The desert goes silent, the shooting stops. Shocked, the men peer around before checking one another for wounds. Soon it becomes clear what happened: The technical vehicles, which were sent to rescue the team, nearly killed them all with friendly fire. It's a miracle that no one was hit by the gunfire. Inza just saved everyone's lives. In the eyes of the men on ODA 3212, Inza just earned his American citizenship. He showed himself to be their only true ally, willing to give his life for theirs.

In the aftermath, a strange feeling overcomes them as they realize that in this moment their ordeal is finally ending. After the vehicles cease firing, the bedraggled men of ODA 3212 cautiously approach the trucks. With pistols drawn, they warily make their way toward the vehicles that just unleashed a fierce attack on them—hoping for salvation, but prepared for anything.

Upon reaching the Nigerien partner-force vehicles, the men realize the trucks were sent from their base in Ouallam by Lieutenant Boubacar's boss as a QRF when he heard they were going to the border alone. Unfortunately, the trucks were many hours behind the team, so their reaction was not quick enough.

As the men approach the Nigerien vehicles they see some oily water jugs hanging from the trucks. The water inside them is filthy, filled with sand, debris, and who knows what else, but in that moment it doesn't matter. The men are desperate for a drink. They huddle together in a circle and share one dirty cup as they fill glass after glass with water and drink deeply. It is the dirtiest water they've had in their lives, and the best.

While drinking greedily, the men remain on high alert, keeping an eye on the village elder who is standing nearby watching them. The

French aircraft finally come down, landing close by and dropping a number of French soldiers into the area before taking off again. Another French aircraft lands to take the injured soldiers on board. Having satisfied their thirst, the Americans shift their focus toward the French helicopter, glad to finally have some backup and partners to coordinate with.

The men who are not injured are desperate to be replenished with ammo and water and then to go back to the kill zone to search for Jeremiah, LaDavid, Dustin, and Bryan. But the team is told they are not being given extra water or ammunition. The French were instructed by their command only to pick up the injured soldiers and then to leave. The entire team, including the injured, begin to protest. Brent and Captain Perozeni refuse to get on the aircraft. They demand that if the French don't share ammunition or water then they better take all the soldiers or none. To leave them in the desert in enemy territory with no ammunition, water, or vehicles is a death sentence. Just as they fought together, they would die together.

An order from the French pilots' command comes over the helicopters' radio, directing the French to take everyone, so the second French helicopter returns for the entire team as the injured are loaded onto the first. Even as everyone begins to load up, Hanson, Ondo, and Brooks refuse to board the aircraft, trying to convince anyone and everyone to turn over any extra ammunition and water so they can go back for the four missing men, but no one will do that.

With no ammunition or water, Smith recognizes that staying is not an option. "I want everyone on the aircraft," Smith says.

Silence falls over the men and they stare hard at Smith.

After an uncomfortable minute, he speaks again. "That is an order. Everyone get on the aircraft!"

At last Hanson shrugs and slowly steps toward the helicopter.

The other men give in and they all file onto the second aircraft, first Smith, then Chester, then Inza. As Inza steps toward the helicopter

Brent Bartels prepped to be loaded onto a rescue helicopter. (*Hanson*)

door, one of the French soldiers shouts, "No, no, no! Not him!" Ondo turns to the soldier, yelling at him that Inza is coming, but the Frenchman stands his ground. Ondo's eyes widen and then narrow with fury as he stares the Frenchman straight in the eye and grabs for his holster, shouting, "He's coming with us!" At this, the French soldier relents. Inza steps onto the aircraft as Hanson gives him a little push, and then Hanson, Ondo, and Brooks follow.

As the helicopter lifts off, the men collapse. Unable to believe they survived, they wonder how long it will take them to replenish their ammunition and water so they can get back out to find their friends.

19

Sorrow

Casey waited impatiently at the AOB in Niamey, hearing nothing from his friends and former teammates after Brent had called in "broken arrow." Once the radios were zeroed out, the AOB command could no longer contact the team.

These men were Casey's teammates and some of his closest friends. A formidable man, standing 6'4" with a muscular build, Casey was no stranger to war. He had been in combat several times and had been part of ODA 3212 as a team member for many years until he stepped back into a support role for this 2017 deployment. He felt helpless not knowing what was happening to the team members and wished he was out there with them. For now, he committed himself to the task at hand, coordinating assets and trying to make contact with those on the ground.

Casey knew through the French pilots and the drone information relayed to them at the AOB that by 4:30 p.m. Zulu time (5:30 local time in Tongo Tongo), all these assets were flying in to where the team was by Tongo Tongo in order to bring them back. Casey walked quickly down to the flight line to await the arrival of the team.

Casey was sitting on the flight line, anxiously waiting, when a civilian helicopter landed. He stared as one Nigerien soldier got off, walking with an IV bag attached and no injuries other than dehydration. This man, who had been "saved," was perfectly fine. Casey still had no idea where his friends were. He felt he was about to lose his mind as he escorted the Nigerien up to the hospital. There, at the hospital triage, Casey found the team had already arrived. The French helicopters they were on had landed far on the other side of the base while he was helping unload the Nigerien from the civilian helicopter. Casey went straight in to see the team as they were tended to—but finding his friends in their current state tore him up inside.

Casey headed over to see Captain Perozeni first, but the captain was busy being attended to by a nurse, so Casey moved on to Brent. Casey had brought Brent to the team, and now Brent was laid out before him looking like he was at death's door. It was crushing for Casey to see Brent so weak.

Casey sat down with Brent for a while before moving on to the other men on the team. Even those without serious physical injuries were not doing well. They were emotionally troubled and desperately wanted to go back out. Their friends and teammates, they said, were still out there. Hanson, Brooks, and Ondo insisted that all they needed was more ammo and some water, and they would head back into the field.

At the same time, Team Arlit left the airfield in Niamey with nine of their Nigerien counterparts. They were ready to search for the four Americans still on the ground in Tongo Tongo; they were at that time known only as missing in action (MIA). It was not long after Team Arlit arrived in Tongo Tongo before the call came into the AOB that they had three known American casualties and one American still missing. Team Arlit found that the enemy had pulled a vehicle up alongside the bodies and had begun loading them into the bed of the truck. If the French jets had not arrived on the scene when they did, the remains of those

soldiers, including my husband's, would have disappeared into the Sahara. This would have left the families with nothing to bury and the fear
that our loved ones had been captured alive.

Once Team Arlit had the bodies of the missing, the Nigeriens responded. They had helicopters loaded with 50-caliber machine guns
ready to fly into Tongo Tongo and search for the remaining missing
American. The French decided that they were going to fly to Tongo Tongo
as well. Just before dark, a helicopter brought the bodies of Bryan, Dustin,
Jeremiah, and one of the Nigerien soldiers back to the base in Niamey.

Casey was still talking with the injured men when the official battle
roster came in with three of his friends confirmed as killed in action
(KIA) and one confirmed as missing. He felt sick as the finality of the
situation hit hard. Casey stood and headed down to the airfield along
with Sergeant Major Kingman to await the arrival of the fallen, stopping
only momentarily to grab a flag from his gear and shove it into his
pocket.

Not only were Casey and the sergeant major there, everyone not ac-
tively engaged with operations was, too. Every man on the team who
had been rescued from the ambush went down to the landing pad, each
unwilling to miss the arrival of their fallen teammates. It was around
7:00 p.m. Zulu time when Casey heard the helicopter approaching; he
gazed out over the horizon and noted the beautiful reds and oranges
splashed across the sky showing off a spectacular sunset. That he was
alive to witness it was something to be grateful for, yet that realization
brought a heaviness to the tragedy playing out all around him.

A blast of hot wind hit his face as the helicopter blades sent the blazing African air swirling around the landing pad. The chopper set down
and the engine and blades slowed to a halt. The sergeant major threw
open the helicopter door. An eerie iridescent green light poured out

onto the landing pad as he reached in to pull the first casualty from the helicopter.

A hush fell over the crowd gathered as the Americans were pulled off first and Casey began to wrap them. In the military, the remains of all casualties after a battle are covered as a sign of respect and honor. It was the job of Casey and the sergeant major to wrap the bodies of the fallen in blankets and flags. It was a job he'd never wanted but wouldn't have allowed anyone else to perform, a job filled with sorrow, one that raised memories of how he had brought Bryan and Dustin to the team. He felt responsible, but he had to push that aside and get the job done.

The first casualty to be wrapped in Niger was Sergeant First Class Jeremiah Johnson, then Staff Sergeant Dustin Wright, and last was Staff Sergeant Bryan Black. The remaining men from the team stood in silence as this was done. The unbearable humidity of the day was waning just a bit, but the sweltering heat was not.

As he wrapped up the bodies, sweat rolled down Casey's back and neck. He tucked the blankets around them and could feel everything, the features of his friends and the injuries they'd sustained. It was gut-wrenching work. Casey stopped for a moment and took in a jagged breath. The body of the man he had brought to the team, the body of his friend, lay before him. Seeing Bryan like this cut him deep, and he was unable to move for a moment. Casey felt the first tear, wet and warm, as it slid down his cheek.

Attempting to regain his composure, Casey asked the sergeant major if he could be given a moment. Casey pulled the flag from his pocket and began to unfold it as tears welled in his eyes. The flag had been a gift from his mother and he had carried it throughout every one of his many deployments and battles. The flag had seen him safely through many bad situations in multiple countries far from home; it meant a great deal to him. He slowly rolled the material between his thumb and forefinger as he said a silent prayer. Casey stepped forward and wrapped his friend's broken body in his beloved flag.

Bryan in black on the left, Casey in white on the right. *(Ondo)*

As Casey turned to walk away, he saw every man—American, Nigerien, French—standing along the walls that enclosed the compound. They all faced the airfield, standing at attention with tears streaming down their cheeks, as they saluted the fallen. Fresh tears sprang to Casey's eyes as he saw their act of respect and the sadness in each soldier's face at the brothers they had lost that day, three Americans, five Nigeriens, and one MIA.

After tending to the bodies of his friends and returning from Mortuary Affairs, Casey continued in his role directing teams out from the base as they searched for LaDavid Johnson, Lieutenant Boubacar, and another Nigerien soldier. Helicopters continued to be sent out throughout the evening and into the night to search for those men still missing.

The search for the missing went on around the clock, Team Arlit working with Nigerien and French teams. The National Mission Force that exists expressly for the purpose of recovering U.S. soldiers flew in almost instantly to participate in the search for the missing, as did many others. There were twenty-one C-17s loaded with teams of men whose only job was to find those missing in action, and they had all flown in within nine hours of the ambush.

All told, there were hundreds of personnel on the ground throughout the next two days, looking for LaDavid. But as Casey noted after returning to the scene with the AFRICOM investigation team, LaDavid was extremely well hidden. "He was smart. He was moving south and he was trying to get to high ground. He was in the best place he could have been to defend himself. When we got to the tree where he made his final stand, there was a huge pile of brass that was outside, like he had edged out a bit to fight, and there was another pile of brass that was right behind the tree as well. He literally died fighting, which all four of them did. And that's all you can ask for."

After LaDavid's body was located, he was wrapped and taken back to the base in Niamey, just as his teammates had been. The young man was removed from the helicopter by Casey and the sergeant major. With his vision blurred again by tears, Casey shook as he draped his friend in an American flag. The entire camp was silent as the multitude of people stood at attention, honoring the fallen hero. The hope the exhausted men and women had held on to the last several days, the hope that had kept them awake and searching, was shattered.

Casey was moved as he saw the nurses at Mortuary Affairs sobbing; they were French and yet they wept for a man who was not their countryman. This loss was felt deeply throughout the camp by those from every country. LaDavid's closest friend and coworker, a noncommissioned officer (NCO) named Chuck, was there to assist. Chuck helped to move LaDavid to Mortuary Affairs and volunteered to identify him.

The wounded men, Brent and Captain Perozeni, were flown to a hospital in Germany, where they would have their injuries tended to. The rest of the men were taken to their base in Ouallam, where they began

LaDavid cutting Casey's hair in Maradi, Niger, during their 2016 deployment. *(Brent Bartels)*

to pack up their belongings, since they were told their deployment was now over. After that, Smith and Hanson headed home, followed a few days later by Brooks and Ondo.

It was there that an ambush of a different kind awaited them.

PART FOUR

Disparities and Dishonor

20

Unjust

That night of October 4, after undergoing a debridement surgery on his elbow, Brent joined Captain Perozeni as they accompanied the bodies of Bryan, Dustin, and Jeremiah on a C-17 to Germany. The bodies were flown to the United States and the two injured men were taken to Landstuhl Regional Medical Center to be treated for their wounds. Brent underwent a second surgery on his elbow to piece the bones back together, and Captain Perozeni was treated for head injuries. The doctors at Landstuhl determined too much damage would be done by removing the bullet lodged in Captain Perozeni's side, so it was left in place.

The men were then transferred to Walter Reed National Military Medical Center outside of Washington, D.C., until the end of October, when they returned to Fort Bragg, North Carolina. Brent would undergo one more surgery later on at Duke University Hospital and months of intensive therapy on his left arm in an attempt to regain as much range of motion as possible.

Captain Perozeni finally had the bullet removed a year after the ambush in the 3212 team room at Fort Bragg. Removing the bullet was used as a training opportunity for the new Special Forces medical sergeant who replaced Bryan on the team. Captain Perozeni lay on a folding table and was cut open for the bullet to be removed from his side while the rest of the team looked on. The bullet now sits on Captain Perozeni's nightstand as a reminder of how close he came to death that fateful day.

In October 2017, Major General Marcus Hicks, the commander of SOCAFRICA, launched a 15-6 investigation (an investigation conducted according to Army Regulation 15-6: Procedures for Investigating Officer and Boards of Officers) into the ambush in Niger. He appointed Special Forces Colonel Mark Bond as the investigating officer, and Colonel Bond put together a team. But General Waldhauser, the commander of AFRICOM, immediately shut down that investigation and launched his own. SOCAFRICA answers to both AFRICOM and SOCOM (Special Operations Command), so they had no option but to comply.

As the investigation got underway, many people at SOCOM became nervous. USSOCOM (U.S. Special Operations Command) is one of eleven combatant commands. SOCOM oversees all of the Special Operations commands, including the Army Special Operations, Navy Special Operations, Air Force Special Operations, and Marine Corps. The generals at SOCOM worried about AFRICOM (another combatant command) investigating and possibly punishing SOCOM's people. SOCOM felt it only right that they would make the final decisions on how to hold their personnel accountable. So an agreement was made in which AFRICOM would conduct the investigation but would not assign blame. Instead, once AFRICOM had finished its investigation and handed its findings over to the secretary of defense, the secretary of defense would then assign various general officers to investigate and take corrective action if necessary.

Military investigations are started for many reasons, but not every death or injury is automatically investigated. If a soldier is injured, dies, or becomes sick as a result of their job, a line-of-duty (LOD) investigation will be carried out. Commanders initiate the investigations, which fall under Army Regulation 15-6. Most 15-6 investigations are informal, as was the case with the ambush in Niger.

Formal investigations name defendants and guarantee them due-process hearings. But informal investigations do not name defendants, so individuals are not entitled to the rights afforded those in a formal investigation, such as legal representation, the right to call and cross-examine witnesses, or the opportunity to participate. However, the investigating officer of an informal investigation may still make findings and recommendations for individuals that adversely affect them.

When General Waldhauser initiated his investigation, he appointed General Cloutier, his chief of staff, as the investigating officer. Informal 15-6 investigations usually have just one investigating officer who conducts the interviews and collects evidence. As the investigating officer, General Cloutier's job was to find all facts relating to the ambush and to impartially consider all the evidence. During informal investigations, the evidence is weighed according to the preponderance-of-evidence standard rather than the more stringent standard that would apply in a more formal investigation. With the preponderance-of-evidence standard, the burden of proof is met when the investigating officer finds that there is a greater than fifty percent chance that a claim is true.

After collecting all the facts, investigating officers issue a report and send it to the commander, who can do one of four things with the findings. The commander can approve them, disapprove them, return them for additional investigation, or substitute the findings and recommendations. In the Niger ambush investigation, General Cloutier handed his report of investigation to General Waldhauser. With AFRICOM running the investigation, it was no surprise when no fault was found on the part of AFRICOM.

Soon after the men from Team 3212 returned to Fort Bragg, they learned that an investigation was underway. During that last week of October 2017, AFRICOM interviewed all of the surviving men of ODA 3212 individually, beginning with Hanson and ending with Captain Perozeni. The interviews were conducted at Fort Bragg at the 3rd Group headquarters. As each man walked into a conference room, they found themselves in the company of General Cloutier, two JAG (military) lawyers, and one or two higher-ranking officials (lieutenant colonel or colonel) who acted as assistants to General Cloutier. A recorder sat on the table as the men were asked to tell their story from beginning to end. The men's stories would be interrupted occasionally while the officers asked questions. The men on the team recall that the atmosphere in the room was casual and their interviews went quickly.

Except for Captain Perozeni's.

Captain Perozeni was the last to be interviewed, since he was recovering at Walter Reed until the end of October. When Captain Perozeni sat down to tell his story, the investigators stopped him over and over again, and the general and the lawyers asked him pointed follow-up questions. It wasn't long before Captain Perozeni became exhausted. He was still battling some of the repercussions of his TBI, and the intensity of the interview wore him out.

During a break that he requested, Captain Perozeni was pulled aside by General Cloutier, who assured him that the interview was not an interrogation. Rather than putting the captain at ease, General Cloutier's reassurance put Captain Perozeni more on edge than ever. The general's use of the word *interrogation* had finally made clear what was happening here. Captain Perozeni still shudders remembering those two excruciating days.

After the interviews with the men of ODA 3212 were completed, the investigative team flew to Germany to conduct interviews with the relevant officers, including Colonel Moses and LTC Painter before going on to Niamey to question the officers and staff at the AOB, where Major Alan Van Saun had returned after his paternity leave. Then the investigative team traveled to Tongo Tongo on November 12, 2017, to start collecting evidence.

In the summer of 2018, from the twenty-three findings of the AFRICOM investigation, five relating to SOCOM personnel were handed to General Thomas, commander of SOCOM, for him to decide what action to take. Some of the findings were as follows:

- Team OUALLAM [3212] was not equipped with a vehicle set that would afford them the operational flexibility to adjust based upon changes to the battlefield.

- The Team Leader [Perozeni] and Team Sergeant [Smith] failed to conduct battle drill and pre-mission rehearsals prior to executing operations on 3–4 October 2017.

- The acting AOB Niger commander [Captain Newburn] failed to coordinate for emergency CASEVAC and personnel recovery support with French and Nigerien partner forces prior to operations.

- The Team OUALLAM Commander [Perozeni], the acting AOB Niger Commander [Captain Newburn], the AOB Niger Operations Warrant Officer [Chief Marshall] and SgtMaj [Kingman] failed to accurately characterize the mission that Team OUALLAM conducted in Tiloa to the SOCCE-LCB Commander [LTC Painter].

- Prior to 4 October 2017, approximately half of Team OUALLAM had never conducted a collective training event [predeployment training] with the team.

The men on the team and the officers, including Major Van Saun, had received briefs by AFRICOM in 2018, just as the families had. Like us, they were waiting for the final report to be released. While the men were aware what the findings were, no one was certain what findings had been approved, since the final report had not been released. While they waited, they worried. In the summer of 2018, Major Van Saun, Captain Perozeni, Sergeant First Class Bartels, and the other members of ODA 3212 were notified that they were going to be interviewed again, their actions reinvestigated. After waiting almost a year to be cleared, they realized their ordeal would continue without end. Fearful of what could happen, some of the men went to JAG, the military equivalent of a law office, to seek legal counsel for the first time. The JAG lawyers told them that since they had already been interviewed, if the details in their narratives differed even a little over the year since the incident, those discrepancies could be used against them. The men feared they could face an Article 92, which is a charge of a violation of orders or regulations under the UCMJ (Uniform Code of Military Justice) or they could be issued a GOMOR (General Officer Memorandum of Reprimand), so many chose to invoke their rights and refused to do a second interview.

A GOMOR is a letter written to a soldier by a general, reprimanding that soldier for bad behavior or actions. While this may not seem significant to people in the civilian world, those in the military recognize that this is a huge obstacle for their future. A GOMOR can become part of a soldier's permanent military file, to be looked at by every person outranking that soldier for the rest of their career. Having a GOMOR permanently in your file means you will never be promoted, and it may prevent you from being able to reenlist when your contract is up.

The only GOMOR that will not permanently ruin a soldier's career is one placed in the soldier's local file. A local GOMOR is temporarily placed in the soldier's file and remains there until the soldier moves to a new base or duty station. Most soldiers move often, so their career is affected for only a short time.

Initially, Captain Perozeni and Major Van Saun were being investigated by SOCOM for dereliction of duty, which is covered by Article 92. The maximum punishment is a bad-conduct discharge from the military, forfeiting all pay and benefits, as well as up to six months in jail. The UCMJ requires a higher standard of proof, which in this instance could not be met.

For Captain Perozeni, who had put in years of training to become an officer, earned his Ranger tab, and completed all training to be an officer and a Green Beret, a GOMOR in his permanent file would be devastating. The same was true for Major Van Saun. They might not receive jail time or lose their benefits, but they would essentially lose their careers.

Alan Van Saun served as a captain in 3rd Special Forces Group from 2009 to 2013, then went to the Naval War College for his Intermediate Level Education (ILE), where he earned a master of arts degree in national defense and security studies. In January 2016, he returned to 3rd Special Forces Group as a major serving as the battalion executive officer for a year and a half. In June 2017, Major Van Saun took command of Alpha Company before their deployment to Niger in August.

The new investigation by SOCOM focused on assigning blame for a lack of pre-deployment training. Before deployment, a soldier must complete such training to be considered ready to carry out their duties. Training is supposed to cover the subjects that relate to a team's missions. A good pre-deployment training exercise, for example, would involve working with fake partner forces and conducting exercises in a tactical environment. The team and partner forces would practice long movements through rough terrain in trucks mounted with guns and maybe working alongside helicopters. But that is not the pre-deployment training Team 3212 was given in preparation for their 2017 deployment to Niger.

In 2016, Lieutenant General Kenneth Tovo, Commander of USASOC, mandated that 3rd Group's 2nd Battalion (which included Team 3212) conduct what is known as the Jade Helm exercise before the next round of deployments to Niger. Jade Helm is an unconventional warfare training exercise. Unconventional warfare is conducted to enable a resistance movement or insurgency to coerce, disrupt, or overthrow a government or occupying power by operating through a guerrilla or underground force. In unconventional warfare, Special Forces are sometimes inserted behind enemy lines, and their job is to train, equip, and advise local people who oppose their government. The goal is to use all means necessary to ultimately bring down a hostile government, and the tactics include destroying military targets while avoiding damage to civilian infrastructure.

The Jade Helm unconventional warfare exercise was completely different from what the teams were going to Niger to do. Jade Helm might have worked for the 2001 deployment of Special Forces to Afghanistan, but it didn't correlate to the mission of Team 3212 in Niger. The government in Niger is an ally of the United States, and Green Beret teams were sent into their country at their request. The teams were not there to build up a resistance to and overthrow a hostile government, but rather to support the Nigerien government and its military.

In 2016, LTC David Painter, the new battalion commander, and Colonel Bradley Moses, the new 3rd Group commander, were told that 3rd Group would be doing the Jade Helm exercise the following year. Despite the fact that Jade Helm had no relevance to Niger, the immediate question LTC Painter and Colonel Moses asked USASOC was whether Jade Helm could count as the validation exercise for deployment to Niger. Using Jade Helm as the pre-deployment validation exercise would be easy, but it was in no way an appropriate validation exercise for the teams leaving for Niger.

The purpose of pre-mobilization training is to validate an ODA for deployment and is known as a "validation exercise." If you read the Army manual on training, you will see that validation must be granted by a commander two levels up. An ODA completes their validation training; the company commander one level up (a major) oversees this; and a battalion commander two levels up (a lieutenant colonel) validates it. In this case, LTC Painter was the battalion commander whose responsibility it was to validate the ODA to deploy to Niger in 2017.

The Jade Helm exercise was conducted in April 2017 under the command of Major Van Saun's predecessor. In June 2017, Major Van Saun took command of the company, and as part of the handover from his predecessor, Major Van Saun was told that all of the ODAs were trained and had been validated. This meant that LTC Painter had validated ODA 3212 as fully trained for their mission in Niger. Major Van Saun was informed that all he needed to do was finish up the pre-deployment planning, then get on a plane and take the company to Niger to start operations.

Bryan did the Jade Helm exercise only to return home and describe it as a complete waste of time. According to Bryan, the unconventional warfare scenario was not realistic, and the exercise was so poorly planned that they spent most days sitting around buildings in middle-of-nowhere Texas with no direction. Uncertain of what they were supposed to be doing, the men kept busy by making videos and drinking. Not only was the exercise not relevant to their upcoming deployment, most of the men Bryan would be deploying with were not present. Only four of the men on the ground during the ambush had actually attended the Jade Helm training, because the rest of the men either were attending other training or were not yet part of the team.

After the Jade Helm exercise, many of the ODA 3212 members left the team. Some were slated to move into jobs elsewhere in the Army and some were retiring from the military. Because of the turnover, new members assigned to the team that summer included Captain Perozeni, who joined just two weeks before they deployed.

Despite the high turnover of personnel and the uselessness of the training event, LTC Painter told Colonel Moses that the ODA was good to go for the 2017 deployment. This fact matters because LTC Painter left the command of the Special Forces battalion after going unpunished by AFRICOM. While Major Alan Van Saun was punished for pre-deployment training and Captain Perozeni was blamed for the ambush, LTC Painter went on to command a newly formed battalion in the Security Force Assistance Brigade, where he would again be responsible for training soldiers as they prepared for a high-profile deployment.

In October 2018, six GOMORs were issued by USASOC.

- Captain Perozeni and Master Sergeant Smith were named, citing insufficient training and lack of pre-mission rehearsals before leaving for Tiloa on October 3.

- Major Alan Van Saun, despite being on paternity leave at the time of the ambush, was reprimanded for "improper training before the team was sent to Niger." Major Van Saun's predecessor was not punished, though he was the one present and responsible for the pre-deployment training.

- Chief Warrant Officer Marshall, who had been at the AOB in Niamey, was cited for filing an inaccurate mission plan that led to the first mission.

- An Alpha Company sergeant major who had left the unit before the team deployed was also cited for insufficiently training the team before they deployed to Niger.

- SOCAFRICA's commander, Major General Marcus Hicks, received a reprimand for insufficient oversight of his subordinate officers in connection with the ambush. He was aware of each CONOP and mission that led up to the ambush and was part of the planning process as he was on the VTCs (video teleconferences) with LTC Painter and Colonel Moses. Although Major General Marcus Hicks was the highest-ranking official punished for the incident, he was also slated to retire, which meant the GOMOR would have no impact on his career.

Major Van Saun and Captain Perozeni were the only two men not slated to retire within two years. In late October, those men receiving GOMORs were notified and given a week to write a rebuttal with the hope of convincing the accusing general to reconsider. Soldiers facing a GOMOR and writing a rebuttal to the reprimand may use anything to support their case. Captain Perozeni included letters from teammates and family members of those who died in the ambush. Henry and I both wrote letters in support of him.

In my letter, I mentioned the fact that the GOMOR for Captain Perozeni indicated that he did not properly train the men for the mission, but he was given the mission late in the evening and spent the night preparing paperwork and the trucks for the trip. This left the captain having to choose between sleep and training for his men and their Nigerien partners. Henry's letter discussed the lack of support the team was given on their mission. How the last leg of the mission called for backup and support, but when that support was unavailable, the team was sent up anyway with no protection. Henry questioned why anyone would believe the threat at the Mali border had diminished significantly enough to justify the lack of support.

Almost a month went by before hearing that Captain Perozeni's GOMOR was probably going to stick. Henry and I decided that if Captain Perozeni's GOMOR ended his career and ruined his reputation, there was no reason not to have our arguments in support of him become public.

On November 14, *The New York Times* published a redacted version of the letter that Henry had written on behalf of Captain Perozeni. It was a poignant and powerful letter lambasting the Army for seeking to punish a man who had pushed back against a mission that left his team in a high-threat situation with profoundly inadequate support. Soon after the letter's publication, Secretary of Defense James Mattis interceded and the GOMOR was dropped from Captain Perozeni's record. We all breathed a sigh of relief.

Secretary of Defense Mattis also demanded that senior-level officers be closely scrutinized for their actions and decisions. On January 16, 2019, Captain Perozeni was again cited for not performing proper pre-mission training. This GOMOR was issued by the head of USASOC and went into Captain Perozeni's local personnel file, meaning it would not follow him and permanently affect his career. Despite this fact, Captain Perozeni once again wrote a rebuttal for the GOMOR he was issued, and once again his punishment was rescinded. Unfortunately, after a year and a half of negative press, doubts cast on his character, and two GOMORs issued against him, Captain Perozeni's reputation was permanently affected within the military community.

The last of the GOMORs went to LTC David Painter, a letter of reprimand to be placed in his local file. His GOMOR was issued for improperly overseeing pre-deployment training. LTC Painter was directed to step down from commanding a battalion slated to deploy just weeks after the GOMOR was issued. His GOMOR has not been rescinded.

LTC David Painter, Colonel Bradley Moses, and others who were not honest with the families of the fallen remain in their positions, commanding men and women, and they continue to advance in their careers. I believe a true leader doesn't lead for accolades and recognition. A true leader does what is right, and if they fail, their job is to bring the families of the fallen the truth—not a scapegoat and a lie. Forcing a widow like myself into a position where she feels compelled to run her own investigation is cowardice. These "leaders" should feel ashamed of their actions, as should every single person who stood by them and knowingly helped cover up the truth.

These people punished their subordinates for what was ultimately an intelligence failure and a lack of sufficient support and assets. USASOC, SOCOM, and AFRICOM should have carried the burden for not having the right assets in the field, but somehow managed to slough off these details onto the men on the ground who were taking their orders.

Even more than Captain Perozeni, Major Alan Van Saun is the person most affected by this incredible miscarriage of justice. Major Van Saun received a GOMOR in his permanent file that ended his burgeoning career even though he was not in command of the company when the pre-deployment training took place. He lost his career over training that his predecessor was responsible for, LTC Painter validated, and Colonel Moses approved. To this day, Alan Van Saun—who is no longer in the military—feels guilty that he wasn't on the ground that October. He feels that if he had been there, maybe things would have been different. Maybe he could have pushed back harder against the mission and

LTC Painter's orders. Maybe he could have done something to save those men.

Alan Van Saun and Captain Mike Perozeni are haunted by the ambush and wish they could have done things differently that day. LTC David Painter, on the other hand, has stated on multiple occasions—including directly to me—that he would still make the same decision to send the team up to the border alone, no matter the cost. I'm left to figure it is easier to come to that conclusion when it has cost you nothing.

21

Final Redacted Report

At the end of October 2018, scarcely more than a year after Bryan's death, I moved out of the only home we'd owned together. The amount of grief those walls and rooms held for me was unbearable, but to leave them seemed equally agonizing. I could not sleep at night, thinking of what we had built together and the things he would never be a part of. People had long since quit stopping by, and I found myself spending the days in deafening silence.

On the one-year anniversary of the ambush, I had hosted all the men from the team at my house. As we enjoyed a good dinner and conversation, I realized that even with these new friendships my old life was gone. It was time to move forward if I wanted to do more than simply exist. My friendships with Bryan's teammates are wonderful, but the men needed to be able to move on with their lives. Remaining in that house left me feeling like my life was permanently on hold, as though I was still waiting for Bryan to come through the door.

I decided to buy a home on the West Coast, up the road from Bryan's parents, in Washington State. Although my family doesn't live there, I understood my children needed to have a piece of their dad still with them while they grow up. I also knew that Bryan would want his parents to be a part of his children's life and that it would be healing for them to have their grandkids nearby. While I might have wanted to be near family in California or Colorado, I decided to be in a place that was beneficial to everyone. After all, we military spouses know how to adapt to living anywhere.

My children and I arrived in Washington just in time for the holiday season. They were difficult, almost eerie. Bryan's absence was like a void at each gathering. As we all stood in a circle to pray over our Thanksgiving meal, Karen and I wept. Christmas morning, Karen and Henry came over early to watch the boys unwrap presents and we forced smiles onto our weary faces, each of us trying our best to recall what excitement looks like when it's genuine.

We expected little of one another, but were immensely grateful to be so close to family who understood the level of devastation that came with losing Bryan. That kind of devastation doesn't go away in a month, or even a year. When I lost Bryan, I lost my future. Figuring out what the future looked like for me was the scariest reality of those first months.

Right before Christmas, *The New York Times* showed interest in an article I had sent them for their *At War* section. On December 21, 2018, the first thing I'd ever written or submitted anywhere was published by *The New York Times*. I was both shocked and humbled. Writing was something I'd always dreamed of doing, but it had felt like a pipe dream. For years, fear of inadequacy and failure had frozen me into inaction. But suddenly at the end of the most tragic year of my life, I found my voice. The freeze thawed and hope began to glimmer. Perhaps a new future was possible for me. Perhaps the stories from the men of ODA 3212 would be heard beyond my dining room table.

I started believing in myself and my story. I began to navigate the world of writing by first making huge mistakes and blunders. Then, with an immense amount of support, patience, and guidance from some of the most selfless people I have ever met, I finally began to make some headway. I learned that, much like raising a child, it might take a village to raise an author.

In the spring of 2019, I returned to Fayetteville, North Carolina, to attend the Memorial Day events held at Fort Bragg. It was almost exactly one year after the AFRICOM brief by General Cloutier and General Waldhauser. Henry and I flew east while Karen stayed behind to work and watch the kids. We attended a stone-laying ceremony for the fallen, a memorial dinner, and various other events to remember the men and women lost in Special Forces both that year and in previous ones.

The last day we were at Fort Bragg, Henry and I were asked if we could stay in Fayetteville longer. The final redacted report was finished, and a general and a colonel were briefing the families on a review of the investigation before handing out the report. Since we were visiting from the West Coast, it would be best for them if we stayed instead of planning to come back. But I needed to get home to my kids and Henry needed to get back to work.

The Army then pressed us to stay in North Carolina—which led me to wonder why there was suddenly so much pressure on immediately doing this briefing that we'd been given no notice of. I discovered they wanted to brief all of the families together. This wasn't a new investigation; it was simply a review of the previous one. Defense Secretary Patrick Shanahan, who had replaced General Mattis, had tapped Army general Robert Brown to review both the AFRICOM and the SOCOM investigations. Hearing this, I had no doubt that the person who had done the reviewing simply read through the executive summary of the report and signed off on it but changed nothing. If the review had been thorough, we wouldn't be receiving a briefing because a whole new investigation would have opened up. By this time, I had interviewed the men of ODA 3212 and knew that there were a lot of things about the AFRICOM investigation that didn't add up.

At last I found out the reason the Army was so insistent about gathering us all together: to create as little publicity as possible. This was the seventy-fifth anniversary of D-Day, so the hope was for our brief to be overshadowed by coverage of President Trump's D-Day events in Europe. An embargoed media announcement—a release of confidential information in advance of its publication with the understanding that the media will keep it confidential until a given date—was set to be released at midnight on June 6, 2019. This put enormous pressure on the Army to make sure the families got the information before the media released it to the public. Once again, the media was shown more respect and dignity than the families of the fallen were.

Unable to stay on the East Coast any longer, Henry and I requested the briefing team fly out to Washington and brief us at home. The burden to inform the families fell on the military, not on us. On the morning of June 5, 2019, the families of Dustin Wright, LaDavid Johnson, and Jeremiah Johnson were all briefed together in Fayetteville, North Carolina. The general and colonel who briefed them, along with two junior officers and an Army chaplain, then boarded a plane and flew to Washington State to brief us.

As we prepared to receive the brief, evening news reports began to pour out about what had transpired in that morning's presentation. It did not sound good. One family had walked out, and all the families present were upset. As I had expected, nothing new was presented. Hearing about the morning's fiasco, I figured the men coming to see us were probably both exhausted and apprehensive about a possible confrontation with our family. When the Department of Defense handed the brief down to be delivered to the families, this group of men had been selected by USASOC to do a job no one else wanted to do. I did not feel shooting the messengers was necessary. Instead, I decided to pretend we were having guests over. The information would be the same whether or not we were welcoming and kind. These men were given talking points, and that was what we'd be hearing.

A minivan pulled into my driveway around 5:30 p.m. The six men who piled out looked both worn and wary. Attired formally in their dress blues, they tentatively knocked on the door. General John Deedrick hesitated as he stepped through the door first, even though he towered over us at 6'5", with a bald head and a commanding presence. Then a colonel who appeared a bit on edge made his way around the room, meeting Henry, Karen, Bryan's older brother, Jason, and me. Next were several noncommissioned officers, an assistant, and the chaplain. Once all the introductions were made, I showed them to the kitchen, where I had laid out a spread of cheeses, meats, crackers, mixed nuts, and olives, along with a carafe of piping-hot coffee.

The men all stared at the table longingly but didn't move a muscle. "This looks delicious," General Deedrick said stiffly, "but you didn't have to do this."

"Nonsense. I will not have you in my home hungry and thirsty. I can't imagine the day you've had."

There was a long, awkward pause and all of the men looked at one another in silence. No one moved.

"Well, grab a plate and get started," I suggested.

All the men looked uncomfortable and pretended not to hear me. Finally, I turned to the general and asked him in a somewhat chastising tone, "General, you wouldn't want to make me grab the first plate in my own home, would you?"

A faint smile finally broke across the general's face and he grabbed a plate. "No, ma'am, I would not."

I laughed and said, "Good!"

Soon, everyone was swarming the table.

Once everyone had gotten themselves food and drink, we settled into the front room for the brief. The small gesture of food and coffee had already eased some of the tension. As the brief started and a few light-hearted jokes went around the room, I realized this brief was going to be less formal—and less informative. As General Deedrick and the colonel took turns discussing some overly broad findings of the investigation and review, it sounded nearly verbatim to what we'd heard from General Cloutier a year earlier—only less detailed. Answers to our questions were vague and gave us little information.

Early on, Henry asked, "General, has Captain Perozeni been recognized in the report for accurately assessing that the resources available to his team were inadequate to conduct his designated mission and for accurately recommending that the mission not be executed? Including his final request to abort the mission and return to base when Team Arlit had to abort the mission?"

The general replied, "A request to return to base was not recorded."

The men who briefed us were all part of the SOCOM investigation and took part in issuing the GOMORs, but they were not part of the initial investigation and findings of fault by AFRICOM. It became clear from their scripted and rote responses that words were being chosen very carefully, as though everyone in the room worried about saying the wrong thing. Still, we asked questions in hopes of getting different answers.

Henry asked, "General, does the report include the second threat assessment, if one was done, by the higher headquarters that ordered the team to execute the Tongo Tongo mission alone? If the higher headquarters did conduct a threat assessment, what was in that threat assessment, and what was the risk or threat that was identified?"

The general responded, "The report does not include a risk analysis for that mission."

"So, General, you are telling me that a second threat assessment was never conducted before sending my son's team up to the Mali border alone?"

"Yes, sir, that is what I am saying. No second threat assessment was done for that mission."

For the first time, we heard a military officially admit this.

Henry, Karen, Jason, and I all looked at one another but did not speak. There was a long pause as we considered the fact that in the AF-RICOM brief Henry had directly asked General Cloutier about a second threat assessment being done and both the general and the lawyer in the brief had lied and said yes, they had conducted a second threat assessment. Now, one year later, we were hearing that in fact a second threat assessment had not been done. Henry asked them one more time about the threat assessment, and again they reiterated that there had not actually been a second threat assessment, despite what we may have been told in our initial brief by the AFRICOM investigative team.

Henry asked, "I was wondering what intelligence failures led to the ambush and have been identified in the report?"

The colonel sitting on the couch seemed to prickle a bit before replying, "There was no intelligence failure. There simply was no intelligence."

Looking over at Henry, who was sitting on my left, I could see a slow smile creeping across his face. "So, no intelligence means no intelligence failure?"

The line sounded so ridiculous that I, too, started to smile.

The colonel remained serious as he tried to explain what he meant. Even the explanation seemed like everything else in this investigation: as if terms had their definitions changed just enough to get the desired answer without it being an outright lie. That, however, did not stop it from sounding completely ridiculous. "There was no intelligence failure. There were gaps in the intelligence, which will be addressed in the future, but there was no intelligence failure. The intelligence we had was used as effectively as possible, and so there was no failure with the intelligence that we had at the time."

Henry smiled. You really could not make this stuff up.

It was clear the men briefing us believed what they were saying, but what they were saying sounded ludicrous. Yes, if there was a gap in intelligence creating a lack of intelligence, you could technically say that officers did not fail to use intelligence that did not exist. But could you really say that there was no intelligence failure when it was clear that you failed to recognize the potential threat because of gaps in your intelligence gathering? I would venture to say that every man who died was failed by the intelligence. AFRICOM and USASOC can call that whatever they want, but I will still call that an intelligence failure.

Halfway through this final brief, I realized I didn't care what they told us anymore. It was obvious I was going to get nothing from this last brief. These men were simply messengers of things I already knew. I had interviewed the men who were on the ground during the ambush, and I already knew more truth than I would ever get from the military about my husband's death and what had led to it. I also knew that most of the fixes that needed to be made to prevent something like this from happening again were senior-level fixes, and yet mostly junior-level punishments were handed out. By now the wagons had been circled and nothing was going to change. I was done caring about getting the truth or anything reasonably close to it from the military.

After the brief was finished, we were handed copies of the final redacted report. Now that it had been given to the families, the way was cleared for the awards process to begin. After the brief was over, I invited the group gathered to stay for dinner. It was a warm Washington evening, so we grilled out on the porch and enjoyed some friendly conversation. Everyone was grateful to have the day and the briefings behind them, and the evening ended on an enjoyable note.

The following morning I awoke excited to dig into the material inside the report. When I opened up the binder, I was shocked by the amount of redacted material. On one of the first pages I turned to was the following:

REDACTED REDACTED When the French Mirages came on station, they performed the first of two shows of force before establishing communication REDACTED REDACTED REDACTED REDACTED REDACTED REDACTED Team

OUALLAM wanted the Mirages to drop ordnance, REDACTED REDACTED The Nigerien response was also immediate. REDACTED of the TIC, REDACTED REDACTED the RE-DACTED commander, launched a ground QRF from REDACTED REDACTED. In addition, he launched a Gazelle helicopter from REDACTED.

This went on throughout the entire report. After flipping through the rest of the pages, I shut the book, laughing. It was so *redacted* that I was going to have to become clairvoyant to read it. Even Captain Pero-zeni's name had been REDACTED throughout the report. I was going to have to take my interviews with the men and piece together what they said with what the report said to fill in as much of the redacted portions as possible.

I understand the need for classified material to remain classified, but this went far beyond that. Much of the redacted information was already common knowledge, like Captain Perozeni's and LTC David Paint-er's names. Whoever had done the redactions had certainly gone above and beyond the call of duty. Except they failed to redact the names of two active Green Beret special operators who were on the ground that day and survived. They had not failed to redact the names of any of the higher-level officers. Funny how after two years of "careful review" and thorough redactions they had missed something that would expose two junior-level team members' identities. Just as in everything else to do with the investigation, the junior-level team members were treated with less respect than the higher-ranking officers.

22

Disparities

The week after the final brief, I eagerly combed through the report, trying to parse the military jargon. One of the very first things I read stated the following:

> I do not find any officer above the company level (above the AOB) was derelict or performed his duties in a clearly unacceptable manner. While the investigation determined the mischaracterization of the original mission to Tiloa prevented the higher headquarters from initially providing appropriate approval and oversight, the subsequent mission and approvals were conducted at the proper levels. The decision to conduct the mission on Objective North near the Mali border was made at the appropriate level in the chain of command and executed within the intent of the SOCAFRICA approval framework.

There are several problems with that statement. Stating that no officer above the company level was to blame sets the tone for the rest of the report. Blame was solely and repeatedly laid on those at the lowest levels using the first CONOP as proof—despite the fact that CONOP 1 was for the first of the three missions, and the only successful one. Buried deep in the redacted report I found the following statement:

> The investigation did not establish by a preponderance of the evidence that the CONOPS [CONOP 1] was deliberately crafted as a "Civ/Military Reconnaissance" in an effort to lower the approval authority to what the Team believed could be approved by the AOB.

The official report states that LTC Painter was not briefed on the "true nature" of the operation in CONOP 1. But as stated above, the investigation also did not find that the mischaracterization of the first CONOP by Captain Perozeni was done deliberately in an effort to mislead those above him. Another thing buried in the report is the statement:

> Team OUALLAM's initial mission was driven by REDACTED that identified the possible location of a named objective in the vicinity of Tiloa. REDACTED Intelligence leading to the potential capture of a high value target drove an urgency from the AOB to exploit a time-constrained opportunity. This urgency drove the hasty planning and shortened execution timeline for this mission . . .

This is an interesting statement considering the investigation focused heavily on the lack of pre-mission rehearsals by the team. Starting in the executive summary and then again multiple times throughout the report the investigation states: "The Team Leader and Team Sergeant failed to conduct battle drills and pre-mission rehearsals prior to executing operations on 3-4 October 2017."

Later the report goes on to say that:

The lack of a coordinated and synchronized response to contact was to a large degree a result of no meaningful pre-mission rehearsals. Pre-mission rehearsals and immediate action drills with the partner force is a fundamental aspect of "good soldiering." The deficiency must be immediately addressed by the chain of command.

It is this finding that was handed over to SOCOM and used to initiate the punishments (GOMORs) for the the team leader (Captain Perozeni) and the team sergeant (Master Sergeant Smith). Ironically enough, buried deep in the report is a lengthy discussion on the failure of leadership to meet the time requirements for notification of missions, which not only limited rehearsal time but also made proper oversight difficult if not impossible. According to the report:

The SOCFWD-NWA commander [Colonel Moses] did not notify the SOCAFRICA commander [Major General Marcus Hicks] that there was going to be a complex operation involving two SFODAs [Special Forces Operational Detachment Alpha] on a partner assisted interdiction operation involving nighttime movement and air insertion, within the notification requirement. Although the SOCFWD-NWA notification of this CONOPS to SOCAFRICA was far short of SOCAFRICA's notification requirement, it was consistent with a standard of practice tacitly approved by SOCAFRICA over the preceding 11 months.

Clearly SOCAFRICA has a requirement that they must receive notification of operations within a certain time frame before the missions are carried out. These notification requirements were consistently not being met by those highest up the chain of command to include, as stated in the report, Colonel Moses. The report continues discussing the issue further:

Although the SOCAFRICA commander, Maj Gen Mark Hicks, testified that the notification requirement is intended to afford his staff sufficient time to look at the CONOPS and to conduct a full staffing process, SOCAFRICA had not implemented any processes to account for time-sensitive or real-time approvals. In the absence of clear guidance as to the approval and notification process for time-sensitive missions the SOCCE-LCB commander [LTC Painter] routinely approved time-sensitive missions, and SOCFWD-NWA routinely notified SOCAFRICA of these missions, over the preceding 11 months.

As seen above, the notification is necessary to afford SOCAFRICA the time to review the CONOPs and properly prepare for the mission. Surely the same would be said for the teams on the ground who are receiving time-sensitive missions but are not given sufficient time to prepare as well as run pre-mission rehearsals. Yet the practice of approving these time-sensitive missions without proper notification had become a routine of LTC Painter, Colonel Moses, and those commanding SOCAFRICA. Still the discussion continues:

Prior to 2 October 2017, SFODAs within the SOCFWD-NWA area of responsibility executed time-sensitive missions for which prior notification was required by the SOCAFRICA approval matrix. SOCAFRICA never denied or objected to any of these missions, and never raised concern over the fact they had not received advanced notification. SOCAFRICA's lack of guidance or corrective action following any of the previous missions, a period spanning the command tenures of both Donald Bolduc and Maj Gen Hicks, resulted in the implicit acceptance of short-notice operations. As a result, SOCFWD-NWA developed a practice of providing immediate notification of time-sensitive CONOPS, then executing the operations, even though such notification did not comply with the prior notification requirement.

With such short notification, the teams on the ground were not given sufficient time to run pre-mission rehearsals and yet they were punished. Those officers handing down the short notification missions went unpunished for the short suspense missions leading to lack of pre-mission rehearsals despite not complying with the notification requirements within their own approval matrix.

Another focus of the investigation that led to punishments was the lack of pre-deployment training, which places blame on those at the company level and below. In June 2017 when Major Alan Van Saun took command of the company, he was told that all of the ODA's were trained and had been validated as part of the hand-over from his predecessor. Major Van Saun knew LTC Painter must have validated ODA 3212 because units in the Army undergo an external evaluation (EXEVAL) to validate training. According to the Army Field Manual for Training [FM 7-0], "an EXEVAL is an evaluation planned, coordinated, and executed by an organization outside the unit two levels up."

The same field manual also states that a key requirement of an EXEVAL is that "the higher commander two levels up approves and resources it." So in the case of an ODA team, the commander one level up would be the company commander (Major Alan Van Saun). The commander two levels up would be the battalion commander (LTC Painter). According to both Major Van Saun and the Army's own Field Training Manual, the company commander (Major Van Saun) was not responsible for validating or resourcing the ODA's training. The individual ODA's training had to be validated and resourced by LTC Painter and the entire company's training had to be validated by the officer two levels up. That officer would be the group commander Colonel Moses. Pulling from the redacted report the families were given by AFRICOM:

Command Training Guidance [CTG] was published in 24 July 2016. The CTG required Battalion Commanders [LTC Painter] to certify and validate SFODAs annually and prior to every deployment.

A few paragraphs later it continues:

Only six of 11 team members participated in the JADE HELM exercise together. The Battalion [LTC Painter] considered JADE HELM to be the validation exercise required by 3rd SFG(A) training guidance, although participating SFODAs do not appear to have been externally evaluated.

A short while later the report excuses LTC Painter:

The 2/3d SFG(A) Battalion Commander [LTC Painter] could not have validated and certified to deploy in August 2017 because the personnel on that team had not conducted the requisite collective training events together.

This doesn't give an explanation for how that conclusion is reached and how the team was able to be deployed if they did not meet the requirement that "Battalion commanders certify and validate SFODAs prior to every deployment." Oddly enough a few paragraphs later the report states: "In August 2017, Company commander [Major Alan Van Saun] validated training to the Battalion commander."

Major Van Saun took over the company just as they were preparing to leave for deployment. I spoke with him at length and according to our conversations he did not validate the training. He could not have validated the training. He was not commanding the company when the training was decided on or carried out and he was not two levels up from the SFODAs, as required by the Army, in order to validate a team for deployment.

So how did Major Alan Van Saun receive a career-ending punishment over the lack of pre-deployment training? And how did the battalion and group commanders, whose job it is to resource and validate pre-deployment training, avoid getting GOMORs during the first round of punishments? Lastly, how is it that LTC Painter only received a local GOMOR and Colonel Moses received no punishment when those below them lost their careers for pre-deployment validation that could have only been carried out by the battalion and group commanders?

Another thing I found particularly confusing in the report is that the investigative team ignored a huge piece of evidence: ODA 3212 was operating off of intelligence for a two-hour window of time on the night of October 2 when the terrorist Doundou Chefou was expected to be in Tiloa. Yet Team Ouallam was told to wait until the morning of October 3 to leave on the mission. The investigation states that the reconnaissance team coming from Niamey was sent to help pinpoint the terrorist's location, so it was a find-and-fix as well as a kill/capture mission. The problem with this is that the team was only told to find and fix the location of Doundou Chefou if possible, but they understood they would need to call for proper approvals on the off chance the terrorist was still in the area. He was not. The team planned for a daylong mission, completed it, and were heading home when those at the AOB found a new location for the terrorist. Only then did LTC Painter get involved.

Another problem with the original statement is that it jumps right into the other theme carried throughout the investigation: that a misleading CONOP for the initial mission to Tiloa provides an excuse for not laying any blame on those officers who created and approved the second and third CONOPs and forced the team on the final two missions. In other words, the two CONOPs that actually led to the ambush. The report does say the CONOP approval process was confusing and needed to be changed by those who decide the details of the process to include SOCAFRICA and those at the battalion and group level, which is to say Major General Hicks, LTC Painter, and Colonel Moses.

Within the report we find the following statements about the CONOPs' approval process:

> The authority level to approve CONOPs is determined by a SO-CAFRICA CONOPs approval matrix, which assesses the nature of the operation and the residual risk associated with the operation. At the time of Team OUALLAM's operation, three conflicting CONOPs approval matrices existed to delineate what authorities had been delegated from the SOCAFRICA commander: SOCAFRICA followed matrix 1227; SOCFWD-NWA and SOCCE-LCB followed matrix 2228; and AOB Niger and its subordinate teams followed matrix 3229.
>
> To add to the confusion, each of the CONOPs approval matrices had provisions to delegate approval authority to command "levels." Several key witnesses articulated different understandings of who could approve an operation that had been delegated, for example, to "O-4 level." SOCAFRICA commander viewed the delegation as tied to rank, while the AOB Niger commander thought the authority was tied to position, and therefore could be delegated to an "acting commander" even if he was below the rank of O-4.

So the team and the AOB followed a CONOP process created by those men highest up the chain of command that was confusing and then were lambasted for not doing it right. It was recommended in the report that Major General Hicks and Colonel Moses fix the CONOP approval process. Yet somehow they are not held accountable for the issue. Senior-level fixes, lower-level punishments. When the team felt they had no other option but to follow orders and go after the terrorist near the border, they requested that Team Arlit be brought in as the lead team. That does not sound like a bunch of cowboys trying to hide a headhunting mission from higher authorities. These men were overruled by those who outranked them multiple times, including those at the highest level who would later be commended by investigators for having done nothing wrong. LTC Painter would push, forcing the team all the way to the Niger border—and when men died, the implication was that the team misled him in a CONOP. A CONOP that was ultimately irrelevant to the mission where the team was ambushed.

But *even if* the team had misled everyone and lied in CONOP 1, it would have made no difference if LTC Painter had not then sent them up to the Mali border in search of the terrorist on an actual kill/capture mission. Everyone on Team 3212 would have been safe in their beds that night instead of stomping through the desert hunting down a terrorist at the request of a couple of officers sitting at their desks in a different country. Maybe those officers were thinking that a terrorist apprehension would earn them a gold star to pin on their shirt, but instead I am the one who got a Gold Star, thanks to their actions.

Further on, the investigation report states: "The SOCCE commander [LTC Painter] then directed a multi-team raid including a second US-SOF Team and their partner Nigerien force out of Arlit, Niger as the main effort, and Team OUALLAM [3212] and their partner Nigerien force as the supporting effort."

This makes LTC Painter sound like a true leader, a man with a plan, even as he takes credit for something his subordinate did. The truth is that Captain Perozeni assessed the risk of his team driving up there alone, recognized the lack of assets, and saw what would be needed for a successful mission. It was Captain Perozeni who first contacted Team Arlit, and it was Captain Perozeni who suggested the multi-team raid to the AOB. Once Team Arlit and Captain Perozeni coordinated, only then did LTC Painter become involved in the plan for a multi-team raid. Clearly LTC Painter did not understand the need for Team Arlit, because only a few hours later he ordered 3212 ahead without Arlit, despite the assessment of Captain Perozeni and Lieutenant Boubacar that it was not safe. Lieutenant Boubacar was so nervous about the mission, he even reached out to his higher headquarters for help. The investigation report kept to the narrative I had heard in my brief that Captain Perozeni was not to be trusted, so to credit Captain Perozeni with a good idea would detract from the narrative.

One of the most ridiculous statements came in the third paragraph of the report: "As thorough as this investigation may be, it was unable to address specific information regarding the precise enemy composition, how the enemy was aware of the location of U.S. forces, and how the enemy planned and executed a deliberate ambush on 4 October 2017."

AFRICOM could not figure out how the enemy was aware of the location of U.S. forces and how they planned and executed a deliberate attack? The team drove for *twelve* hours in the dark in a large, noisy convoy of trucks through a remote desert area known to house terrorists. The team, under orders from LTC Painter, were looking for one of these terrorist leaders. The terrorist they were searching for was known to carry a cell phone, and the village elder of Tongo Tongo had that phone number stored in his phone. That same terrorist had just been to Tiloa and LTC Painter had the team chase him to his campsite. While clearing the campsite, the team spotted men on motorcycles. Yet AFRICOM is completely stumped about how the enemy found the U.S. and Nigerien forces.

In the sixth paragraph, the report states: "SOCAFRICA's assessment of the operational environment leading up to the events of 4 October, 2017 was informed by all available sources of information, and we do not assess any intelligence was overlooked, withheld, misinterpreted or otherwise mishandled that would meet commonly-accepted definitions of the term 'intelligence failure.'"

Perhaps commonly accepted definitions for the term *intelligence failure* are different in the upper echelons of AFRICOM than everywhere else in the world. Researching intelligence failures, I found it consistently defined one way. According to the *Oxford Research Encyclopedia*: "Intelligence failures are commonly understood as the failures to anticipate important information and events, such as *terrorist attacks*. Explanations for intelligence failure generally include one or more of the following causal factors: organizational obstacles, psychological and analytical challenges, problems with warning information, and *failures of political leadership*." (The italics are mine.)

But when an investigation is run by the very leadership that failed, that leadership needs to find a different definition in order to acquit itself of wrongdoing. Hence there were no intelligence failures, just intelligence gaps, as the officers claimed in Washington State during our second family brief.

The findings in the report essentially let AFRICOM, SOCAFRICA, and those in leadership off the hook for something they would later blame the team for being unable to accurately evaluate. The report criticizes the team for not assessing how high the risk was for their mission to Tiloa—a successful mission that did not lead to the ambush.

Regarding CONOP 1, which was put together by Team 3212, the report states:

> Although this CONOPS [CONOP 1] properly identified the risks associated with this operation, the risk mitigation measures were inadequate, resulting in an inaccurate residual risk determination. For example, the CONOPS identified an ISIS-GS attack on the team as a moderate risk to force but the measures listed to mitigate that risk REDACTED REDACTED. These mitigation measures are pro-forma, and do not reflect a deliberate assessment of how to actually mitigate risks. In fact, the operation posed greater risk to force than Team OUALLAM [ODA 3212] or the AOB fully appreciated.

And yet the team was not attacked on its mission to Tiloa, nor were they attacked *en route* to their base in Ouallam. Nowhere in the report was there anything about the risk to force on the two following missions, which directly led to the ambush and loss of life. The report also fails to bring up what the risk-mitigation measures were for those missions.

Considering what occurred on the ground, I would venture to say the risk-mitigation measures put into place by LTC Painter for CONOP 3 were a failure. I'm also curious how those conducting the investigation could recognize that the team failed to identify a high-risk situation if AFRICOM claims they were "unable to address specific information regarding the precise enemy composition and how the enemy planned and executed a deliberate ambush," even after an eight-month investigation.

Despite what General Cloutier told my family in our first family brief, no second risk assessment was done before sending the team to the Mali border alone. Regarding the second risk assessment, the report states:

> Notwithstanding the changes in Team OUALLAM's [ODA 3212] directed task and purpose, neither the AOB nor the SOCCE-LCB [commanded by LTC Painter] developed a CONOPS detailing Team OUALLAM's [3212] modified concept of operation. The SOCCE-LCB notified the SOCFWD-NWA [commanded by Colonel Moses], who in turn notified the SOCAFRICA J33 via email, of the revised plan through a short description of the five-W's [Who, What, When, Where, Why]. Missing from the five-W's description was a modified [second] risk assessment for Team OUALLAM given the team's new task and purpose, including the nearly 24 hours with little rest, no quick reaction forces assigned, an execution timeline that would put the team near the Mali border approaching daylight hours, no CASEVAC [Casualty Evacuation] plan, and an ISR [drone] platform without sufficient fuel to cover Team OUALLAM's return to base.

It seems to me the operation posed greater risk to force than LTC Painter fully appreciated, but the report lays that claim only at the feet of Captain Perozeni and the AOB. LTC Painter failed to have a second risk assessment done before sending the team to the border. This second risk assessment would have taken into account critical facts, many of which Captain Perozeni had been arguing about for hours. There was a lack of close air support, the soldiers lacked sleep, and their partner forces lacked both food and water. There was no casualty evacuation plan in place, no quick reaction force, and a drone that was running out of fuel. Not running a second threat assessment, supplying a QRF, or putting support into place showed a cavalier attitude.

That LTC Painter did not have his command conduct a second risk assessment is barely mentioned in the investigative report. But mentioned several times and discussed in depth throughout the report is that the *team* had set up insufficient risk mitigation for their mission to Tiloa the first day. This shows the clear focus on those lowest down the chain, when the failures that led directly to the ambush were higher up.

This language may sound like nonsense to most readers, but I am pulling it directly from the report:

> Global collection prioritization, collection platform availability, REDACTED REDACTED and other issues all generate significant gaps in intelligence regarding REDACTED in Niger and throughout Africa. These gaps have been thoroughly documented by USAFRICOM and briefed to the Joint Staff and Congress in USAFRICOM's 2017 Posture Statement and the 2017 Commander's Annual Joint Assessment. USAFRICOM'S 2017 Counter-VEO [violent extremist organizations] Campaign Assessment stated "only a fraction of USAFRICOM's ISR requirements are met. This limits situational understanding, support to operations, and fails to offer adequate threat indications and warnings."

While this statement clearly reveals an inability to adequately collect intelligence by AFRICOM, they still stand by the claim that it does not equate to an intelligence failure.

After the report let AFRICOM off the hook for intelligence failures, the next paragraph blames the team for failing to gather intelligence:

Team Ouallam and AOB Niger had full access to the intelligence resources and assets available to them at the time they planned the 3 and 4 October 2017 missions. Working with their Partner Forces, Team Ouallam and AOB Niger were aware of the VEO attacks in the Tillabéri region in the previous 12 months, as well as the sophisticated tactics, techniques and procedures (TTPs) demonstrated by VEOs. Despite this precedent for attacks against security forces in the region, no information existed to suggest a specific threat of ambush by VEOs against U.S. forces. Consequently, Team OUALLAM and AOB Niger did not believe the enemy would attack U.S. forces.

Much of the above statement is misleading and parts of it are a lie. The report never discusses what knowledge of militant attacks in the region LTC Painter, Colonel Moses, and other leaders involved in the VTCs on the night of October 3 had, despite the fact that they were responsible for planning and ordering the team to head to the Mali border. It states that the team had full access to intelligence resources and assets "at the time they planned the 3 and 4 October 2017 missions"—but they didn't plan the October 4 mission and they didn't have access to those resources or assets when the mission was planned. The team was on the road, driving through the night—not at a computer in an office like LTC Painter, Colonel Moses, and all of the other leaders. LTC Painter, Colonel Moses, and the others had access to those resources and assets but failed to see the danger involved and still ordered the men to go. They then claimed not to have failed—and allowed the men they sent on the mission to be punished for that failure.

In my first family brief, I had questioned General Cloutier if there had been previous attacks in the area and he had said yes, just never on

Americans. Henry and I had dug deeper, researching attacks in the region prior to the ambush. In the twelve months prior to the ambush on my husband's team, there were a total of sixteen significant attacks in the region. Five of the sixteen attacks occurred within a hundred miles of Tongo Tongo. Two of those attacks were ambushes; one of the ambushes occurred only fifteen miles from Tongo Tongo and was carried out on a Nigerien army convoy. In that attack, sixteen Nigeriens were killed and eighteen wounded, while seven vehicles as well as arms and ammunitions were seized.

How is it that Henry and I can do a simple search on the Internet and come up with this information, and yet AFRICOM claims their intelligence did not fail? It is not only their job to know what is happening on the African continent but to use that information to protect the soldiers on the ground who risk their lives every day. The officers running AFRICOM, SOCAFRICA, and SOCOM have the responsibility to set up their men and women on the ground to succeed, and that includes passing vital information all the way down the chain. That includes thorough risk assessments and recognizing and admitting when you have failed to accurately assess the risk so you can learn not to fail the next team.

Moving beyond the executive summary and reading through the redacted report while referencing my interviews, I began to notice a pattern. There were clear discrepancies among the story I had heard from the men of Team Ouallam, the story recounted in the family brief, and the story told by the redacted report. It was clear that the investigative team did not trust the members of ODA 3212. It seemed that from the outset, General Cloutier decided Captain Perozeni had done something wrong, and that he and his team were untrustworthy. I could come to no other conclusion than the entire investigation was conducted around the preconceived notion that the team was guilty and AFRICOM's job was to figure out what they were guilty of. The accounts from the team of what had transpired October 2 through October 4 seemed to have carried very little weight in the investigation and in its findings.

Bryan's parents and I had been told multiple times by AFRICOM in both the first and final brief by the USASOC general and colonel that the team did not resist any portion of the three missions. We were told that Captain Perozeni did not push back. The exact wording in the final redacted report states: "Given that distance to travel, and the fact that his partner force had been up for over 18 hours, REDACTED expressed to REDACTED his preference that the force return to base (RTB). REDACTED relayed REDACTED preference to REDACTED but REDACTED directed that REDACTED move to Objective NORTH and conduct the raid."

After completing my interviews, my best guess is that the above statement should read as follows:

"Given the distance to travel, and the fact that his partner force had been up for over 18 hours, [Captain Mike Perozeni] expressed to [the AOB] his *preference* that the force return to base (RTB). [The AOB] relayed [Captain Perozeni's] *preference* to [LTC Painter] but [LTC Painter] directed that [Captain Perozeni] move to Objective NORTH and conduct the raid."

According to every official in two separate briefs, Captain Perozeni never pushed back against any part of the mission—he simply preferred not to go. But according to every man interviewed, both those on the ground and those back at the AOB, Captain Perozeni vehemently protested going to the border and made it clear he did not think it was a good idea. They said this without my prompting when I interviewed them individually and without knowing what others had said. Captain Perozeni requested to return to base more than once and was willing to leave Mangaize and head north again only when it was agreed that Team Arlit would lead the mission. Casey, who was running communications at the AOB in Niamey, said the same thing: Captain Perozeni pushed back several times and requested to abort the mission and return to base more than once.

In the first days after the ambush, Colonel Moses came to my house and told my family and me that he knew very little about the ambush except that the team had been on a routine patrol and had not expected to encounter enemy forces when the ambush occurred. None of that was true. The truth is that Colonel Moses was involved in a series of video teleconferences on the night of October 3, with LTC Painter and Team Arlit, as well as other leaders, as they planned the mission. Colonel Moses had the authority to stop the mission if he did not agree with it, but he did not stop the mission. This leads me to the conclusion that he approved the mission.

It was not true that the team had been on a routine patrol. Both the men on the team and the final redacted report state that Team 3212 was on a raid to capture/detain an enemy target. As AFRICOM has pointed out several times, the team was in-country to advise and assist Nigerien partner forces on missions, essentially training them. The team was not in-country to create their own missions and conduct raids, but that is what they were ordered to do by those highest up the chain of command on October 3.

Colonel Moses told my family that the team had not been expected to encounter any enemy forces. After Team Arlit was turned around, the men on Team 3212 were read the Rules of Engagement—which they had never been read on any previous missions in Niger. The team explained to me that the Rules of Engagement are read when contact with the enemy is expected. So why did Colonel Moses tell us the team had not been expected to encounter enemy forces? It has since been explained to me that whenever venturing out near the border, Special Forces teams must expect the possibility of contact with the enemy.

All of this leads me to one obvious conclusion. The men were sent—underprepared—on a mission they were not in-country to do by a chain of command with a cavalier attitude toward the enemy they knew the team might encounter. When the team did in fact encounter the enemy and events turned out far worse than those highest up the chain expected, everything was downplayed. The conclusion I was left to draw was that those involved in ordering the mission needed a good explanation to cover themselves, so they came up with that one.

That good explanation, according to LTC Painter, was this: "We had received intelligence that a known terrorist had been up in that area and we were searching for an American kidnapping victim that we believed may have been held at that site."

It was spring 2018 when we began to hear about a kidnapping victim possibly being held in Niger. According to media reports, Christian humanitarian worker Jeffery Woodke had been kidnapped and may have been held by the terrorist Doundou Chefou. Then LTC Painter informed my family that intelligence led him to believe Jeffery Woodke may have been held at the campsite near the Mali border. Rescuing him would have been a noble and justifiable reason to send a team up to the terrorist campsite. But the problem is that not one person on Team Arlit or Team 3212 ever heard mention of the name Jeffery Woodke relating to that mission until they saw his name pop up in news reports six months after the ambush. How can you send a team to look for a hostage or to find clues of his presence without ever telling that team of his existence? To me it seemed clear that this explanation for the raid was crafted after the ambush. The way I see it, the team was sent on a poorly planned mission to chase after a terrorist who instead tracked them down first.

According to General Cloutier in the first brief, there was only one tree at the campsite near the border and the area was empty. But according to the men on the team, there were numerous trees covering the area, and after clearing the campsite two militants on a motorcycle rushed out from under one of the trees and headed north.

General Cloutier told us: "Before leaving, the team commander, Captain Mike Perozeni, ordered their only ISR drone up to the Mali border in order to gather intelligence on possible enemy routes leading into Mali." General Cloutier said they pushed it north to look for crossings into Mali, never mentioning that the drone was going to run out of fuel and was pushed north to follow a motorcycle with militants to make sure they did not circle back around and attack the team. General Cloutier used Captain Perozeni's decision to send the drone north to once again make Captain Perozeni look irresponsible when in fact whoever had left the underfueled drone with the team as their only support had been grossly negligent. Aware that the ISR could not make it back to the base in Ouallam with the team, Captain Perozeni made the best decision possible and sent the drone to follow the militants. I would find out later in reading the final report that the drone had recorded that the men on the motorcycle had met up with several other men on motorcycles.

In our original family brief by AFRICOM, General Cloutier told us that Captain Perozeni had chosen to stop the convoy when the first shots rang out in order to get out and conduct a bold flanking maneuver. The general made it clear he thought stopping in the kill zone was a bad choice—and conducting a bold flanking maneuver was another bad choice. But Captain Perozeni's choices were explained differently to me by the men who were there. When the first shots rang out, the Nigerien partner-force vehicles backed into Truck #1 and caused a collision that forced the convoy to stop. Captain Perozeni ordered the flanking maneuver because it was going to take a minute to sort out the trucks after the collision, and at the time the team thought the enemy comprised a small group. If Captain Perozeni hadn't done the flanking maneuver, the team would not have known that the enemy was growing and trying to trap them on the road. What Captain Perozeni did that day was textbook tactics given the situation and saved the lives of most of the team. Yet in the report, these choices by Captain Perozeni are said to have cost lives.

The final report makes no mention of the collision but lists the decisions to stop the convoy and to order a flanking maneuver as two of the factors that led to fatalities. Ironically, in the same chart of contributing factors, the decision by LTC Painter to send an ill-equipped team to the Mali border is listed as an *attenuated* contributing factor.

If LTC Painter had listened to the team in the first place and allowed them to return to base as requested, the Nigeriens would not have been in a position to panic and back up, trapping the trucks in the kill zone. Was Captain Perozeni expected to ram the panicked Nigeriens' truck when they stopped? Would more team members be alive today if Captain Perozeni had not organized the flanking maneuver and realized the enemy was maneuvering on them? Would more or fewer members be alive today if LTC Painter hadn't ordered the team up to the border? I don't need misleading charts to see what led directly to the ambush.

The team members were also criticized by the media, in the AFRICOM brief, and in the final redacted report for not wearing their PPE (personal protective equipment), such as helmets and bulletproof vests. What everyone fails to mention is that it was not standard operating procedure in Niger to wear PPE. The men were doing what they had been taught was appropriate, considering the hundred-plus-degree temperatures in Africa and the low risk of combat. As soon as the incoming fire picked up, they all put on their PPE. According to all standards, at that time on the ground in Niger it was neither required nor expected for the men to always wear their PPE. As Finding Three in the report states: "There are no clearly defined standards for the wearing of personal protective equipment during combat operations in Niger." Even so, once the battle began the men quickly put on their PPE, and only after their PPE was on did anyone die. Not one man was killed *without* their PPE on.

The final report recommends what should be done in relation to PPE: "Recommend Commander, SOCAFRICA [Major General Marcus Hicks], and Commander, SOCFWD-NWA [Colonel Bradley Moses] review PPE requirements in Niger to ensure they are appropriately tailored to the threat and issue a clearly defined standard for wearing of PPE."

This statement of recommendation is telling. The team had been held accountable for not wearing PPE, though they were not required to do so. The SOCAFRICA commander at the time, Major General Marcus Hicks, and the SOCFWD-NWA commander, Colonel Bradley Moses, are called out in the report to fix the situation. Even so, Colonel Moses never received any formal reprimand, but allowed the team to be blamed for something that was ultimately his responsibility.

There were many discrepancies as I read through the final redacted report that had to do with what the team did on the ground. In the report's executive summary it states: "The front two U.S. vehicles and three partner vehicles moved approximately 700 meters south and consolidated at what the investigating team calls 'Position Two.' Realizing that the third vehicle and their associated personnel were not present, and after repeated attempts to contact them by radio, four U.S. soldiers moved on foot back to the ambush site to find them."

According to my interviews, the men had actually done two bounds of three hundred meters each. It was after the first three-hundred-meter bound that they noticed that Truck #2 and the three men from that vehicle were missing. Ondo and Brooks immediately left their truck and ran back. After the vehicles bounded another three hundred meters, two more men—Hanson and Smith—went back to assist. The only vehicles that did bound seven hundred meters initially were the Nigerien partners, and all but one of the trucks drove off into the desert.

This difference between the report and the men's accounts matters for two reasons. First, for accuracy of the information and timeline. From the beginning, it bothered me that there was no detailed timeline of events given by AFRICOM in our family brief. Without a detailed timeline, inaccuracies could easily go unnoticed. Small inaccuracies can lead to wrong overall conclusions, especially where punishments and awards are concerned.

The difference between bounding seven hundred meters at once versus doing two three-hundred-meter bounds matters because of the marked difference in distance. Seven hundred meters is not quite half a mile, whereas three hundred meters is .18 miles. Imagine being on a dusty road and throwing a smoke grenade, then gunning your truck for nearly half a mile before stopping and realizing you have a vehicle missing. That sounds negligent and fits with the narrative of the team being irresponsible and Captain Perozeni making poor tactical decisions. Bounding less than a quarter of a mile, on the other hand, means that the men of ODA 3212 would still have been able to see Truck #2 if it weren't for the smoke grenade. They did not ditch their friends, as the brief and the final redacted report make it appear.

The redacted report says the vehicles bounded seven hundred meters and "four members of Team Ouallam and approximately 25 partner Nigeriens remaining at Position Two continued to engage advancing enemy forces." The fact is that, after bounding seven hundred meters, only one Nigerien partner-force vehicle stopped, not three. The other two were gone by the time the U.S. trucks had done their two three-hundred-meter bounds. That leads to the other issue. Rather than twenty-five of the thirty-two partner-force Nigeriens remaining at Position Two to help combat the oncoming horde of militants, there were in reality only nine remaining Nigerien partner-force members assisting in the fight. Why are these basic and important facts wrong in the final AFRICOM report? I am left to surmise that the accounts from the men on Team 3212 did not hold much weight with AFRICOM.

The report also downplays the team members' suspicions about the village elder in Tongo Tongo being complicit in the ambush. The report states that "while the Team members' theory about the village elder is plausible, the investigation could not determine his complicity by a preponderance of evidence."

The village chief later admitted pointing out the team to the QRF trucks, yet denied directing fire on the team, saying that he was just pointing in their general direction. The report states that the team opened fire first—but this makes no sense. By that point the team was down to one hundred rounds of ammunition among all of them, there were several men badly wounded, and they were walking out to be rescued. Why would the team stop, pull out their M4s, and drop their remaining rounds on trucks armed with mounted machine guns unless they were already being fired on?

In Finding Five of the report it says, "Team OUALLAM was not equipped with a vehicle set that would afford them the operational flexibility to adjust equipment based upon changes to the battlefield."

The vehicles the team used were long known to have mobility issues and weak engines. They were lightweight vehicles with no armor, and they could not maneuver well in the sand and constantly changing terrain in Niger. The vehicles could not handle carrying more than four people each and all of their equipment without getting stuck or having engine trouble. The Nigerien partner-force vehicles—which could easily maneuver through the desert and carry up to ten soldiers and their equipment—were often needed to pull the American vehicles out after they got stuck.

The vehicles were an issue that the American leadership was well aware of. In my interviews with the men, several of them brought it up. It was something I was aware of because Bryan had mentioned it after his first deployment to Niger and had sent a request for better vehicles up his chain of command, as had other team members after their 2016 deployment. Those requests were ignored.

In the final redacted report it is recommended that "USSOCOM and SOCAFRICA conduct a holistic review of vehicle requirements in theater based on mobility, protection, and weapon utilization. Consider implementation of a theater motor pool concept that will allow commanders the flexibility to choose vehicles based on mission requirements, changing terrain/climatological conditions, threat assessments, and partner force capabilities."

Once again, a failure that easily could have been fixed years before the ambush by senior-level officers. A failure that those highest up the chain were aware of but didn't bother to address until people died. Considering all of the money the U.S. pours into the military and its operations overseas, how is it that we have elite soldiers whose vehicles are so lacking they often get stuck and are forced to rely on their partner forces' vehicles for help? Niger is one of the poorest and most underdeveloped countries in the world, yet their soldiers have the vehicles they need to properly conduct operations in-country.

Finding Twenty-three is the only finding in the entire report that was disapproved by General Waldhauser of AFRICOM. It says: "The contracted MEDEVAC/CASEVAC capability in Niger does not meet USAF-RICOM's Personnel Recovery requirement for operations against VEO's [militant organizations] operating in West Africa."

This is the one finding that directly laid blame on AFRICOM for a specific failure.

It has been extremely difficult for me knowing Bryan's teammates as well as I do and processing the details the public hasn't learned. The inaccuracies in many of the reports, blame poorly placed on lower-level people, and disparaging remarks made about the team and Captain Perozeni made watching the news an infuriating experience. Knowing what I know and how off base many remarks and reports were, I regularly felt as if I was losing my mind.

It is hard enough to lose your husband, but to watch the media report inaccuracies told to them by high-level officials placing blame where it should not be placed—that is gut-wrenching. My husband, I can say with certainty, would completely agree with me that Captain Perozeni did a phenomenal job under the circumstances. His CONOP had nothing to do with the ambush or a lack of training, and the team was not intentionally trying to mislead higher authorities. It is truly a shame that the military and press reports disparaged Captain Perozeni on a national stage as though he were a war criminal and that the battalion commander, 3rd Group commander, SOCOM, and AFRICOM allowed it. I would choose him again to lead that mission, just as I'm sure Bryan would.

The issue was not the man leading the team, the issue was that no one higher up the chain of command listened to what the man on the ground leading the team was telling them. Captain Perozeni was hung on a technicality, but that is what happens in a world where leaders are guided by their concern for politics instead of their concern for people.

Nor was the issue training. If it had been, the same men who ordered the mission would have been the ones held responsible. LTC Painter validated and Colonel Moses approved all pre-deployment training. The decision made by men higher up the chain of command was to send ODA 3212 into a dangerous situation with woefully inadequate support. This decision put the team far from help with no assistance for many hours in the dark.

The one positive thing that has come out is that every possible promotion for LTC Painter and Colonel Moses has been blocked thus far. All I can do is hope that continues to be the case.

During my search for answers I visited General Don Bolduc, who had handed the command of SOCAFRICA over to General Marcus Hicks just months before the ambush. I asked the general from his experience working on the continent of Africa if he thought AFRICOM should have been investigated.

He replied, "Yes. I think someone from the outside should have come in and investigated AFRICOM. However, they would have found out very quickly that SOCOM and USASOC and the regiment and Colonel Moses and LTC Painter did not prepare that team for that mission properly. And they had just as much a responsibility to do that. A bigger responsibility. We [SOCAFRICA] told them [the battalion and 3rd Group commanders] what we needed them to train on and said, 'Pre-mission training needs to consist of *this*.' We insisted on a validation process for a reason: I didn't trust them," he said, meaning the commanders. "That's why we have generals—not to meddle in what these guys do, but to provide proper oversight through experience to make sure guys are prepared. And there was a cavalier attitude among the general officers stateside about Africa, and it cost these guys their lives. And like you said, we're not doing any of this to be vindictive, we're doing it because we don't want this to happen again. And it will happen again. It will."

If the lessons from the ambush are not learned, General Bolduc is right in stating that AFRICOM should not have been conducting the investigation. If General Cloutier and the investigating team lied to us in our family brief about conducting a second threat assessment, it leaves me wondering what other things they might have lied about throughout the investigation. It makes me wonder *why* they would lie. Were they trying to cover for someone? Did General Cloutier not know the answer, so he lied to cover his tracks? Why did the lawyer step in and help him lie? In the end, the truth was clear from the start: AFRICOM should never have been conducting the investigation into those under its command. AFRICOM should have been investigated by someone entirely outside of their ranks and authority who had nothing to lose.

When I think through this entire process—from losing my husband to wanting the truth—I always find myself coming back to one thought. Things happen in war—people die, unexpected attacks and ambushes occur, and there are failures along the way—but we must learn from those failures. It wasn't the families wanting punishment that led us here, it was the families wanting the truth. It felt to many of us as though when those in positions of leadership realized the truth might cost them promotions, they began lying to us and searching for someone to punish who they felt wouldn't be a great loss to the regiment. It seemed they gave us the version of the truth that felt safest for them and their futures—forgetting that Jeremiah, LaDavid, Dustin, and Bryan didn't lose a star, a career, or a reputation. They lost everything. And so did those of us who loved them.

23

The End of the Line

After the ambush, the investigation, and all of the controversy, the one bright thing everyone hoped for at the end were proper medals awarded, both to the fallen and to the survivors of the ambush. The Army uses awards to recognize men and women for acts of heroism in combat and in non-combat-related service. The top medals awarded in the Army, from highest to lowest, are the Medal of Honor, the Distinguished Service Cross, the Silver Star, the Bronze Star, the Purple Heart, the Meritorious Service Medal, and the Army Commendation Medal.

The Medal of Honor is presented by the president of the United States. It is given only to those who have distinguished themselves through conspicuous acts of valor while risking their lives and going above and beyond the call of duty. The act of heroism and risk to life must be performed while involved in combat. It must set the soldier apart from their comrades and there must be incontestable proof of the act.

The Distinguished Service Cross is given for extraordinary heroism in battle. Actions that merit this award are of such a high degree that the act of heroism must be notable enough to have involved risk to life and sets the individual apart from other soldiers.

The Silver Star is awarded for heroism and valor in combat. It is primarily awarded to soldiers for gallantry in action against an enemy of the United States and does not require an act in which the soldier risks their life.

The Bronze Star is awarded for heroic achievement, heroic service, praiseworthy achievement, or exemplary service in a combat zone—but not necessarily engaging in combat. Civilians are authorized to earn the Bronze Star, since it is meant for any person who has distinguished themselves from their comrades by brave or admirable achievement or service. The Bronze Star with a "V" is awarded for valor or bravery during combat. The Bronze Star may also be awarded to military members of foreign countries.

The Purple Heart is awarded for wounds or loss of life in combat.

Next is the Meritorious Service Medal, which is awarded to a soldier for having set themselves apart from their comrades by way of outstanding non-combat exemplary achievement or service.

The final award, the Army Commendation Medal, is awarded to any member of the military other than general officers. Those awarded this medal are distinguished by heroism, exemplary achievement, or admirable service. Acts justifying this award may also entail flight or non-combat-related acts of heroism. Military members of foreign countries may also be awarded the Army Commendation Medal. The Army Commendation Medal is sometimes referred to by soldiers as the "PCS" medal. PCS (Permanent Change of Station) is when a soldier is relocated to a new military base. Most military members and their families PCS every few years. Soldiers are often awarded the Army Commendation Medal before moving to a new base after serving their unit well. A "C" is attached if it is given for a good job in a combat zone, and a "V" is given if they displayed valor while in a combat zone.

For the families of the fallen, the medals would be a way for the military to publicly recognize the men who died—a way to acknowledge their accomplishments and bravery in the face of certain death. Our family hoped that the military would recognize that Bryan's actions on the ground merited him a Silver Star. Bryan's father, Henry, had run investigations during his long military career as an officer, so he well understood the process and decision-making behind military awards—and he was certain Bryan would be awarded nothing less than a Silver Star.

Numerous people on multiple levels are involved in the nomination process. In this case, the original nominations were made by a collaboration of people within 3rd Special Forces Group, then handed up the chain of command to be approved or downgraded. The final approvals or downgrades were decided by a collaboration of commanders: four-star SOCOM commander General Raymond "Tony" Thomas, three-star USASOC commander General Francis Beaudette, two-star 1st Special Forces commander General John Deedrick, and senior representatives from 3rd Special Forces Group.

SOCOM carried the most weight when it came to the final decision on the awards to be handed out, because the general of SOCOM outranks every other general involved in the process. General Thomas, who had overseen the second investigation, claimed he wanted to oversee the awards for the team as a way to set the record straight on the battle. Those involved in the process claim that most of the awards the men were originally nominated for were downgraded one or two times under pressure from General Thomas.

Over the next several months, it became known to the families that most of the awards the team members were nominated for were being downgraded. Captain Perozeni, who had been nominated for a Silver Star during the original process, had his award downgraded to a Bronze Star once the nominations were sent up the chain of command. Then Captain Perozeni's award was outright rejected by General Thomas. In a note on the rejection, General Thomas stated: "While I do not discount the bravery of Captain Perozeni in the face of overwhelming enemy force, I am opposed to awarding a commander whose poor tactical actions directly led to a tragic outcome."

In July 2019, USASOC contacted us about the presentation of an award for Bryan. He was to be awarded a Bronze Star with a "V" device for valor. While it was not what we had hoped for, we were still grateful. The military wanted to first present the families of the fallen with medals before then presenting the surviving team members with theirs. We were asked where we wanted the award presented. Initially I thought we should have the ceremony where we all lived, in Washington State, but after I thought things over it felt wrong to do the awards ceremony anywhere other than Fort Bragg. It also felt wrong to have his award presented apart from the brothers he died defending. We decided that my sons and I would stand in Bryan's place alongside the rest of the men from Team Ouallam as they received their awards. I couldn't imagine missing the medal presentation for the team members, and I couldn't imagine Bryan having a ceremony separate from his teammates.

On August 13, we attended the private ceremony at Fort Bragg for the families of those receiving awards and the families of the fallen. Jeremiah Johnson had received his Bronze Star with "V" for valor a few days before, but his father and stepmother came that day to support the others. As each man went up to receive their awards, we watched with somber faces. Sergeant First Class Brooks and Sergeant First Class Brent Bartels were presented with Silver Stars, and Staff Sergeant Hanson was presented with an Army Commendation Medal with a "V" device for valor.

When they called us up to receive Bryan's award, I was sure I wouldn't cry, but as Bryan's name and acts of valor were read, the tears began to flow. Watching Ezekiel and Isaac—now thirteen and eleven—receive the Bronze Star with a "V" device for valor on behalf of their father, I felt overwhelming heartbreak.

The day after the ceremony, we drove with the team from Fort Bragg to Santa Claus, Georgia, where a crowd of friends and family had gathered for Dustin Wright's ceremonial presentation of a Silver Star for his valorous actions on the ground. That day's powerful speeches brought many of us to tears.

While my children and I attended Dustin Wright's ceremony, my father-in-law made his way to Florida. That Friday he attended a ceremony for LaDavid Johnson in Miami Gardens, where the Army presented LaDavid's family with a Silver Star to recognize his heroic actions during the battle.

On the second anniversary of the ambush, October 4, 2019, the final medal was handed out in Phoenix, Arizona, to Ondo. I flew there to see him presented with a Bronze Star for his heroic behavior during the ambush. Ondo—who had lost Dustin Wright, one of his best friends, in the ambush—had become disillusioned with the military. He felt deserted by the leadership above him—so only a few short years after earning his green beret, Ondo left. He chose a new career as a firefighter in Arizona, and his graduation from the fire academy was to be held on the same day as the award ceremony. The team and I wanted to be there as his dad welcomed him into the Phoenix Fire Department.

I loved seeing everyone and the guys from the team seemed so happy to be back together. The awards ceremony was short but powerful, as Ondo was presented with his Bronze Star with a "V" device and read his citation of heroic actions on the ground.

After returning home to Washington State, I felt as though that chapter in my life had closed. I found myself in a new city, without a social circle, without Bryan. Going back to what I knew from years of being a military wife, I went to the local military base, a joint Army and Air Force base called JBLM (Joint Base Lewis-McChord). There I found an office designated for people in my situation: widows. I managed to make a few friends before too long and began to build my new life. Slowly, life after Bryan has become easier to cope with.

Certain times of year the pain of losing Bryan and the sacrifice of so many comes back to me. One of the hardest times each year is Memorial Day, which most people think of as the exciting start of summer. Last year I was at the grocery store picking up items, and as I laid them out on the belt the checker cheerfully asked if I was doing something fun for Memorial Day. I was about to travel east to attend several memorial services for the men and women killed that year and in previous years. I thought about the stone bearing my husband's name, birth date, and date of death, and a towering wave of emotion hit me. I looked down at my purse, pretending I'd dropped something, so she wouldn't see my eyes filling with tears.

"Well . . ." I faltered.

I thought of a friend who had lost her husband the week prior and was about to bury him. I would be seeing her at the bar where Bryan's picture hangs. Together with other Gold Star families, we would toast those we are meant to remember on Memorial Day.

"No," I said, "I'm not doing anything fun. What about you?"

"Just relaxing and barbecuing," she said. "I love having a long weekend!"

Not so long ago I was just like her. Memorial Day was the beginning of summer, it was big sales and sunshine. Barbecues, swimming pools, laughter, and drinks. It has something to do with celebrating our free-dom, right? Happy Memorial Day! Happy. Memorial. Those two words merged together create an indescribable level of pain for those of us who have lost a loved one to war.

My children lost their father. Bryan's parents lost their youngest son. I lost the love of my life. So I will not have a happy Memorial Day. That's simply not possible for those who understand what Memorial Day is. It is not a happy day; it is heavy and somber and gut-wrenching.

The last time I was happy on Memorial Day was May 2017. I remem-ber looking at Facebook and seeing a picture of a woman at a cemetery with her young children. They were taking flowers to their father's grave. It was the first time I truly took the time to consider that Memorial Day should not be thought of as happy and that people need to learn the difference between Veterans Day, which honors those who have served or currently serve in the military, and Memorial Day, which is for remembering those who died in service to this country. I stared at the picture, unable to comprehend how this woman had the strength to do what she was doing with her children. Little did I know that just six months later I would be doing that very thing with my two sons.

Looking back, I am so grateful for the time I had not knowing that a gravestone is the closest we will ever get to Bryan. Not knowing that you go to the cemetery not because you are strong but because he is there, and it hurts, but so does not going. So does breathing. Everything hurts, so you go because maybe he'll know you were there. You go and face your biggest fear over and over again, and in facing it there is strength and healing.

The pain doesn't end, but the darkness dissipates over time. The tears are still there, but now I see the flowers laid on the headstones and am grateful for the passing of time. I go on Memorial Day to the graves and honor those who gave their lives in service to our nation. I say their names, and I remember what they did and why. Dustin Wright, Jeremiah Johnson, LaDavid Johnson, Bryan Black. It is not happy, but it is right. It doesn't make me feel good, but Memorial Day is not about me. I have plenty of days to learn to feel good again. That's the beauty of being alive. Memorial Day is for the fallen. That is the lesson I didn't expect to learn as I stared at the photo of the widow in the cemetery. A lesson in sacrifice I now can never forget.

Neither can the men of ODA 3212 who survived the ambush but were left with the scars of war on their bodies and their souls. By the summer of 2019, most of the men from ODA 3212 had settled back into their lives and work at Fort Bragg. In February 2019, Brent left ODA 3212 after three surgeries to repair his arm. He continues to serve in Special Operations Forces. Not long after returning from Niger, Hanson proposed to his longtime girlfriend and she moved to North Carolina, where they were soon married. He continues to serve on ODA 3212 as the senior weapons sergeant and is currently deployed to the Middle East.

Casey proposed to his college sweetheart after his return and soon they, too, were married. Sergeant First Class Casey Wilbur returned to ODA 3212 in 2018 and is serving as the detachment's intelligence sergeant. He has deployed three times since returning to the team, once back to Africa, and is currently on a second six-month deployment to the Middle East.

Sergeant First Class Brooks left ODA 3212 in 2018 but continues to serve in Special Operations. Master Sergeant Smith has retired from the Army. Chester the JIDO analyst continues to work as an analyst and currently resides in the Middle East.

Captain Perozeni married the love of his life a short time after returning from his ordeal in Niger. After successfully rebutting two GOMORs, Captain Perozeni finished his time as the detachment commander before he left ODA 3212 in September 2018. He was selected to be the HSC (Headquarters and Support Company) commander for 1st Battalion, 3rd Special Forces Group (A), where he deployed in support of combat operations as a support center commander in the Middle East. Following HSC, Captain Perozeni moved to SWC (John F. Kennedy Special Warfare Center and School), where he is currently an instructor at the 18A Course Committee for Special Forces, using his experiences to teach young Special Forces students.

Sometime in the summer of 2019, while walking through 3rd Group headquarters, Captain Perozeni was spotted by a warrant officer. The officer pulled Captain Perozeni aside to hand him an Army Commendation Medal with a "C." It had been sitting on the warrant officer's desk for a while.

Like tipping a waitress a penny, the award seemed to be more of a slap than a recognition. By that time, no one was surprised, and very little outrage was left in any of us. We had come to expect those at the highest level to stay true to the narrative they had forged. We have all moved on and the fallout of the ambush no longer has much bearing on our day-to-day.

Our lives have scattered us all around the globe, but the bonds we built through loss cannot be broken. I see the men at least once a year and we all talk often. Their wives are wonderful women and I am lucky to have their support. Their families have become mine, and in the absence of Bryan that has meant the world to my boys and me.

I have watched my boys begin to emerge from their pain and repair their lives in a new place. Ezekiel has started attending middle school at the same school where his grandma teaches. The support given in Washington State to children on the autism spectrum is leaps and bounds above those given at schools in Fayetteville. After only a few months, Ezekiel has gone from failing nearly every class, being constantly bullied, and being regularly in trouble to suddenly passing every class with A's and B's and earning a "leader of the pack" award at school for his exemplary behavior. The school administrators who had initially been hesitant to allow him to transfer into the district after reading his school records from North Carolina now sing his praises and cannot understand how he'd ever gotten into trouble before.

It does my heart so much good to see my child treated with kindness and grace by the adults in his life. I have seen my son, who once hated going to school, growing in confidence and happily walking out the door every day. I do still see the effects of the trauma from his previous school pop up occasionally. I've received multiple calls from him panicking over small things that he is certain he'll get kicked out of school for. He's had to learn that telling a teacher about an issue is a good thing and will not lead to him being blamed and suspended as it often did at his previous school.

Isaac is also thriving in his new town. Within a month of our move, he made new friends at school. He attends more birthday parties and social events with friends than ever before, and both boys spend lots of time with their grandparents. Together, Karen, Henry, Ezekiel, and Isaac have started learning archery and are members at a range up the road from our house. They've learned to snow ski and found that they love it. With each passing day, both boys look more and more like their father, which is both wonderful and terrible. I love seeing Bryan in them, but it makes me sad for all that has been lost and all that Bryan will miss.

As I write this, it's been nearly four years. Isaac is thirteen and Ezekiel is soon to be fifteen. The last time they saw their dad they were nine and eleven. They deserve better and so did he, but I am grateful for the time we were given. My children got to know their father before he was gone.

For me, there will always be the pain of losing Bryan way too soon. People always expect you to recover quickly from losing someone you love, but grief is complex and multifaceted. It is not just missing Bryan that is terrible, it is the isolation, the anger, the fear, and for me it is the lack of feeling safe after many years of having a protector. People pass judgments on widows. By the standards of our society, I am expected to be an old maid now, to wear black every day and live my next sixty years shriveled up in mourning. There is no longer someone who fights for me, and I have to do all the fighting for myself. And oftentimes I'm seen as an easy target by predators. When I fall apart, I do it in private when no one is watching, and my kids don't see or hear me. There are places a widow knows are safe: the shower, the car, walking the dog late at night. Those haunted hours are when I can let the painful cries I can no longer contain escape while the rest of the world sleeps.

When we use the word *sacrifice*, we often imagine one act. Really, sacrifice is a way of life. Sacrifice goes on and on once you've committed to it. We began sacrificing the day Bryan signed on to the Army and left me alone with two babies while he went to boot camp. That is when sacrifice begins for all military families. That first year, Bryan missed my birthday as well as Isaac's second, and he was given three days' leave to fly from Texas to California and back for my dad's funeral. Each year, there were sacrifices made with the understanding that one day our family might have to make the ultimate sacrifice.

We give up so much when we commit to a life in the service to our country. We give up our home and our friends as we move multiple times, wherever the Army tells us to go. We give up attending family members' weddings, funerals, and births because it does not fit into the deployment schedule.

Sacrifice does not even end when your husband's life does. For my sons, they have lost the father who would teach them how to throw and catch a ball, tie a tie, be a good sport, time a good joke, catch a fish, talk to a girl they like. The sacrifice of the fallen is a long and painful list. Do not be fooled into thinking the sacrifice of the fallen ends once the final shot is volleyed.

The sacrifice made by the men and women protecting our freedom plays out over generations. Their husbands, their wives, their children, their grandchildren. Their mothers, their fathers, their brothers, their sisters. It also plays out in the lives of those who stood beside them in battle and had to carry the news and the scars back home with them. But more precious than the lives lost is the freedom that sacrifice afforded, and no one understands that more than those who have worked to free those who live under tyranny.

De Oppresso Liber.

Acknowledgments

There are so many people to thank for helping me along the way as I sought the truth and set out to write this book. First, everyone at Putnam who made this book possible, especially Mark Tavani, my editor, for believing in me and the importance of this story; your support has meant the world to me. I am deeply grateful for the tireless hours you put in helping me through many drafts to perfect each sentence of *Sacrifice*. To Danielle Dieterich, I am immeasurably grateful for all you have done. Without all of your help, hard work, and coordination *Sacrifice* would not be what it is today. Also many thanks to Alexis Welby at Putnam for helping me navigate all things publicity; I would have been lost without you. And to Karen Mayer, thank you for the time and patience you showed me while offering your invaluable insight. I can't thank you enough.

A special thank-you to my agent, Bonnie Nadell, for your unwavering belief in my ability to write this story. All I needed was one agent—the right one—and I'm so glad I found you. Without you, I could have never navigated the world of book writing so boldly. Your advice and encouragement on some of the hardest days of telling this story brought me both peace and the confidence to move forward. Thank you. I would also like to thank Austen Rachlis for all of the time you poured into editing my early writing and roughest drafts. Thank you for helping shape the narrative by providing insightful notes and editorial comments.

To Thomas Curwen at the *Los Angeles Times*, for being the first person to encourage me to write this book and for introducing me to Bonnie Nadell. Without your support I may have never found the courage to begin this project or the right agent to help me see it through. The day we met over my misfortune a little silver lining was brought back into my life. So from the bottom of my heart, thank you.

Thank you to my in-laws, Henry and Karen Black; my brother-in-law, Jason Black; my children, Ezekiel and Isaac; the men of ODA 3212; and everyone who believed in me and this project. Henry, thank you for all of the hours of time spent reviewing details of this story and your patience in explaining all things military to me; your guidance and input were invaluable. Thank you to my dear friend Megan Corbett for sitting with me in those early days and sifting through my very rough first draft; your input and support meant the world to me. I'm grateful to the men who were willing to be interviewed and patiently answered my questions even months later as the book progressed. To General Don Bolduc, thank you for the hours spent patiently walking me through the command center and inner workings of the upper echelons of AFRICOM and SOCAFRICA. Without your knowledge I would have been lost. To Alan Van Saun for generously sharing with me your depth of knowledge on the military, Green Berets, and Special Forces Command, and giving so much of your time. I'm immeasurably grateful for sharing your invaluable insights with me. To have found an officer consistently candid and trustworthy during this process has meant the world to me.

To each man on Team 3212. You trusted me with your story and walked me through each excruciating minute of the ambush; though you all would have preferred to remain anonymous, each of your names will forever be etched on my heart. Thank you for your patience with me as we spent countless hours going over endless details. I will forever be indebted to each of you for your many sacrifices and you will forever be a part of my family.

Finally, to each person who helped me along the way but asked not to be named, thank you. Your guidance, assistance, and support were invaluable.